VALUES SHIFT

The New Work Ethic &
What It Means for Business
John B. Izzo, Ph.D.,
and Pam Withers

Prentice
Hall
Canada

A Pearson Company

Toronto

Canadian Cataloguing in Publication Data

Izzo, John B. (John Baptist), 1957-
    Values shift: the new work ethic & what it means for business

ISBN 0-13-028669-9

1. Work ethic. 2. Organizational change. 3. Personnel management. I. Withers,
Pam. II. Title.

HD4905.I99 2000   658.3'14   C00-931462-8

ISBN 0-13-028669-9

Editorial Director, Trade Division: Andrea Crozier
Acquisitions Editor: Nicole de Montbrun
Copy Editor: Lisa Berland
Production Editor: Lori McLellan
Cover Design: Bill Douglas/The Bang
Art Direction: Mary Opper
Interior Design: Mary Opper
Production Manager: Kathrine Pummell
Page Layout: Janet Zanette

1 2 3 4 5 WC 04 03 02 01 00

Printed and bound in Canada

Visit the Prentice Hall Canada Web site! Send us your comments, browse our catalogues, and more. www.phcanada.com

Prentice
Hall
Canada

A Pearson Company

"*The need to be a preferred employer and a competitive force makes this book a great investment of your time! This book will raise your thinking above the daily turbulence, better enabling you to better comprehend what's impacting your organization's culture*"

PAUL RUSHFORTH, CEO, STRAFFORD FOUNDATION

"*John Izzo is at the vanguard of helping leaders understand what people want from work and how to win their loyalty. Put this book on the top of your reading list!*"

FRED BARNES, PRESIDENT, DMG WORLD MEDIA

"*Extending the reach of an organization's potential can only be done by passionate and empowered employees. Today's workforce is trading in management layers for a clear vision that fosters personal ownership. Values-Shift offers refreshing views on creating heart-felt passion in the workplace!*"

TODD EDMONDSON, PRESIDENT & CEO, TLV INC.

"*This book is long overdue! Values-Shift provides a blueprint of the future, as no longer is it sufficient for managers to just recruit talent to their organizations but more importantly, managers must find innovative ways to retain the workers they need to achieve their corporate goals!*"

GEORGE MADDON, PRESIDENT , PINTON FORREST & MADDON
EMA PARTNERS INTERNATIONAL MANAGEMENT SEARCH
CONSULTANTS – HEADHUNTER FIRM

"*John Izzo has special insight on how attitudes and personal and business values can either co-exist or conflict. This perception allows business leaders to develop a company culture that is nurturing both personally and professionally.*"

RICHARD ADAMS, CEO, HUMAN SERVICES CONSULTANTS

"*This is a 'must read' for all leaders who want to maximize people performance and corporate success! Values-shift meticulously describes the six trends which are changing the face of work.*"

PETE MAKOWSKI, CEO, CITRUS VALLEY HEALTH PARTNERS

"To turbocharge retention, you must first know the hearts and minds of your employees and then undertake the tough and rewarding task of sculpting careers that bring joy to both."

— HARVARD BUSINESS REVIEW

Dedicated to those companies and leaders for whom creating a great place to work is an end in itself.

Contents

Acknowledgments

Acknowledging people can be a challenge. On the one hand, you don't want to be like the Oscar winners who must be removed with a hook or stopped with music. After all, we authors are generally more interested than readers in acknowledgments. On the other hand, you will always forget someone who contributed in ways you forgot to mention. With both dangers in mind, here goes:

- To Leslie Nolin for her ongoing support and tireless efforts to move this work forward.
- To my co-author Pam Withers, whose openness to feedback and willingness to give are the mark of a true professional.
- To my children, who interrupted me enough for basketball games and bug watching to keep the process fun.
- To our research assistants, Janet Freeman and Julie Burtinshaw.
- To David Lavin for believing in the book and to Prentice Hall for publishing it.
- To the many companies and leaders who have taught me/us by example about what it means to create a great workplace. Special thanks to Synovus Financial and TDIndustries, two companies that remind me of what heights can be achieved at work.
- To Pete Makowski and Paul Rushforth for their own leadership and ongoing personal support.
- To Steve Sreb and Jeremy Ball, who continue to be trusted friends and fellow believers in this work.
- To my assistant Alison, who keeps the office sane and focused.
- To the leaders and companies who gave freely of their time so that we could get their perspectives on the changing ways we see work.
- As always, to my clients, who have taught me as much as I have taught them.
- To the millions of North Americans who go to work every day desiring what my grandfather called a "good tired."

John Izzo

Above all, I'm indebted to my co-author for his vision, accessibility and professionalism, not to mention his talent for modeling every one of the concepts in this book. I'd like to give special thanks to our researchers, Janet Freeman and Julie Burtinshaw. They're worth acknowledging again because without them, this book would never have made its deadline. Julie in particular went above and beyond the call of duty in grasping the concepts and giving us a rich amount of data from which to work. I'd also like to salute Bonnie Irving, editor of *BC Business* magazine, for her support and friendship over many years, and for her generous permission to use material from my past *BC Business* magazine articles for this book. I'm grateful to Robin Roberts and Sue Dritmanis for their moments of "sushi sanity," and to my clients, who put up with my "leave of absence." Thanks to Leslie, Alison, David Lavin, Nicole de Montbrun, Peter Frost and George Madden. And on a personal level, to Heather Pringle and Tish Sears. Last but by no means least, I am deeply appreciative of the patience and support my husband and son have given me through months of being rather too attached to my keyboard. It has been a journey well worth taking!

Pam Withers

PART ONE

Winning the changing workforce

1

The retention game: Why bother with values?

"As boomers retire, employers find they're fishing for talent in a puddle instead of a pool."

— SEATTLE POST-INTELLIGENCER

"Good morning. This is Sandra at Technology Consulting Inc."

"Hi there, Sandra. This is Great Wings Promotion Company, and we have twenty-five free tickets to next week's super-glam concert for all your information technology staff. Just fax us their names, and we'll have their personalized invitations delivered by courier this afternoon."

"Wow. What's the catch?"

"No catch. It's just their lucky day. Oh, and you get a ticket too."

"Awesome. I'll get that information to you right away."

Oops. Hopefully, Sandra doesn't work for your company, because she isn't tuned in. She failed to suspect that Great Wings Promotion Company is working for I.T. Executive Search Firm, and soon, each and every one of your hard-won information technology stars will be receiving tempting job-interview offers.

Thirty years ago, when headhunters were interested only in candidates for management, and job hopping was frowned upon, employees tended to stick with one employer for a lifetime. No one needs to tell today's leaders that both they and the workforce are now playing an entirely different game, one that involves revolving-door employment and never-ending recruitment at all levels.

But chalking this up to the old versus new economy (empowered workers in a flatter, faster organization), or a temporary demographic twist (more openings than qualified candidates), only supplies half the picture. There's also the much less explored phenomenon of a fundamental shift in workers' values and expectations. Why and how are employees changing? Let's begin with a quick summary of how the workplace has been put through the wringer.

Over the past two decades, workers have gone from secure jobs, lifelong careers, and predictable ascents up corporate ladders, to a world of temporary jobs, lifelong learning, and highly competitive industries in which they're only as good as their last gig, regardless of rank or experience. All this has triggered a deluge of words on how workers had better adapt or die. But even as career counselors scurried to re-educate the masses, two more powerful changes sneaked up from behind. First, workers began seeing work through a new shade of tinted glasses. By that we mean that, virtually unnoticed by corporate leaders, work itself has been devalued in the bigger picture of life as seen from the eyes of today's talent. And second, almost overnight, a severe skilled-labour gap has begun to put applicants in the driver's seat and to turn employers from confident recruiters into groveling pursuers desperately holding their fingers in the dike of employee turnover. US unemployment is at its lowest rate in thirty years, and given baby boomers' impending retirement (which officially starts in 2011), and the likelihood that they'll retire early (60 percent by the age of sixty-two), the skilled-labor gap will begin building to a crisis starting in 2005. Either the current strong economy will start to suf-

Seventeen percent of American MBA students polled by Stockholm-based Universum planned to leave their first position after one or two years.

fer for the lack of skilled labor, or workers fifty-five and over will have to increase their labor-force participation by 25 percent just to maintain a constant employment–population ratio.

The hunter has become the hunted—not yet in all industries or regions, but with gathering force. Nor, as we'll explain many times in this book, is this a temporary phenomenon. And even if it were, the workplace and worker have changed too much to go back to where they were. Today, the secret to winning the loyalty of professionals is understanding their shift in values. Fortunately, that concept is easy to grasp if one takes a quick journey back into the annals of modern business history.

Twenty years ago, much of the business world was taken by surprise when the proverbial work pyramid was up-ended. Suddenly, customers were on top, and a flattened hierarchy placed the responsibility on front-line workers to study, understand, and satisfy the customer's every whim. Keeping the customer satisfied was now more than a mantra; it was a matter of corporate life or death. The roots of the customer service shift are well-known to everyone: speeded-up business cycles, increased international competition, and a growing assertiveness on the part of customers.

Today, we're poised for the natural sequel to that revolution: It's time to focus on keeping the worker satisfied—or at least, engaged in his or her work. The factors triggering the pyramid's final meltdown may even sound familiar: warp-speed business cycles, a borderless world, and a degree of employee assertiveness that makes demanding customers of the 1980s look docile.

For years, analysts have freely acknowledged the following:

- Work processes are changing at a frantic speed to keep pace with ever-faster business cycles. This puts tremendous pressure on workers *at every level*, which in turn invites a degree of burnout previously known only to top executives and entrepreneurs.
- "Worker motivation" has become an antiquated and paternalistic concept. Today, workers at every level must be more responsible, autonomous, and self-motivated than ever before, with the authority to make quick and important decisions. They work across time zones, often connected only by e-mail for short periods before joining a new team. Of course, the entrepreneurial qualities they need to succeed are precisely those that tempt them to leave their company and start their own enterprises.
- Top-flight contract workers and consultants that leaders wish to attract are even more slippery to hold onto than employees.
- Workers, salaried and otherwise, are becoming ever more certain and demanding about what they want from the work experience. Ranking highest on their wish list—regardless of age, gender, or culture—are a work/life balance, constant personal and career development, exciting work, and a sense of contributing to their

community. Responding to such values, previously considered "fuzzy" or extracurricular, is in some respects a greater challenge in our electronically-linked, revolving-door workforce than it was in the old economy. (In other ways, it's easier.)

Put these together and the message is clear: Worker motivation now ranks evenly with customer service as the key to holding market edge. Never has it been so important to see the workplace through workers' eyes and to cater to their beliefs and needs, which represent nothing short of a sea change from worker values of even ten years ago. Besides, there's a frequently overlooked link between employee retention and customer service. As the director of human resources at Kinko's Inc. put it, "Our customers told us they wanted to see a familiar face taking care of them."

How content are workers these days, and how likely are they to stay put? Although surveys show that most people like their jobs, this has little to do with whether they'll stay. Two-thirds of North Americans say they are actively thinking of leaving their present company in the next two years. In our own engagement and retention assessments, we have discovered many companies where employees are satisfied with their jobs but still plan to leave. Understanding what drives people to stay and what drives them to leave is more critical than ever.

"It's a more educated, affluent workforce. They don't feel that a job is an asset they're lucky to have. They have greater expectations," says Mark Sussman of Jackson, Lewis, Schnitzler & Krupman, a New York employment law firm.

When consultants like Tom Peters first started suggesting that the "search for excellence" aimed at customers would drive results, his inverted pyramid was controversial. Now people take the link between customer service and profits for granted. This book suggests that a similar and equally profound shift is happening. The work experience will now have to be organized around the worker, and not vice versa. Converting a company to be worker-driven is a daunting but unavoidable task for every forward-thinking organization. Fortunately, it becomes less daunting as you read on.

Albert Einstein once said, "History has changed everything except our way of thinking." This book is about how, in the world of work, history has now changed everything, *including* how individuals think. A new set of values is emerging, a new way of thinking about work and what employees want from it. These shifts cut across generations, and gaining an understanding of them is fundamental for any leader or company wanting to attract, keep, and maximize the performance of the changing workforce. What's more, understanding the shifts is not enough. So this book also helps readers *respond* to them in practical and tangible ways.

Tumultuous change at a speed unprecedented in history is the definition of today's workplace. In a business world that shrugs off international boundaries, where companies live or die by their ability to keep increasingly fickle and demanding customers satisfied, old-fashioned values like loyalty, patience, and deference to one's elders have been tossed overboard like excess baggage. Newer competencies, including intuition, risk-taking, and mercenary résumé-building, are today's currency. And yet, precisely because they must live life in the express lane, winning employees learn early on when and how to pause and refuel. Baby boomers, missing the irony of what their own era has taught younger workers, often look askance at younger workers' determination to add balance to the mix, chalking it up to slackness or unreliability. In truth, a work/life balance is just one of several items that has graduated from an asset to a survival tool in this new era.

Perhaps least-recognized and most significant of all the changes the new economy has wrought is the abrupt end of the employer's "buyer's market," which has existed (with the exception of occasional war-induced shortages) since at least the mid-1800s, the dawn of the Industrial Revolution. In other words, for more than 150 years, there have always been more workers than positions available, which means there was never any doubt as to who set the rules and who was in control. Even where desired skill sets failed to match applicants' experience, there was plenty of time to train them—in contrast to today's hit-the-ground-running environment.

The triad of a global economy, the information age, and skewed demographics (98 percent of population growth is occurring in countries that do not have a strong education system) has changed all that. Now, not only do skilled workers increasingly have their pick of employers, they've learned to negotiate salaries and benefits with all the aplomb of yesterday's executives. Candidates with the right stuff are being head-hunted by firms that once filled only corner offices. In contrast to their less skilled workmates, skilled employees are also being granted regular access to the training they crave. As the self-serve economy extends into every corner of life, today's job applicants are even able to conduct highly efficient comparative research on prospective employers' corporate culture and benefits by Internet, and once in the door, design their own benefit packages by Intranet.

Retention: The new game

Here is the paradox of employee relations for the new century: Companies need good people more than ever, and yet loyalty as we know it is dead or hardly breathing. According to a worldwide study in 2000 by Watson Wyatt, the global human resources consulting firm, only 49 percent of Canadians are committed to remaining with their present employer, down from 62 percent a short nine years ago. Two in five Canadians always have their résumés up to date, according to a Royal Bank of Canada study in 2000. Curiously enough, the same study identified another major shift among workers: They aren't scared anymore. Whereas the workers of the early 1990s were painted as cowering victims of downshifting, worried about whether they could make a living away from the corporate trough, the Royal Bank study found that two-thirds of Canadians today feel strongly that they have the skills necessary to compete in the new century. That's evolution and adaptation within a very tight timeframe. It is also a reflection of new worker values.

Unfortunately, many of today's employers don't "get it." They don't believe their buyer's market has ended, or they believe the current situation is very temporary and restricted to a few elite industries. They don't want to pander to spoiled kids with quirky notions of benefits, like the team of young high-tech stars that demanded, in absolute seriousness, that they be located beside a certain cookie-franchise outlet to enhance the sugar-highs of their breaks—and were granted their desire. Wizened companies are in a bending-over-backwards contest, barely able to keep up with the new limbo positions demanded as the bar slowly falls. A 1999 study indicates that human resources issues—staffing, recruitment, retraining, and morale—have leapfrogged to employers' No. 1 concern, notably ahead of sales and growth, profits and cash flow, macroeconomic issues and competition. And justly so, for a skilled labor shortage in a knowledge industry means that those who catch and keep the best will thrive; the rest will shrivel and die.

The proportion of people currently unemployed who left their last job voluntarily is now at 15 percent, the highest in almost ten years. The average job tenure in information technology has shrunk to thirteen months from eighteen months two years ago. The cost of losing and replacing an employee can reach between 100 and 250 percent of the salary of the leaving employee—or more: Taco Bell's research found that their outlets with the lowest employee turnover produced up to 50 percent more in sales.

A significant improvement in recruiting new talent can produce a 10.1 percent increase in a company's market value. That's according to Watson Wyatt, which also found that honing key human resources practices—especially recruiting—led to a 30 percent increase in shareholder values.

Earlier this year, co-author John Izzo was present when the CEO of a company that had been receiving all kinds of accolades for its products and services reviewed the returns of an employee survey. He literally looked as if someone had plunged a dagger into his heart. Especially given that his company is not in the high-tech sector, and is not part of an industry for which professionals are highly sought after, he could hardly believe his eyes: Employees had indicated that they liked their jobs for the most part, and believed in the company, but more than 50 percent of them were actively looking for another place to work!

"Screw it," he muttered.

Welcome to the new world of retention, and to a set of workers with a whole new outlook on work. In the old days, a growing company with relatively happy employees could count on most of them staying. But today's workers bring a new set of profound, if at times unrealistic, expectations of what work should be like. Here are two bold guesses: A lot more of your people are thinking about leaving than you think. And by taking to heart the strategies outlined in this book, you can help stem that tide.

As *Inc.* magazine recently proposed, "Smart companies don't think only about filling jobs anymore. Nor do they add one perk here, one perk there, ending up with a patchwork approximation of what their competitors are already doing. Instead the companies immerse their employees in an experience they'd be hard-pressed to find anyplace else."

We call it a *values match.*

Hard time finding good people? Get used to it!

Is the current retention scare temporary? Decidedly not. Sixty percent of large employers say they are having difficulty attracting workers now, but the struggle has only just begun. As much as 30 to 40 percent of the managerial workforce is currently on the verge of retirement, prompting a rising panic to retain some of these graying leaders for a smoother transition, as outlined in Beverly Goldberg's *Age Works: What Corporate America Must Do to Survive the Graying of the Workforce.* Research shows that baby boomers, by far the largest pool of workers—the largest by far—plan to stop working full-time much earlier than did their parents.

According to a study by International Data Corporation, western Europe faces the same growing talent gap: About 510,000 full-time information technology jobs are vacant, a number expected to grow to 1.6 million by 2002. Given that by 2006, half of all workers will be employed in information technology positions or within industries that intensively utilize information technology, products, and services, this shortfall presents a crisis. In other words, companies are shortest on help in the fastest-growing sector, one that promises to swallow other sectors whole. Training will help, but how can it help fast enough? What about importing professionals? Although the US Congress raised the number of visas from 1999 through 2001 for skilled technology workers by 142,500—a 73 percent leap—the stark truth is that birthrates have fallen below replacement level in countries that stress education. Also, as we said earlier, most population growth is occurring in countries where education is not widely available.

Meanwhile, Western-style consumerism is racing to establish itself in every corner of the globe, a process that requires a skilled workforce. Clearly, only companies that excel at retaining skilled workers can compete in this race; those that also manage to "engage" the hearts and souls of their workforce will come out at the head of the pack.

The concern for "intellectual capital" is new and pervasive. John recently arranged a major consulting project, involving an employee retention assessment strategy for a high-tech company, on his car phone during a fifteen-minute initial conversation. The client had never even met John face to face. It was almost as if the simple words, "This could help you attract and keep people," were sufficient unto themselves. It's not that the client was completely convinced a retention strategy would help. It was more like a dying person being offered a drink of water: The need was greater than the rationality. Such is the world of business today. People are the only real asset, and they are harder than ever to find and keep.

> Eighty-six percent of US employers surveyed found recruiting qualified workers difficult, and 60 percent reported problems retaining employees.

At a *Fortune 500* company's corporate event, John spoke about the need to organize business around the changing worker. Afterwards, an executive approached him to comment, "Ten years ago, we'd have laughed you out of the room. But today, everyone was riveted." Such is the shift in today's workplace: from requiring the worker to organize around corporate needs, to a place of more equality, where a company ignores the deepest needs of workers only at its peril.

The shortage of skilled workers is beginning to reach much further into the workforce than a few years ago, when only high-tech industries were most affected. A recent survey conducted by the National Manufacturers Association found that 48 percent of respondents were concerned that their workers would be unable to read and interpret drawings and diagrams.

So, demographics, the global economy, and the information age together dictate that the overturning of the employer's "buyer's market" is far from a temporary situation. Only companies that have moved their human-resources staff front and center into strategic planning will survive this trend. Success in this new environment relies on three simple premises: Know your employees' needs and desires. (This book reveals what they are.) Meet their needs and desires. (We show you how.) And never assume you know what they want.

For example, companies have found they can increase productivity, revenue, or both by 20 percent simply by implementing a work/life balance program for staff. Likewise, it's possible to reduce turnover by as much as 50 percent by introducing any of the following: dependant care leave, childcare subsidies, eldercare programs, counseling and referral, and flexible working hours.

Here's the bottom line: The era of analyzing economic changes in terms of how workers must adapt to survive is over. Instead, this book explores how companies must adapt to keep workers, how economic and societal shifts have literally changed the way workers see work.

The new economy and society have changed what people want from jobs and employers, and what they want rests on changing values. Values are the primary source of energy that drives behavior. Inwardly, we know our values as beliefs. Outwardly, they are manifested as behaviors and choices. When our values and work drift apart from one another, we experience a commitment crisis. When they're neatly tied into a bundle, we put our hearts and souls into our work.

Values Shift identifies six major expectations, all based on those changing values, that affect what workers of several generations now want from work. We also help leaders by suggesting practical strategies for winning commitment from the changing workforce. This new outlook represents a force to which organizations must respond if they want to attract, motivate, and keep talented people of all ages and backgrounds. We help forward-looking organizations and leaders understand exactly what it takes to maximize people performance in the new economy.

The six trends discussed throughout the book, which apply to workers of all demographics, include:

1. An expectation of partnership in a collapsed hierarchy
2. An expectation of a work/life balance and synergy
3. An expectation of work as a noble cause
4. An expectation of personal growth and development

5. An expectation of community at work
6. An expectation of trust

But are these shifts new?

Some business leaders will suggest that the "shifts" we discuss in this book are not, in fact, new. When we interviewed Paul Hollands, chief operating officer of A&W Canada, for this book, he commented, "These are the things people have wanted since human beings have been around." Wanted? Yes. But in a position to demand? We think not.

As we move deeper into the new century, "wants" are becoming "expectations." Just as workers' attitudes towards work have changed radically in key areas—their view of authority, their more entrepreneurial orientation, and their attempts to achieve a work/life balance, to name a few—so too have their values. The two are clearly intertwined, each impacting on the other.

These value shifts are the result of several decades of change in the family, society, and work itself, as explained in the next chapter. What we are saying is simple: The six expectations outlined here form a template for companies that want the best employees to flock their way. Companies that align themselves with the new worker values will achieve great things. Knowing how people see work is critical. Knowing their dreams and highest hopes is paramount.

A tongue-in-cheek Monster.com advertisement illustrates this shift in values. The ad features young children talking about what they want to be when they grow up. Through a series of vignettes, the kids say they want to be a brown-nose, a yes-man, a middle manager in a large organization, a downsized employee. The ad ends with the poignant question, "What did you want to be?" It strikes a timely chord in North America because our views of work and what we want from it have changed dramatically (although not as dramatically as the kids' lines would have us believe!). Ironically, Monster.com is a Web presence devoted to helping people—maybe your people?—find employers highly tuned to workers' shifting dreams.

Years ago, sociologist Studs Terkel wrote *Working*, a collection of interviews with people about work. In talking with people who laid bricks and cleaned floors, Terkel quickly discerned that work was not just about earning a living; for these folks, it was about making a difference, making a contribution. Echoing that insight, 80 percent of North Americans today say they would continue to work even if they won the lottery. Why? Because work has never been just about pay, and in a society relatively satiated with material goods, pay means ever less. Study after study on employee retention shows that while money is often a factor in an employee's decision to leave, it is rarely the primary reason. So, we'll say it once more: Knowing what *else* today's workers expect from work is sure to keep your business competitive. But before we talk about the six shifts, let's explore the forces that have changed the way we see work and what we want from it.

2

Four forces that have changed how we see work

"Rather than thinking of the economy as something that operates independently of our culture, history and community values, think of them all as interwoven."

— ANGUS REID, *SHAKEDOWN*

In a finely polished boardroom, the senior executives of a large chemical manufacturing firm have gathered to ponder an uncomfortable question: What can they do about the increase in turnover at their research facilities and the growing difficulty in recruiting the kind of talent they need? During the heated discussion, the senior vice-president of human resources draws vigorous nods of approval when he says, "Look, employees today want exciting work, a corporate buzz. They want to believe in our products and services."

"No, they're not willing to stay in one place for long no matter what we do," someone else objects. "Not even for a secure job."

Now the CEO, who has been tapping his fingers impatiently, speaks. "Once things get slow, people will just want a paycheck again," he asserts.

If only it were so simple. Leaders and business owners may be tempted to see the shifts in worker values as temporary responses to a red-hot labor market that is sure to alter during the next economic slowdown. But the truth is, four broad forces have been at work for a number of decades to shape a brand-new work ethic. We'll discuss those forces momentarily. For now, suffice it to say that long-term loyalty is long gone, and attracting, retaining, and motivating skilled workers has risen to a new art form. It's an art we guarantee you can master by the end of this book, and one that promises more payback than any other business investment you could make.

The trick is to put away all those personnel department how-to-hire manuals and to head into the realms of sociology and psychology. Values are not just the fancy of academics. Rather, the underlying values of a society and its workforce shape the contours of business strategy. Put more simply, understanding the core values people have about work is the key to winning their commitment. And acting on that understanding is far more powerful than learning a series of recruitment techniques. In the end, it is the fit between an individual's values and the perceived values of his or her company that determines how long that company and worker will stick together and whether the worker is putting in time or giving her all to move the company ahead.

This chapter identifies four fundamental forces that together have reshaped what workers want from their work and the workplace. Understanding these shifts and building your company around the needs that they have spawned are the keys to attracting and retaining people.

FAMILY

Today's leaders underestimate changes in the family at their own risk, for this is where each and every one of us forms our values. As author and speaker Stephen R. Covey says, the new economy needs leaders in every rank, and leadership abilities may have more to do with how we were raised than with our training, or how we were mentored early in our careers. While Covey is perhaps ahead of his time—still a voice in the wilderness on the family–leadership link—the Western world's tendency to draw a strict divide between work and home is relatively new in historic terms. Indeed, it is still unusual worldwide, as we discuss in greater depth in Chapter 4. Turning our backs on the work/life connection is also ironic given that technology is increasingly blurring the distinction between home and work time.

Leaders must recognize that over the past thirty years, the family has undergone major changes that have reshaped the values of workers from baby boomers to the so-called Net generation. Here, we describe some of those changes and how they have affected what we want from work.

Changing parenting and family patterns

Now that most married couples are dual-wage earners, and a large contingent of employees are single parents, it's no longer possible to pretend that childcare considerations never impinge on work. Today, half of women with *young* children work, while 77 percent of all women with children work.

Family size, structure, and values have all changed markedly in recent decades. Essentially, smaller families and a more egalitarian and permissive parenting approach have contributed to individuals' sense of autonomy and the decline of rigid hierarchies and paternalism. Anyone who visits the local supermarket will find aisles filled with young children debating with their parents about everything from cereal to acceptable behavior. This new style of parenting, combined with smaller families, has helped spawn a ferocious distaste for hierarchies and paternalism at work, as Chapter 7 discusses. At the same time, rising divorce rates, dual-worker couples, the latchkey experience, and a lack of time with hardworking parents have introduced a feeling of insecurity, which in turn is contributing to workers' desire for a more personal relationship with bosses than would previously have been acceptable. The need for recognition has made a steady rise up the list of workers' reasons for job satisfaction, as reflected in human resources surveys over the past decade, in part due to such changes in parenting approaches.

Plante & Moran, the firm that ranks first in its percentage of female partners and boasts a turnover rate of 6 percent, compared with the accounting industry's average of 25, provides free on-site Saturday childcare during tax season.

"Generation X feels robbed of time with their parents. Managers inherit life issues that weren't resolved in families. The manager now becomes the parent," writes Claire Raines in *Beyond Generation X*. The successful leader accepts this new, if not always comfortable, role while learning to garb himself or herself in the same protective gear that more professional listeners—such as therapists—have learned to wear.

Peter Frost and Sandra Robinson's *Harvard Business Review* article, well worth reading, recently dubbed such leaders "toxic handlers."

German software firm SAP AG provides each employee with mentors for the first month of the job.

Warning: Special training is required to avoid encouraging dependency or burning oneself out in the process of trying to help.

Ironically, these changes in the family have created significant paradoxes in winning workers' loyalty. More time spent alone and less experience with a hierarchical parenting style has created workers who are fiercely independent and resent being told what to do. At the same time, all that time spent alone has created a hunger for mentoring, recognition, and a deeper experience of community at work. Is it any wonder many managers have expressed to us their bewilderment at how to win workers? These are issues tackled in Chapters 6 and 8.

The affluence factor

Societal changes have altered family values in other ways, too. Decades of commercials enticing us to buy unnecessary goods on impulse have taken a toll on society, especially on families with more money than focused parenting time. The bombardment has intensified over the years: Americans were exposed to six times as many advertising messages in 1991 as in 1971. Baby boomers can be seen as the first truly post-materialistic generation. They came of age in a time of rising affluence and expectations. Most of them assumed that they would be better off than their parents, and many of them are. This shift to an expectation of affluence led many boomers to see work as more than a paycheck. Work became an expression, if not the central core, of their identity. But that was only an interim stage. With the shift to knowledge work and their basic material needs met, a growing number of baby boomers came to expect even more from work than a salary and self-identity. As it turned out, the rise of affluence and hard work had not bestowed upon them the requisite sense of fulfillment. So they've since focused their sights on a life/work balance, meaningful work, a sense of community, and more. Meanwhile, the next generations are crowding the workforce and bringing their own values, formed in part from watching the boomers' overemphasis on work and materialism, and the undignified manner in which they were downsized.

Thus, the Information Age, into which boomers and Generations X and Y have moved, has been characterized by a dual focus—on materialism and soul. Today's workers arrive at work daily with that subconscious paradox. On the one hand, they have been indulged with material things all their lives, a situation that has bequeathed to them a distorted sense of "entitlement." Highly educated Generation Y (also known as the Net generation) workers have this in concentrated form, having arrived at the work world's doorstep at a unique time in modern history, when companies are so desperate for knowledge workers that they greet them and treat them like royalty. What twenty-something's head *wouldn't* swell?

> Stonyfield Farm, said to be the only yogurt company with a growing market share, has taken on a broad range of social and environmental issues, from an anti-dumpster drive, to promoting gun safety by handing out thousands of free trigger locks.

But remember, these same workers were raised by parents who often felt demoralized by the blessing and bane of high salaries that came without deep fulfillment. Both Generations X and Y, having taken the boomers' often unspoken ambivalence to heart, move through the workforce focused on wealth, but with a deeply held belief that work should offer something more meaningful. Yet, however much boomers, Xers, and Yers may crave a soul/work connection, they remain inclined to see work as demeaning and pointless, say family therapists John C. Friel and Linda D. Friel, authors of *The Worst Seven Things Parents Can Do*. Turn them around on that score with all the patience, tough-love attention, and positive reinforcement that a skilled mentor would engage, and they're yours. Social workers in at-risk teen programs do it all the time. They slowly win the respect and loyalty of individuals suffering from

> At CDW Computer Centers in Vernon Hills, Illinois, the human resources department was renamed "co-worker services."

an inner clash of fierce independence, cynicism, and insecurity. A skilled leader does what it takes, including boning up on parenting texts to help finish an unfinished job.

Robert Bly, author of *The Sibling Society*, adds the following theory to this discussion: The turbulent period of adolescence (marked by insecurity and a lack of impulse control) has more than tripled in length since before the Industrial Age, now extending well into one's twenties. The reasons may be partly physical and partly cultural, Bly posits; the cultural aspect is best explained by consumerism, a growing lack of intimacy with one's parents (due to diminishing family time), and little contact with grandparents, who have traditionally offered youth a steadying hand. This trend, Bly and others warn, offers serious repercussions for each succeeding generation, as relatively immature adults become parents. Top that with the fact that the percentage of twenty-somethings living with their parents has doubled since 1960. Are current demands in the workplace for more balance a natural attempt to readjust this scenario?

If there is a silver lining to a pampered or demanding employee, of course, it is that they have an intuitive understanding of today's increasingly pampered and demanding customer base. Regis McKenna has much to say on this in *Real Time: Preparing for the Age of the Never Satisfied Customer*.

Changing family structures

If today's employees are riddled with insecurities because of gaps in how they were parented, business leaders need to understand that this has created a backlash against workaholism. The last two decades have taken a measurable toll on family life, and today's workers are trying to take a stand against that toll. Half of Generation X comes from divorced families, and the divorce rate has shot up since they were growing up in the 1970s, according to Meredith Bagby, author of *Rational Exuberance*. Time and family are now the gold of the new millenium worker, regardless of age or professional status. Now that they're in the driver's seat, job candidates can and will decline work where the company has a reputation for burning out practitioners in six months. Lest you think that such a reputation could not possibly belong to your company, or

McCormick, the spice company in Sparks, Maryland, has banished time clocks.

that dissatisfied ex-employees could not broadcast their feelings very far, check again. The Internet is full of sites that do nothing but let people with too much time and angst vent their spleens. These freedom-of-speech sites cost little to hoist, and can be discovered from anywhere in the world with as little as one keyword (your company's name?).

The point is that today's workers have witnessed firsthand what an over-focus on work can produce. Consequently, they come to the workplace with their guards up and often with a personal pledge not to fall into the same pattern. A recent survey of graduating MBAs showed that a large percentage has vowed never to let their work life overwhelm their personal life, a clear backlash against an overdevotion to work.

THE ECONOMY

The new economy has influenced workers' values in two primary ways. First, finding satisfactory work and building a career have had to become constant concerns; no longer can these issues be placed on autopilot. Second, with work having become so all-encompassing and the number of hours individuals are working having risen dramatically, employees are looking to the workplace to meet needs they once fulfilled elsewhere.

At St. Louis brokerage firm Edward Jones, new brokers are immersed in seventeen hours of classes at a cost of $50,000 to $70,000 per head. "We consider training an investment rather than an expense," explains the principal.

Thanks to global competition, mergers, downsizing, upsizing, and longer and more demanding work hours, today's workers understand that if they are not growing and learning, they can quickly become obsolete. When they do have a job, it now seems to follow them around everywhere. Witness the back seat of their car filled with work they intend (*intend* being the operative word) to do in their leisure time. As we mentioned in Chapter 1, 40 percent of employees always have their résumés up-to-date. The same study found that 60 percent have taken courses to upgrade their skills in the last year alone.

Contrast all that with the experience of John's grandfather, a Nova Scotia shipbuilder who settled in New England during the 1930s. For thirty-five years, he worked at the same shipyard, weathering occasional layoffs and furloughs, but never questioned the concept of a lifelong job that began each day at nine and ended at five, when the whistle blew. He never had to change careers, and as far as we know, never even considered it. His work days generally ended on time, and weekends were always his.

John's fourth-grade son, Carter, on the other hand, recently came home from school and announced that he would have to tackle four to five careers during his lifetime. Children are being indoctrinated very early in the realities of the new economy. Not only is this boy correct in anticipating constant change, but already he understands the importance of learning as a pursuit for a lifetime.

What does all this have to do with workers' values? It means that career development and résumé enhancement are now a way of life. Regardless of their age, nearly all workers today regard the notion of hitching their wagon to one company for life as an unrealistic if not unwise career choice. Companies are lucky to keep an employee for the current average of three and a half years (men, 3.8; women, 3.4), and some say the Net generation's average is closer to two years.

Today's youngest workers learned from their parents' layoff experiences that corporate loyalty is nearly obsolete in a global environment. The boomers learned it firsthand when security guards showed them the door during "reengineering." So, the worker as mercenary is now a natural part of the landscape, as we'll discuss in Chapter 6.

But while the new economy has bred mercenary workers, it has also created new and more human desires among workers. Thanks to mergers and acquisitions, and the growth of super-large companies, we're seeing two opposing trends: more small and home-based businesses, and more mega-corporations. Both of these trends have spelled longer and more intense work hours, shorter career ladders, and shrinking buying power. Even when combined with greater job flexibility, this creates a need for something to make all the stress worthwhile: work-sponsored socializing, career-building courses, and community causes. The all-encompassing nature of work today means we want more from it.

Ideas rather than tasks are the currency of the new economy, and the so-called knowledge workers, who can work anywhere and anytime, often feel compelled to work everywhere, all the time. Again, a level of burnout once reserved only for business owners has been passed on to the entire knowledge workforce, along with a dare to shoulder the risks of decision-making in a high-speed business environment. The good risk-taker is served up every day with large portions of ambiguity, uncertainty, and vulnerability, and too much of this diet eats away at one's sense of character. This sense of character, which includes values, can only be built back up through leisure, family time, and comradeship, all of which can and should be openly supported by the new-economy employer who wants to retain and inspire valued staff.

Now that work is life, it had better be a good one

Before modernism, we lived in the country, worked largely in crafts with our family in close quarters, and were deeply religious. When a new age of economics shoved us into city factories with strict supervisors, we felt depersonalized but at least we still had income and an after-work life. At five p.m., we could leave work and experience life through the traditional means: church, family, and geographical neighborhoods. As mobility further loosened our ties with family and neighborhood, however, and as divorce rates rose and work began claiming us for longer and longer hours, work and self-identity fused. The result: Social behavior is now affected primarily by chosen interest groups (for instance, sports or environmental). For better or worse, we're now free to create our own lifestyle group identity. With so many of the traditional sources of fulfillment outside of work crowded out by longer work hours and the dual-worker family, people seem to be focusing on work as a primary source of personal fulfillment. This is a role that the workplace did not have to meet in previous generations, as we discuss in depth in later chapters.

Increasingly, workers want and expect the workplace to meet needs it never had to meet in the past. Business leaders ignore this trend at their own risk of high turnover and waning performance. Wise companies understand that their role, like that of society, has shifted, and that the word *values* no longer needs to be whispered in the cloak-rooms.

Ninety-three percent of corporate and human resources executives believe that a strong corporate values system has a positive impact on financial performance, according to a study conducted by Blessing/White, an international human resources consulting firm. But only 64 percent of those executives said values are part of their companies' performance management systems. Only 54 percent said their companies practice "personal–organization" fit as part of recruitment. Only 46 percent said senior management was involved in the development of their companies' values. Perhaps most discouraging of all, only 19 percent said that all employees participated in values development.

We'll bet the farm on this: Companies unafraid of tackling the values shift, unafraid of fully embracing the new responsibility for employees' greater welfare—with employees' input—will be around in the next decade. And they will discover that this approach offers more than one kind of payback.

SOCIETY

Societal values, like everything else, have shifted with the times. Let's begin with two that have had particular impact on *work* values.

Consumerism and spiritual hunger

One of the ironies of the new century is that in North America, we are wealthier than ever and yet less at ease. The signs of our angst are everywhere, and they profoundly influence our view of work. Since the mid-1960s, there has been an unprecedented increase in clinical depression in advanced and rapidly advancing economies, generally attributed to individuals' increasing lack of friends or confidantes (or quality time spent with them). People born after 1945 are ten times as likely to suffer from depression as people born fifty years earlier, in a less materialistic era. A 1999 Novratis study found that the most prescribed drugs in North America treat depression and ulcers. Other studies show that since 1960, there has been a steady downward trend in the percentage of respondents who say they trust most people. Meanwhile, the global economy's consumption rate of material goods has doubled in the past twenty-five years.

Simon Zadek of the New Economics Foundation believes consumerism and loneliness are linked: "The market in general and rage to consume in particular have crowded out or undermined friendship," he wrote in a fascinating book entitled *The Good Life*, from Demos, an independent think tank in London, England.

Two-thirds of experts at the Open University's Futures Observatory in England believe that materialism will be replaced by ethics within twenty-five years, and three-quarters believe that organizations in general will stress ethical values within twenty years. The following chart, measuring students' definition of success over two decades, agrees:

PRIMARY MEASURES OF SUCCESS

(according to graduating MBAs of Duke University)

1989	1991	late 1990s
power	successful relationships	marriage
prestige	a balanced life	health
money	leisure time	ethics

Source: Making a Living While Making a Difference, p. 3.

Regardless of whether the experts are right, it's certainly true that the old paternalistic, controlling, and bureaucratic system is neither necessary nor tolerated in an age of educated masses and instant information—especially when serving the customer means being empowered to make fast decisions, often as part of an ever-changing team.

Meanwhile, more independence and customer focus has, for some, uncorked a longstanding desire for blurring the line between one's personal and work self. As the Duke University and other surveys show, our society is shifting towards a focus on things of the spirit. For instance, what of the plethora of books, magazine columns, and

Internet chat groups about "bringing one's soul to work"? A quick review of recent bestsellers in North America is strong evidence of this movement. From the proliferation of converts to Zen Buddhism (now the fastest growing religion in North America, according to *Time* magazine), to the phenomenon known as "Chicken Soup for Every Kind of Soul," to the remarkable popularity of the anti-advertising magazine *Adbusters*, there is a backlash happening against modern consumerism. Call it shifting values.

English poet David Whyte, popular on corporate speaking circuits for this topic, has written, "Work is not and never has been the very center of the human universe.... Continually calling on its managers and line workers for more creativity, dedication and adaptability, the American corporate world is tiptoeing for the first time in its very short history into the very place from whence that dedication, creativity and adaptability must come: the turbulent place where the soul of an individual is formed and finds expression." Without encouragement to contemplate what spirituality is and how it might be connected to work, he says, workers experience a "dehydrated workday."

This growing desire to respect things of the spirit (discussed in Chapters 5, 6, and 8) is having a profound impact on how we see work. As Michael Hammer declares in *Beyond Reengineering*, "It is thrilling to be part of a revolution that replaces meaningless work, petty bureaucracy and dead-end jobs with a workplace to which people enjoy coming, knowing they will be challenged and appreciated." What leaders must understand is that people are looking for these things on work time, not just on vacation time!

Democracy and the Internet

All over the world, there is a nascent democratization happening, albeit punctuated with backslides into dictatorships. The Internet is part of this shift in societal values, proving that information and decision-making are not the realm of a privileged few, but the right of all. (On a recent trip to the mountains of Costa Rica, John was taken aback to see a lineup of Internet cafés bearing witness to this trend.)

Thanks partly to the instant accessibility of information, we've moved closer to a "direct democracy" than ever before. According to a study conducted by the University of Zurich, the ability to have a say in how one's region is run ranks right up there with a giant hike in income for ensuring personal happiness. Certainly, speaking one's mind—to parents, bosses, or co-workers—is tolerated far more now than in previous times, for better or worse—and the Internet has proven a highly popular vehicle for soapboxing.

This worldwide shift towards democratization and access to information, coupled with more permissive parenting and teaching styles, has accelerated the values shift against hierarchy. Here's a simple way to frame it: "If I can speak to anyone in the world via the Net, and even the Berlin Wall can't stand up when the people want it to come down, I surely should be able to challenge my boss."

TECHNOLOGY

Technology has both changed the workplace and made it easier for people to stoke a long-held desire to leave and work for themselves. Technology has become so integral a part of our society that expenditures for it in the United States have grown from 5 percent of total capital spending in 1970, to nearly 50 percent in 1999. In workplaces, there is now one personal computer for every 1.3 employees. At home, more than 60 percent of households are expected to have personal computers by 2003. Internet access, totaling 14 million in 1995, is expected to reach 320 million users in 2002. Cutting-edge technology is also one of the most cited reasons for employees to stay with a company.

Technological innovations have brought us faster product cycles; changing work processes; a smaller, more skilled, and internationally competitive workforce; and seemingly inescapable communication devices. Those devices contribute both to efficiency and to burnout. In our worship of the former, we often drive ourselves blindly into the latter. Americans are working 163 hours (about one month) longer per year than they were in 1969, and this is not just a North American phenomenon. Just over one-third of Britons work on weekends, and 54 percent work into the evenings. Americans are even outworking the

> In an Internet chat group about "electronic leashes," a participant suggested putting dead batteries into one's pager to have a "valid" excuse for not returning the boss's call.

notoriously workaholic Japanese: 1,966 hours per year in the US compared to 1,889 in Japan.

By 2010, one in five American workers will telecommute. Although telecommuting has been hailed as a positive technological development, a less welcome result, as far as employees are concerned, is electronic monitoring and surveillance. With this, all the advances a more democratic and open work environment seems to offer are sent reeling. Employers can now check out job applicants' Web surfing to examine their hobbies, interests, and attitudes. Several British companies are discussing implanting microchips in employees to monitor their whereabouts and for timekeeping. Employers can read their employees' e-mail, access their computer files, track their Internet traffic, and listen to their voice mail. They *can* do all this, but when and how often *should* they? Do technical advances in this arena endanger the trust on which employee motivation sits? We discuss this issue in Chapter 9.

Much has been written about the effect of the World Wide Web on society's values, but one effect in particular should make savvy business owners sit up and take notice. Successful Web masters discovered early on that one of the keys to attracting the maximum number of visitors to their sites was to offer a sense of personal service and customization. If this meant inviting e-mail questions and responding personally to each and every one, such a policy proved worthwhile. If it meant, as with the Barbie doll site (**www.barbie.com**), allowing buyers to choose their model's hair color, outfit, lip tone, and personality (we're not kidding!) before shipping out the order, so be it. Certainly, Levi's, the jeans company, surged back to power through offering custom-made jeans—a feat made economically feasible only through Internet technology.

"Customers have become empowered, engaged and actively integrated into the business organization's decision-making process," states Richard W. Oliver in *The Shape of Things to Come*. We say *workers* have also become empowered, engaged, and actively integrated into this process.

Make no mistake: Employees who've grown up with custom-ordered Barbie dolls and Levis *expect* employers to extend such privileges to work benefits. Why should they have to stroll into the personnel office to ask how many vacation days they still have coming, when logging onto a password-accessed intranet site can give them the same information twenty-four hours a day, seven days a week? Why shouldn't they be able to custom-design their own benefits package on the same self-serve basis (within spelled-out guidelines), or suggest ways to renovate work systems and expect a speedy response from the powers that be? The US software company Oracle, for example, uses its Intranet to help retain staff by offering them the choice of various employment perks, such as benefits packages, longer holidays, sportier company cars, or better retirement packages. In summary, keep an eye on Internet/intranet developments for potential applications to employee retention. What works to keep the customer satisfied is bound to build employee loyalty.

"Technology's effects on us today are different from those of the Industrial Revolution," writes Regis McKenna. "They are more democratic, more personal, more subtle and profound. They are changing our very perceptions of judgments of value, our loyalties and relationships. They are changing who we are, even as we casually press each new technological device into service, taking it for granted."

In other words, technology is helping to change our values, especially when it comes to our workplaces.

Putting it all together

This chapter began by asking whether the shifting values discussed in this book might be merely a symptom of the current "hot" economy. Although workers naturally become more demanding when times are good, our thesis is that this shift goes much, much deeper. The values underlying these demands—the very way we see work—is what has begun to shift. And only by understanding the forces that have shaped the shifts can one begin to see how robust they will remain, even when the economy slows down.

Change has become the watchword of the twenty-first century. We are living in a world that is radically reshaping the human experience. From biotechnology to information technology, from the way we work and the way we shop to the way we connect with one another, no traditions from the past can be taken for granted any longer. Families, the economy, society, and technology have all undergone radical change—unquestionably the most profound upheaval since the Industrial Revolution. The values of today's workers are changing along with that upheaval, and in the chapters that follow we focus on how companies can respond to workers' changing needs.

3

Understanding demographic differences in work values

"There is a thin line between a twenty-something 'slacker' and a forty-something convert to 'voluntary simplicity.'"

— BARBARA MOSES, *CAREER INTELLIGENCE*

As we've said, there are six clear shifts in the way workers see work, and these shifts cut across age and gender lines. The latter first became obvious to John when individual listeners approached him after his talks to corporate audiences about what younger workers want from work. In his lectures, he emphasized younger workers' desire for community, constant development, integration between personal and work life, and a higher purpose to work. Afterwards, young employees would bound up to him and say, "Hey, bang on, you really know us! Thanks for helping these old guys understand us." More intriguing, however, was the response baby boomer listeners would offer: "You know those things you said younger workers want? Well, I want them too."

After months of such feedback, John was able to determine that while there are demographic differences in why and how workers arrive at these goals, the similarities are stronger than the differences. That is why we have chosen to spend six full chapters on the shifts that are universal to workers of all ages, genders, and ethnicities—shifts that matter if an organization wants to attract and keep good people.

But before we launch into those chapters, we've chosen to pause and reflect on some of the demographic differences that are worth paying attention to. First, there's the age factor: Different age groups have somewhat different views of what the ideal work life looks like. Next, there's the gender gap. Clearly, men and women have different takes on how to improve the workplace experience. Finally, there's the cultural diversity factor: workers of differing cultures define workplace issues differently.

Everyone knows that today's North American workforce is more racially and ethnically diverse (20 percent of workers are non-white), older (the median age will surpass forty in the year 2003 for the first time ever), and comprised of more women (48 percent) than it was twenty years ago. But are they aware that far more Generation X than baby boomer workers are toying with the idea of starting their own business (54 contrasted with 36 percent)? That's a *generational* issue. To employers concerned about losing young talent or facing competition from ex-employees, surely that means catering to younger workers' more searing need for independence and flexibility. We call it the search for partnership. Boomers want partnership, too, but in different ways and for different reasons, as discussed in Chapter 7.

How many employers know that far more boomers than Gen Xers (born 1963 to 1977) identify their jobs as "an expression of themselves" (56 compared with 46 percent)? While all workers are putting the desire for balancing work and personal life near the top of their lists, there are real generational differences in the role work plays in one's life. Work is central to the self-identity of boomers and Netters, perhaps because, unlike their Gen X cousins, they came of age in times of economic prosperity.

Of course, the age gap is only one aspect of diversity. When it comes to the *gender gap*, knowledge of Mars-versus-Venus perceptions about work is no longer a luxury. For instance, both women and men identify balance as an important issue for them at work, but survey after survey shows that this balancing act is the *overwhelming* concern for working women, especially when they become parents. Addressing balance in a way that allows women, and a growing number of men, to deal with family and negotiate the "opportunity" ladder is critical to retention. This means flex time, job sharing, no glass ceiling installed during maternity/paternity leave, and tackling the childcare issue with more enthusiasm (ideally in the form of on-site facilities).

Ellen Gee, professor of sociology at Simon Fraser University in British Columbia, Canada, says that employers looking for optimum performance need to pay particular attention to the young female employee's requirements. Whereas early boomer career women sought flexible hours and daycare, when such perks were not forthcoming they often hired nannies or dropped out of the workforce. Many Generation Xers and Yers aspiring to motherhood—and women remain the primary parents—have less relative income, pricier housing, and no dropout option. They are delaying parenthood significantly longer than boomers did. For some, lack of flexibility in the workplace is causing them to sacrifice the parenting experience altogether—or it's heavily affecting employee loyalty and the health of the next generation's children.

"They need not just flexibility, but recognition by the employer that there is this family/work conflict," says Gee. "They need provisions for when a child gets sick. They need not to be punished attitudinally." Mortgage assistance plans and paternity leave are also on Gen X's and Y's wish lists.

Finally, awareness of the *cultural diversity factor* means understanding and communicating across different frames of reference, and tailoring rewards to the context and culture of individuals—not according to traditions based on a more homogenous workforce. Today, one in three Gen X workers belongs to an ethnic minority, and that doesn't even account for overseas-born workers who, by dint of being "white," may not be considered "ethnic," yet come with their own distinct frames of reference. (Immigrants from former communist regimes are just one example.)

PricewaterhouseCoopers—selected as one of the 100 best companies for working mothers in a *Working Mother* magazine rating—has a mentoring program, a new mom's lactation program, workplace flexibility, adoption leave, non-primary care parent leave after birth or adoption, sick leave for family care, and a focus on promoting diversity.

Building a more diverse workforce and training staff in intercultural sensitivity pays, and with ever greater dividends in our increasingly interlinked world, as numerous studies have shown.

The age issue: A tale of three generations

Three generations of workers currently dominate the halls of the work world: the baby boomers (born 1947 to 1966), Generation X (born

1963 to 1977) and the newest graduates from adolescence, often known as Generation Y or the Net generation (born 1978 to 1998). Boomers total more than sixty million Americans, Xers make up forty-seven million, and the Net gen has roughly 12 million so far in the workforce. The major differences between generations—each with potential for conflict—involve work ethic, technical competence, company loyalty, and people skills.

To understand the unique differences in attitude that define generations, we need to contemplate the concept of "value imprinting"—the notion that our experiences between late childhood and early adolescence have a particularly strong influence on how each of us continues to view the world, especially in relation to cultural values. Value imprinting has ensured some sharp differences between how the three generations view work today, although it's crucial to note that the generalizations we make here do not necessarily apply to workers raised outside of North America—a fast-growing segment, to say the least.

Baby boomers received their value imprint during a time of great optimism; the 1960s saw significant economic expansion in North America. Jobs were plentiful and opportunities abounded, most of them nestled within the corporate structure. Due to the sheer size of their segment, boomers were focused on and doted over. Alongside the youthful questioning—the sexual revolution, the bra-burning stage of women's liberation—old values stood their ground. As youngsters, boomers largely experienced stay-at-home moms, and dads who finished work at five o'clock. In their early careers, the sense of long-term rewards for company loyalty was still intact. A deep respect for the longstanding institutions of society—church, education, corporations, and government—was under challenge but not dismantled. Hence, baby boomers still see public service as a legitimate career choice, whereas a recent study by the Nexus Group in Toronto found that public service is not even on the radar screen as a preferred career option for the Net generation.

The baby boomers were imprinted with a few contradictions: Question authority but climb the corporate ladder. Think for yourself but the company will take care of you. And above all, affluence is your destiny. What did not imprint was the notion that finding a job could be a problem.

The views of today's boomers reflect these values: They rebel against authority but instinctively desire it. Deep down, they believe companies should be loyal, and they feel betrayed that this appears to be no longer the case. And after years of working to achieve the good life, they find that the definition of the good life they bought into appears to exclude what they valued most as children: family and leisure time. Having hit midlife, they feel guilty about what their work has done to their home life, and they feel a tug towards the ideals of their youth. They are focused on defining and achieving a work/life balance, a new priority induced by work burnout and/or the sense that they can now afford to rebel against long hours.

The boomers' dilemma is in direct contrast to younger workers' determination to achieve balance for the sake of family and health, even if it means taking a hit in terms of career and earnings so that they don't turn out like their out-of-balance parents and older siblings. (Besides, they've correctly assessed that two-way corporate loyalty and long-term payback is no longer there.)

Finally, baby boomers in the United States also experienced the civil rights and anti-war movements, the birth of the Peace Corps, and the "save the world" activism that these movements spawned. Boomers often have a nascent desire to be involved in pursuits more profound than the bottom line. Many feel that they "sold out" on several fronts, and want to correct that before it's too late.

When it comes to imprints, Generation X, on the other hand, got a rough start. They were imprinted at the height of a brutal recession in the late 1970s and early 1980s and took dead-end jobs outside their field, or entry-level positions with promises, but few prospects, of moving up. This early work experience confirmed or strengthened that imprint. Corporate cost cutting ensured them lower pay than their predecessors received for many years. Underemployment was their middle name, living at home their nightmare. They delayed long-term relationships and parenting, watched their pre-boomer parents get downsized with no regard for a lifetime of loyalty, and observed older boomer siblings working sixty-hour work weeks with little job security and less life to show for it. Again, this early imprint formed the tendency toward what boomers often describe as cynicism. (Perhaps it's actually a reality check.)

Then there is the Net generation. By the time they arrived at their imprint age, a new world of work was emerging. Many grew up in single-parent or blended families, and their mothers were very likely to work outside the home. Time spent alone and independently was common to these latchkey children, who observed the dawn of the entrepreneurial age and, unlike boomers, viewed corporate loyalty as a thing of the past.

Like John's elementary-school son, the Net generation accepted from a young age that they would have to learn and fend for themselves. They glimpsed the formation of a two-tier system, one that treated skilled workers like gold and all but discarded those without technical skills. By the time they entered college, a college degree had the same value as their parents' high school certificate. Throughout their growing-up years, technology was a favored companion. When the game got boring, they simply pressed reset. Likewise, since yesterday's big issues—the ozone hole, global warming—had become so big that no individual could be expected to change them, they learned to focus on local issues and tune out grand schemes.

> The key to training the younger generation, according to Marc Prensky, CEO of games2train.com, is to create hip, "twitch-speed" experiences with the newest technology.

Indulged by their wealthy and materialistic boomer parents as children, the Net kids have less experience than Xers of deferred pleasure and deferred career attainment. This has given them both more confidence and a sometimes overblown sense of entitlement. Also, while Gen X was the first generation to experience an epidemic of parental divorce, Netters learned to view various family configurations as normal. They're also more apt than any previous generation to embrace cultural diversity and flattened hierarchies as the norm. This in itself may heighten their sensitivity to age-related issues, especially subtle X–Y divisions that boomer bosses may fail to see or address.

Members of the Net Generation, like their older boomer coworkers, share a world of contradictions. All their early independence has made them averse to rules and hierarchy, yet they long for mentoring, community, and recognition. They want the benefits of community—belonging—without its bane (rules, procedures, and structure).

How do all these generational differences determine retention strategies that work? Above all, establish flexibility in the workplace, through and through. That's No. 1. It speaks to all three generations, albeit for different reasons. A policy that says, "This is the schedule. Take it or leave it," worked for boomers years ago, but as more of them reach the option of early retirement, they may just leave it. Generations X and Y are even more likely to leave it, or to feel "less engaged" with their assignments in such a regime.

The No. 2 retention strategy should be attempting to bond this disparate workforce. Multigenerational conflicts, like multi-ethnic tensions, must be addressed proactively, through policies that promote mutual respect. From sending around magazine articles or Web site items on the topic, to encouraging a discussion group or sending departments off to seminars, there are many options for heightening generation-gap awareness and meeting the challenge head-on.

Ensure that teams are multigenerational, and that one segment is not inadvertently trampling on the others' potential input. Keep in mind that Gen Xers tend to see boomers as making decisions and then calling for a pseudo-discussion to secure a stamp of approval. Further, Xers' history and their sense of detachment from a company's long-term plans make them reluctant to speak up at all, let alone in multi-generational meetings. Why should they waste time on a done deal, and why should they care if they're only investing a year or two in the company to grab some experience before setting up their own business? Perhaps the boomers' tendency to "over discuss" and the Net generation's cockiness and naive belief that they can change the world annoy Xers. Perhaps they feel outnumbered, outranked, or sandwiched between an army of oldsters and post-teens. Perhaps, like Netters, they'd be more vocal in an intranet discussion group, or through e-mail.

On the other hand, boomers may feel that no one pays attention when they offer an opinion, especially if it involves a high-tech issue. They may feel discouraged that no one else seems to care, and stop offering valuable input as a result. They may resent reporting to the increasing number of supervisors younger than themselves, an issue that can be dealt with through good leadership (see Chapter 7).

Boomers may hanker for a full team effort accomplished through face-to-face brainstorming meetings, while X and Y employees prefer to puzzle things out through a series of e-mail discussions, or each take away a portion they can call all their own, and bring it back resolved, in an entrepreneurial fashion.

We reflected earlier on the irony of younger workers possessing both hard-edged cynicism and a fire to change things. Here's a boomer manager, quoted in *Civilizing the Workplace*, who has acquired a positive spin on this issue: "Some of our younger employees are an odd mixture of pseudo-sophisticated cynicism and high ideals. I try to find a way to break through the cynicism and capitalize on those ideals. I don't always succeed, but I try to let them know that it's their job to put meaning back into the workplace. Nobody else can do it for them."

There have always been generation gaps, but back when each segment was relatively homogenous, and change occurred at a snail's pace, the gaps were more easily bridgeable. Today, it takes a skilled leader—and one who is well aware of all the potential rifts just named—to pull more from teams than the sum of their individual parts. This is particularly true when each group has a radically different receptivity to the concept of hierarchy and the career as self-identity in the first place.

Workforce magazine recently advised managers on how to better retain employees: Tie rewards directly to performance, offer rewards closer to the time of the actions deserving them (immediately being ideal), create varying kinds of financial rewards, and consider pay-increase cycles. Also, increase employees' control over their physical workspace and address work/life balance and training needs.

In short, today's business leader, like today's marketer, is faced with a more fragmented "customer base," requiring more use of intuition and developing-technology to keep the ranks satisfied in precisely the manner to which each would like to become accustomed. Embrace the possibilities, lose workers or let polarization and mayhem rule. In today's super-competitive market, is there really a choice? In the end, he or she with the best leadership skills for bringing together a diverse employee-base wins.

Let's contemplate the biggest differences between the generations:

TREND: Younger workers are more entrepreneurial.

RETENTION STRATEGY: It's wise to give younger workers more autonomy, and to reward top performance with the training for which they yearn (gradually, like slices of a carrot stick)—training they see as eventually allowing them to go out on their own. To those who think, "But if I do that, I'll lose them," we reply: "If you don't do that, you'll lose them anyway, and you just *might* keep them." Provide plenty of opportunities for them to ask questions, adapt information to the scenarios they present, and re-engineer titles to help them feel more entrepreneurial. (At a Richmond, Virginia, marketing agency called Play, some of the more unusual titles include "Voice of Reason" and "What's Next Strategist.")

NOTEWORTHY: Fifty-four percent of eighteen- to twenty-four-year-olds are highly interested in starting businesses, compared with 36 percent of thirty-five to sixty-four-year-olds. Eight of ten US adults trying to start a business are in the eighteen to thirty-four age group. In contrast, only 2 percent of the Harvard graduating class of 1942 showed any interest in self-employment. Also, one out of eight employees moonlights, and the fact that between thirty-five and fifty-seven of these own their own moonlighting business means it's likely that many are "incubating" an enterprise they hope will one day support them.

TREND: Older adults are feeling increasingly insecure, because for the first time in history, the tables are turning; layoffs are now more likely to hit boomers (people in their forties and fifties), whose fat salaries and—in some cases—lack of technological expertise appear to make them easy targets. And don't expect Gen Xers to feel like pulling out the violins for them. The shoe was on the other foot last round.

RETENTION STRATEGY: Wise leaders go out of their way to make boomers feel their positions are secure, and offer them training that keeps them up-to-date technologically. Incidentally, although fewer older than young adults are currently set up to go online (19 percent of the fifty-plus crowd compared with 30 percent of under-thirties), users fifty-five and older *spend more time online* than their younger counterparts.

Retention-savvy companies are inaugurating mentoring programs, which serve not only to ease the leadership transition, but also to make both older and younger workers feel more valued. Managers need to encourage oldsters to tell stories of "how it was done" to counteract their fear of looking stupid or outdated. Remember, too, to present change in a positive manner, explaining its benefits to overcome many older workers' risk-averse natures.

NOTEWORTHY: Young adults suffered an unemployment rate twice the national average for most of the 1990s, but now age discrimination is catching up with boomers, counterbalanced only by a strong economy that asks some of them to stay beyond retirement age to ease the transition. By 2003, for the first time ever there will be more workers over forty than under forty. Also, computer ownership among individuals over fifty has grown 38 percent in four years. In fact, 40 percent of over-fifties own a computer. When management firm Watson Wyatt Worldwide asked close to one thousand CEOs at what age they felt people's productivity peaked, the average response was forty-three.

TREND: Younger workers are less likely to wrap up their self-identity in work.

RETENTION STRATEGY: Spend more time explaining the importance of a particular project or training session, discussing how it fits with the company's corporate culture and what it will do for one's career. Also, allow them to express skepticism without generating disapproval, and take pains to make work fun.

NOTEWORTHY: Only 46 percent of Gen Xers identify their jobs as an "expression of themselves," compared with 56 percent of boomers.

TREND: Younger workers process information fast, intuitively breaking down big chunks into smaller bites.

RETENTION STRATEGY: Switch them to new projects faster than has been done in the past, and when holding meetings or soliciting their input, keep in mind the following statistics: Television programs change scenery every twenty seconds. Trainers speaking to younger crowds have been advised to change their message or activity every eight, ten or fifteen minutes.

TREND: Since young people have a strong interest in "making a difference" in the world, companies inclined to help them with that goal will garner more loyalty. Boomers once felt that way too (remember Sixties idealism?), and in their later years, their material desires largely satiated, they're more than inclined to rekindle some of that fire, especially if the company initiates a strategy.

RETENTION STRATEGY: See Chapter 5, which deals with expanding a company's activities to serve a noble cause.

NOTEWORTHY: Three-quarters of college students say that making a difference in the lives of others is very important, and more than half say doing volunteer work is a worthy cause. Gen X volunteers more than any other generation in America. One expert has said of the Net generation, "They want spirituality incorporated into the company culture, more flexibility than even Generation X wants, and more information, more quickly."

TREND: Boomers enjoy competition and tend to be extroverted. Gen Xers are less inclined to stand out or speak up. The Net generation is particularly comfortable socializing and communicating via the Internet.

RETENTION STRATEGY: Instead of calling on people in a meeting, have people pick one another, perhaps via a talking stick. No one likes being put on the spot, and requests for a volunteer to "go first" may encourage the same few extroverts to set the tone every time. Generate other ideas for making participation feel safer. Involve younger workers right away and cater to older people's preference for interaction and discussion without frustrating younger people's desire to resolve an issue and get on with it. (Give workers the choice of participating in face-to-face or e-mail discussions, then link the two discussions to ensure a full flow of communication and input overall.)

TREND: Boomers have grown up with more structure and rules than younger generations.

RETENTION STRATEGY: Introduce plenty of ground rules and make expectations clear to prevent projects and meetings from turning into a party, while leaving room for enterprising behavior. Check regularly to ensure that everyone is helping to keep a project or session on track and relevant.

The gender gap

Which has more power to determine a pay gap, ethnicity or gender? The correct answer is gender. In fact, while seven out of ten human resources professionals believe minorities encounter barriers to career advancement, nine out of ten believe women do.

The five primary stumbling blocks for women are:

1. corporate cultures that favor men
2. stereotypes and preconceptions of women

3. a lack of women on boards of directors
4. exclusion from informal networks
5. management's perception that family responsibilities will interfere with work

After founding an "Office of Retention" to reduce high turnover, Ernst & Young in New York began helping women network and find mentors.

The key to counteracting these obstacles is gaining high-level support for women in professional and senior roles, and putting more dedicated efforts into recruiting and retaining senior female managers.

Note that pay and advancement are not the top priority of working women. At a recent Los Angeles conference for women graduates in business, 48 percent of participants said balancing work and family represented the largest issue facing women today. Equal work for equal pay ranked a distant second, and the glass ceiling placed third. Ninety percent of attendees said they planned to start a family, and 78 percent of those said they would keep working when they had children.

Given these statistics, is it any wonder that women today can't fathom why employers continue to panic when they become pregnant? Unlike fifty years ago, the vast majority remain in their jobs, take minimal leaves of absence and stop at one or two children. Most women return to work within six months after giving birth, according to Catalyst, a research organization specializing in women's careers. Yet one-fifth of all complaints received by the Canadian Human Rights Commission in 1998 involved allegations on the basis of sex, and a disproportionate number of those concerned women who suffered adverse consequences when their employers learned they were expecting.

Even as achieving a work/life balance moves up the priority list of male workers, there's no disputing that it's a hotter button with working women, whose numbers have grown exponentially. Fifty years ago, only a third of working-age women in the United States (and far fewer in Europe) worked outside the home. By 1990, the number had leapt to 57 percent, and today, it stands at 61 percent. Meanwhile, two-thirds of unmarried mothers with a child under three are now in the labor force, compared with just over half in 1995. While only 3 percent of the most senior jobs in Fortune 500 companies are currently held by women, more than four hundred of the Fortune 500 companies have at least one woman on their board. And in Canada, two of every five managers and one in five senior managers are women.

Given the combination of a strong economy, growing labor shortage, and high number of educated women in the workforce, gender-based glass ceilings and walls may well shatter of their own accord. According to US Bureau of Labor statistics, the pool of talent that will supply the next generation of workers will soon be dominated by women and ethnic minorities. Indeed, the book *Megatrends 2000* reports that women have taken two-thirds of all the new jobs in the information economy. That will make their demands difficult to ignore.

> In an effort to stem a tide of departing women, Deloitte & Touche in Wilton, Connecticut launched a cultural revolution called Women's Initiative, which dramatically changed the environment to one more sensitive about the need for balancing work and home.

As *Megatrends 2000* states, *"There are not nearly enough people with college degrees or advanced vocational and technical training to fill the more than two million new managerial, administrative and technical jobs coming on-line annually. Without mass immigration from Western Europe (unlikely since it is entering its own boom years) or mass liberalization of immigration laws, there is no way the United States will have the optimum workforce needed in the information economy."*

While balance may be women's biggest issue (59 percent of working mothers would relinquish a day's pay for extra time off, while only 43 percent of fathers would do so), savvy business leaders slip other insights into their toolboxes. For instance, "When it comes to praise in the workplace, women like it in writing, boomers like it more than they get it, and small companies are quickest to hand it out," quips *Inc* magazine, explaining an *Inc.*/Gallup survey.

Research has also shown that women are more receptive to and appreciative of detailed feedback and assistance from others, and that female managers in organizations that offer flexible work hours experience a significantly higher level of organizational commitment and job satisfaction.

As mentioned previously, women also value relationships in different ways than men. According to a US Bureau of Labor study, the No. 1 predictor of job satisfaction for women is the relationships they form at work. Therefore, employers are wise to encourage social mixing by creating places for it, and to put as much effort into evaluating how employees work together as they do for what work employees are accomplishing. It's a subtle distinction, but so effective in keeping valued female employees.

Diversity

The North American workforce is increasingly diverse in terms of ethnicity and national origin, as earlier statistics in this chapter indicate. Given this diversity, it is reasonable to wonder whether the shifts discussed in this book are a fair representation of the needs of that diverse workforce. Although a broad exploration of this issue is beyond the scope of this book, there are two key points to be made. First, John has made presentations on the shifts discussed in this book in Europe and throughout South America over the past year, afterwards asking audiences how relevant these shifts are locally. And most of the managers with whom he spoke suggested that these expectations hold true for their workforces, too.

> Companies with diverse boards reap greater market returns, according to a recent study.

AES, a global power company with offices from China to Central and South America, has conducted a worldwide values study for a number of years. According to Dennis Bakke, CEO of AES, "There are no differences on [the results] of those values surveys from all over the world." That is, what an increasingly educated workforce wants from work appears to be reaching a point of convergence. Although our experience and that of AES is largely anecdotal, together they point in the direction of alignment. Having said that, we'd like to add that the key for your organization is to manage diversity in a way that both values and responds to the differences that do exist, not only because it is the right thing to do but because it makes for a sensible human resources strategy.

"Effective management of a diverse workforce translates into bottom line results. That's different from saying just because you are diverse you are going to get the benefits of that diversity," David Thomas, a professor of organizational management at Harvard University, has said.

As much as North Americans boast of being a melting pot or mosaic of cultures, their cultural sensitivity has a long way to go. And yet, as a region with a long history of accepting immigrants, North America is well positioned to capitalize on global connections as the Internet and increased global trade all but melt international boundaries.

Theoretically, a skills-based economy abolishes class, gender, ethnic, and racial divides and judges people purely on merit.

"Many computer companies don't bother with affirmative action programs. The attitude is, 'Let's just get the best talent,'" says Phyllis Swersky, executive vice-president and chief financial officer at Artificial Intelligence Corporation, a software maker for IBM mainframes.

Certainly, young Asians who felt their career ladders blocked by Asia's more hierarchical system streamed into Silicon Valley, where almost a third of the region's scientists and engineers are now Asian-born. That's Asia's loss and North America's gain, proving that in the new economy, a work environment seen as democratic and supportive of diversity wins the talent pool. Another example: Of the 36,000 Chinese students who have gone to the US to study since 1979, only 8,800 have returned to China.

> Alagasco of Birmingham, Alabama, recently offered a $500 prize to employees for an idea that address is diversity problem in their area.

As the current skilled-worker shortage grows more acute, educated immigrants and minorities—especially from such youth-filled countries as China and Mexico—will soon be sought after. They'll be catered to with all the intensity that North American information technology workers currently experience. Companies that get a head start on this process will be tomorrow's winners. A reputation for actively supporting minorities today is the ticket to success tomorrow.

For now, however, efforts to retain minority workers typically lack bite. As *Organizational Dynamics Magazine* has put it, "Current corporate attempts to address the specific needs of these new workers tend to consist merely of isolated programs…managed at relatively low organizational levels and rarely connected to larger strategic initiatives.

Hence, the benefits of these programs to organizations go largely unrecognized, while the benefits to individuals may be overstated."

Moreover, as groups of new immigrants arrive each culture brings its own age and gender issues, causing old battles to be fought all over again, and new views or solutions to be heard. Managers who tune into these team-dampening undercurrents are well advised to meet diversity challenges head-on, after securing plentiful resources and support.

Companies that have introduced initiatives for helping workers deal with the tension and conflict created by differences among them tend to include any or all of five approaches:

1. Multi-cultural and skill-building workshops that focus on group norms and behavioral do's and don'ts.
2. A program of "Celebrating Differences" that offers a calendar of cultural and educational events.
3. "Cross-cultural" or "inter-cultural" workshops that help participants learn the norms and practices of different countries.
4. Organizational development activities that focus on team building and values clarification.
5. Personal development through dialogues in small, ongoing groups.

Finally, there's a new trend afoot, often called the reversal of the melting pot syndrome, which fosters the sense that each interest group must be catered to on its own terms. If that sounds unreasonable, think again. As discussed in Chapter 2, technological developments have allowed us to "customize" marketing messages, an edge highly applicable to retention if human resources professionals want to reach different groups of employees with different messages. From an intranet bulletin board for Hispanic employees to custom-delivered holiday messages, the possibilities are endless.

> Companies with greater diversity make better business partners and merge more smoothly with other companies.

Apply the following comment from a 1993 article in *Advertising Age* to employee retention, and you're on the right track: "Marketers must start from scratch in the language of each target market, work within the context of the original culture and formulate copy and design rooted in the culture itself. And if you end up with ten different campaigns, so be it."

As with most of the shifts covered in this book, we're talking about a hope having become an expectation: "In education, minorities once thrilled to have their languages on schools' curricula at all, are now insisting that their children be taught the history, literature, myths and music of their cultures of origin," says Regis McKenna in *Real Time.*

Etec Systems, a manufacturer in Hayward, California, is a company that emphasizes cultural training as a customer service skill. Employees attend courses in communication, culture, and customer service. "Passport Day," an optional activity, immerses workers for ninety minutes per day in each of three cultures. Cultural training touches on geographical location, geopolitics, cultural values, roles and relationships, communication styles, and the effect of culture on business relationships. The bottom-line message: Diversity is appreciated.

Why spend all the money and effort to promote such a message? "Minority-friendly companies tend to be superior performers," states a *Fortune* article. "Diverse groups make better decisions. If everybody in the room is the same you'll have a lot fewer arguments and a lot worse answers.... Diversity is a competitive advantage."

When John first began speaking to business audiences about the generational differences in values at work, he received plenty of feedback confirming that the differences are real. That is why we've taken the time to identify how gender, age, and ethnicity affect perspectives. And yet, age, gender gap, and cultural factors are not as profound a force in today's work world as the six shifts we describe next—shifts that largely transcend demographic influences in the long run.

The bottom line is that today's leader is faced with a new kind of worker, one whose fundamental values and desires about work is changing. We now move on to deal with these shifts, and to offer ideas for leaders who are anxious to respond to them in ways that promise significantly higher retention and engagement.

PART TWO

The six expectations of the
new workforce

4

The expectation of balance and synergy

"The key to the good life lies in balance and integration in all facets of our lives."

— *THE GOOD LIFE*

At a large health organization in Western Canada, the corporate culture was so linked with overwork that all 18,000 employees regularly pushed the envelope of how much work and how little life could be fit into a day. Leaving the building late at night and carrying bulging brief-cases home appeared to be *de rigueur* for managers of all levels. One day, however, the CEO stood before his entire management team and announced, "I don't want to lead an organization where no one feels they can have a life. We can't sustain it. I want each of you to push back on me, and on each other, when the demands are unreasonable."

Did the corporate culture change overnight? Of course not. But recognition by senior leadership of the tension building at this company was a critical first step.

The desire for greater balance and harmony between work and one's personal life comprises the first of the six shifts in what today's workers want from work. More than any of the other shifts, this one cuts across all demographic differences, even though its permutation varies. At first glance, this newfound desire appears to stem from longer work hours and demands. But a deeper look suggests that not only will workers today sacrifice a great deal to have more flexibility and personal time, they harbor an unmistakable desire for these two aspects of life to become more synergistic. By this, we mean that they want less compartmentalization of their lives, more flow across the boundaries, and a deeper trust that being their "full" selves at work won't be held against them. A boss who understands this desire and taps into it for boosting retention gives time off freely to allow employees to nurse a sick relative, comes through when asked unexpectedly for advice about a romantic entanglement, or organizes a surprise staff party to celebrate the recent tennis trophy they mentioned winning.

"There are companies that don't want people to talk about their personal lives, but I say, 'Bring it on.' If people can get something off their chests for an hour, then I've got them for the next ten," says Paula Lawlor, founder of Medi-Health in King of Prussia, Pennsylvania. Employees there are allowed to bring their children to work and to arrange their schedules around their families' needs. Anyone can take a three-month leave of absence without risking job security.

A wise company not only supports but proactively steers employees towards getting and maintaining a life outside of work. Old-style, old-economy leaders will be initially uncomfortable with this approach. We promise, however, that they'll be with the program and brimming with original ideas by the end of this chapter.

In Japan, divorced men lose work promotions on the assumption that if they can't manage home life, they are poor bets for managing work life. In contrast, our culture since the Industrial Age has been

rather proud of the way it has partitioned work and the rest of life. Surely this church-and-state-style separation has led to more work efficiency and personal privacy, has it not?

Let's counter that question with three others. First, were the two ever successfully separated, even in the old economy? (Hint: Back in the 1950s, wives of executive candidates were sometimes interviewed along with their husbands, and the CEO's wife could tell lower-ranking corporate wives how to decorate their homes.) Second, since technology and the new economy have blurred the lines between work and personal life, and societal changes have seriously wounded former after-work support systems, how valid remains the notion that the separation serves efficiency and privacy? And third, in whose interest were the two sides separated, and who's in the driver's seat now? (Hint: Answers to choose from are management and employees.)

Workers want more balance and synergy, and they want it now. Emerging signs of the "balance revolution" are everywhere. Workers say they'd be willing to give up a whopping 21 percent of their work hours *and salary* to achieve more balance—nearly double the amount they reported being willing to sacrifice just seven years ago. A lack of balance between work and personal life is one of the top six reasons why new managers fail. But perhaps most telling of all, a poll of all employees on flexible schedules at one major company found that 65 percent of them would have left the firm without the flex time.

Younger workers are especially inclined this way. Sixty percent of men and women under age twenty-five with children say they would make "a lot" of sacrifices in money and career advancement in order to spend more time with their families. Fifty-five percent of eighteen- to thirty-four-year-olds identify the freedom to take extended leaves or sabbaticals as a key workplace benefit.

Having control over one's time ranks ahead of everything but making money and using one's brains, according to a 1995 report of "the new work ethic" by Demos, a public-policy think tank in London. And the desire for flexibility is not generation-specific. Workers close to or past retirement age want flexibility to catch up on all the things that a lifetime of work has put off. In any case, when the boomers' mass retirement begins to wreak havoc with an already mushrooming employee shortage—spawning a need to increase the labor participation of those over fifty-fives by 25 percent—flexibility will be the key to wooing some of them to stay a little longer. The alternative is convincing younger workers to put in longer hours (good luck) and/or opening immigration floodgates, which is more expensive if immigrants lack the proper education and skills training, in any case.

There is a growing awareness in North America that home life and work life impact each other in significant ways. In *The Corporate Mystic*, Gay Hendricks and Kate Ludeman write, "Many people mess up by trying to get their home needs met at work, and vice versa. A person who is hurting because he does not know how to communicate

with his kids becomes a blustery communication obstructer at work. Another person walks in the door at night so full of undigested work issues that no one in the family can get through to her. This problem, unless corrected, becomes a self-fulfilling spiral downward. He or she spends more time at work to get away from home problems, which creates more conflict at home, which causes them to withdraw into work more."

Leading-edge companies have begun to tackle the tricky business of creating a workplace that respects workers' personal lives. At the center of this shift is the need to see work through the lens of personal life. Work affects personal life in a myriad of ways, from the time away from home on business trips to childcare issues. There is also a growing body of evidence that when employers demonstrate sensitivity toward these issues and move to help employees resolve conflicts, retention and productivity rise accordingly.

Who's trying it out?

- At Capital One, vacation days are now available on half an hour's notice.
- The eye-drug maker Alcon Laboratories gives employees up to $10,000 for transportation costs to be with ill family members.
- If you get married while at credit card company MBNA (No. 34 on the Top 100 to Work For list), you get an extra week of vacation. And should you have kids, there are six childcare centers and college scholarships of up to $32,000 for employees' kids.
- Intel offers an eight-week sabbatical after only seven years on the job because employee surveys showed that workers view sabbaticals, which offer the ability to pursue one's dreams, as especially compelling.
- At AFLAC in Columbus, Georgia, employees can take up to twelve weeks at full pay to care for an ill spouse, child or parent.

Clearly, each of these companies believes there will be a payoff in the form of retention and engagement. Or maybe they feel they have no choice but to try *something*. For employers the critical question is, when people say they want balance and synergy, what does that mean? How do employees view these issues, and what do they really want from leaders? What are the components in life in need of balancing, and what constitutes synergy between work and the rest of one's life, anyway?

According to a MORI survey conducted in both 1981 and 1991, the four major factors that contribute to happiness are health, family life, employment, and financial considerations. Yesterday's employers felt they could influence or support only one of these—employment—but today's forward-thinking companies are expanding that frame of reference.

A balanced "diet"

Above all, today's worker wants a balanced "diet." If the four "food" groups have always been work, family, leisure, and health, society has been bingeing with growing intensity on work at the expense of the other three since the 1950s. Of course, if work and the material goods it buys weren't rewarding, society would never have reached this point. But it has to stop somewhere.

Time spent on the job in a given year has increased by 163 hours in the last twenty years, translating into about an extra month of work time, while leisure has declined by one-third. All this at a time when a stable family life and community involvement (still our best stress-busters) appear to be unraveling right along with job security. Like bodybuilders who get muscle-bound from overdeveloping one set of muscles in relation to another, we need to back off, reflect, and build a new program. Workers are way ahead of management on this, and as the power dynamic between them shifts, only the companies that understand and respond will succeed.

After three years on the job, store managers at San Francisco-based Jamba Juice receive three weeks of paid time off toward a sabbatical of up to two months (as well as a retention bonus).

It's time to rebalance for overall, long-term health and happiness. If this means taking a few days off, joining a volleyball team, or doing a bit of volunteer work, employees who can do so guilt-free and on work time—maybe even at their manager's suggestion—will reward their company with a loyalty that no money can buy. If workers also get positive reinforcement for it from a boss who appears to genuinely care, just watch their dedication soar.

At Ernst & Young, employees have permission not to answer their voice mail and e-mail over weekends and while on vacation, and committees monitor employee overtime and redistribute work when the total workload consistently registers more than fifty to fifty-five hours per week.

Workers need company brass to take the lead on the balance issue. Forty-one percent of British managers say they are disappointed with the work/life balance they find in their current job and 85 percent believe vacation should be compulsory. Yet 48 percent of people say they feel guilty when they leave on time. The culprit here is the outdated "face time" tradition, in which work is measured by presence rather than output.

> Six weeks of vacation time is standard at the German software firm SAP AG, and employees—who are allowed to accumulate time off—sometimes take months off after completing a project.

At the workplace of one of John's clients, an international real estate investment firm, employees told us that they felt it was more beneficial to play solitaire for an hour on their computers around leaving-time, than actually to exit at five o'clock. This company's entire corporate culture is built around the belief that putting in long hours signals commitment. The first step for this client was to recognize the company's dysfunctional focus on long hours over productivity. Such a focus is often based on the misguided notion that working more hours leads to greater productivity.

Benjamin Hunnicutt, a historian at the University of Iowa, has spent a lifetime advocating the six-hour workday as optimal for human performance. Whether or not he is correct, today's leaders are well advised to seriously question whether long hours devoid of personal time can truly lead to better performance.

Here are a few findings that suggest this is not the case:

In a recent survey, 43 percent of junior managers said they value their home life more than work time, while only 20 percent of chairpeople, chief executives, and managing directors said the same. And yet, 55 percent of *all* these managers admitted that long hours actually made them *less productive*.

Similarly, a 1998 Watson Wyatt Canada survey of managers and employees found that half of middle managers believe that working long hours has more to do with inefficiency than workload. And only one-third feels that companies do enough to help staff maintain a healthy work/life balance. Current policies are shrugged off as mere window dressing.

Dr. James Mass, author of *Power Sleep*, advocates allowing workers to take power naps during their breaks as a healthier alternative to caffeine-laden drinks. He also believes that employers who ensure that shift workers receive sufficient sleep reduce accident rates by 40 percent.

As a thirty-six-year-old employee told us, "It's normal in my company to hear negative jabs about people who leave at five, or who take lunch, even if they have incredible output. If your boss works until ten, you feel coerced to do the same. I want the flexibility to spend time with my family, and I get frustrated that face-time is valued over accountability or actual quality of work."

The solution, of course, lies in senior managers sending an important message to employees by focusing on results rather than hours worked—and role modeling some balance themselves.

There are indications that company leaders are rising to the challenge of workers' need for balance:

- Large companies report that over the past five years, the percentage of their workforce who share jobs has risen by 81 percent, while the number that work from home has climbed 70 percent. Ninety percent of large companies expect more employees to work from home in the next two to three years, and three-quarters predict more job sharing.
- Retailers, law firms, and management consulting firms in the UK are using sabbaticals for retention with increasing popularity.

Angela Brown, policy advisor for the Institute for Personnel and Development, says, "Rather than lose them completely, you eventually get them back, hopefully happier and more skilled."

- A study of eight hundred employers indicates that 79 percent of corporate employees have formal policies for regular part-time employment, and 38 percent have flex-time arrangements. Another 34 percent provide for compressed work schedules and 26 percent have job-sharing programs. Telecommuting programs are offered by 17 percent of employers, with an equal number considering or developing them.

- Worker satisfaction with workplace flexibility has risen substantially over the past decade, from 39 to 56 percent "completely satisfied" in 1991 and 1999 respectively, according to a 1999 Gallup poll.

- As already stated in Chapter Two, by the year 2010, one in every five Americans will be a telecommuter, experts estimate.

All this is just as well, considering that job stress is estimated to cost US industry $200 billion to $300 billion annually in absenteeism, diminished productivity, employee turnover, accidents, workers' compensation, and direct medical, legal, and insurance fees. Not to mention that Employee Assistance Programs typically save employers between $5 and $16 for each dollar spent, and are correlated with alcohol-abuse recovery rates of 50 to 75 percent.

Responding to the shift towards balance

Gemcom Services in Vancouver, a mining software producer that employs primarily Gen Xers and Yers, views employee retention as a life-or-death matter, and supervisor Mark Metin attributes the firm's low turnover to its relaxed management structure, flex time, social atmosphere, and emphasis on honest communication and positive feedback. Above all, he stays vigilant for burnout, actively discouraging sixty-hour weeks.

"This industry tends to burn people out extraordinarily quickly. Programmers are a different breed, more artists than scientists. Sometimes the inspiration strikes at three in the morning. We have core working hours here, but many special arrangements for people not good at getting up at seven in the morning, myself among them."

A Gen Xer himself, Metin has found that mentoring younger employees with personal problems also goes with the territory. "We make an extra effort to feed people's souls as well as pocketbooks," he explains. "They could get as much money working somewhere else, but we have a family relationship with most people in the company."

Dangerous? Perhaps, although mentoring training should make it less so. Necessary for retention? Absolutely. Untraditional? Who cares? Times have changed, and Metin is a new-millennium manager with his finger on the pulse of the new workforce's needs.

There are employers who scoff at the notion of letting personal matters creep across the office doorstep. But companies mindful that it can cost 150 percent of a worker's salary to replace her understand that boundaries between work and home began fading with the introduction of the cellular phone, laptop computer, and fax. These are the companies that will attract, keep, and maximize the performance of the best workers today. The rest will maintain the necessary number of warm bodies in their ranks while failing to tune in to high turnover and the "B-grade" aspect of their workers.

> In return for completing a health assessment and attending a group counselling session on the results, employees at Fannie Mae receive a "Healthy Living Day" off.

In an age where there is a shortage of educated and self-reliant workers, responding to workers' desire for balance and synergy is a surefire way to win loyalty. A *Fortune* magazine poll of headhunters recently determined that the employees most likely to turn down job offers had flex time. Other studies show that flex time isn't enough on its own; employees are often hesitant to use it if they feel it may sideline their careers. Leaders who are serious about using flex time to increase retention must ensure that no ambivalent messages seep into the process. When a low percentage of workers appears to be taking advantage of such policies, it's time to broadcast a "no strings attached" message and live by it.

John once worked with a company in which a senior manager was denied a promotion because during her interview, she expressed the opinion that taking one's allotted vacation time is key to staying sharp enough to excel. So ingrained was the culture of imbalance at the company interviewing her that no senior person openly challenged the thinking behind rejecting her. When word got out as to why she wasn't hired, lower-ranked employees were reluctant to take vacation time. While we have no statistics on how this affected retention in the long term, we're willing to bet it wasn't positive.

One of the best predictors of retention for women is whether they sense that they can attend to personal life and still develop in the company. That is, flex time and parental leaves mean little to ambitious women who find that exercising these policies puts them on a "mommy track" against their will. Again, double messages and hidden agendas are the usual reasons that expensive perks sometimes have little impact on retention or employee commitment.

Deloitte & Touche, well known as a progressive company, clearly walk their talk. The company boasts at least ten part-timers who have achieved partner status. This remains highly unusual. In most companies, the only part-time person with status is the chairman emeritus!

When Dawson Personnel Systems conducted an in-house survey, they found that their employees rated two items—making a contribution toward the good of the company and spending time with their families—above earning more. Based on this, executives formulated a daring new policy. First, they met with the sales team and assigned it productivity goals 20 percent higher than the previous year. Then they informed these salespeople that as soon as they hit their target, they could go home each day at two o'clock for the rest of the month. Also, the first salesperson to sell more than $50,000

> The service provider DDC Inc. has teamed up with Medela, a supplier of breast pumps and breast-feeding accessories, to offer a new lactation program call M@W (Mothers at Work). M@W offers prenatal training, twenty-four-hour counselling services of a certified lactation consultant, and equipment and support for employers who are introducing the lactation program. The program also provides a guide for managers that explains the benefits of workplace lactation programs and the manager's critical role in the mother's return to work. The program has proven positive for both employee retention and productivity.

would have the last two days of the month off. The result? The team broke every record in the company's fifty-two-year history as members focused like never before and worked well together.

Next, senior management allowed other departments to set their own goals and hours, and promised that for particularly productive weeks, everyone could go home early on Friday. They also mandated a noon closing on holiday weekends. Sales for the year increased by 20 percent, and profits shot up 40 percent.

Roots of the balance revolution

Today's search for balance and synergy has deep roots in North American society. Poet and social commentator Robert Bly has a theory as to how we've reached a point of gross imbalance. As mentioned in Chapter 2, he has written a book called *The Sibling Society*, named for the way in which the parent-child relationship has become a sibling dynamic. Bly says that when the Industrial Age removed men from the home (where, in the Agrarian Age, they mixed work with family and enjoyed more intimate relationships with their children), it eroded their "soft" side and led them to overvalue work and devalue family life. Eventually, they learned to stake their identity, sense of contribution, and self-esteem on the job, which led to increasing hours at work and fewer at leisure and home.

As the Modern Age dawned, women flocked to the world of work, where a "higher" status—compared with the devalued work of parenting—seemed to be waiting. Birth control, liberalized divorce laws, the siren of consumerism and a sense of "pioneering" a new role for womankind all encouraged this. But women became ensconced in the work world just as the global market accelerated business demands to an astounding degree. This, combined with a lack of flexibility for childcare, gave them pause for thought. They applied pressure on male partners to shoulder more household responsibility, only to learn that males (both boomers and Gen Xers) were also growing weary of an overemphasis on achievement and were hankering for intimacy.

Fast-forward to 1993, when Joe Dominguez and Vicki Robin published a book entitled *Your Money or Your Life* that instructed readers on how to live well for less and better align their financial priorities with their values. It has become a national bestseller. Employers who equate salary with retention need to bone up on this text because it represents where things are headed. Example: In the last five years, 28 percent of workers have voluntarily made changes in their life that resulted in making less money, primarily in pursuit of a more balanced life.

New fathers and adoptive parents get six-week paid leaves at Republic Bancorp in Owosso, Michigan.

The graph shown below that charts the relationship between spending and fulfillment says it all. The fulfillment line moves steeply upward, hand-in-hand with money spent, until it reaches a point called "survival." Here, it slows but continues to journey upward in relation to spending until it reaches "comforts." Now its climb tapers significantly, as it wanders toward the peak labeled "luxuries." Here, things get interesting: Fulfillment is now inclined to free-fall unless its owner begins giving *away* time or money. Yes, volunteerism and charity are all that can exert upward lift on fulfillment once it has drunk its fill—even though, curiously enough, individuals continue to believe otherwise for quite some time, according to surveys.

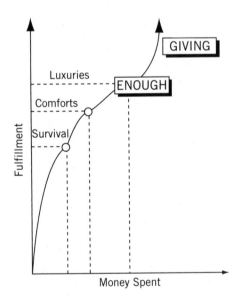

Source: *Your Money or Your Life: Transforming Your Relationship with Money and Achieving Financial Independence.* Joseph R. Dominguez and Vicki Robin (New York: Penguin Books, 1993).

While not everyone in North America has arrived at the post-luxuries dot on the graph flagged "enough," plenty of evidence points to star performers shrugging off raises and gravitating to companies that seem to represent a higher cause. We believe this is occurring with more regularity than in the past, and across generational lines. We'll get into "boosting retention through noble corporate causes" in Chapter 5, but for now, remember that individuals don't always know when they're satiated, or what will re-ignite their fervor. Workers who have been racing blindly for years toward that illusive spending peak often get felled by burnout before they see the light. Leaders who've made note of the graph just described have a canny new insight for retaining and engaging those workers.

Not only do today's workers want synergy between work and non-work hours; they are launching a deep-rooted, unstoppable rebellion against statistics like these:

- In 1935, the average working man had forty hours a week free. By 1990, it was down to seventeen hours.
- Twenty-six percent of males under age forty-five feel that they cannot have a good family life and get ahead in their current job.
- Full-time employees under age thirty-six rate the work/life balance issue above the challenge of their job, the quality of their immediate manager, and the opportunity for promotion.
- The number of managers working forty-nine hours or more a week has risen by 37 percent since 1985.
- Seventy-two percent of British managers surveyed said that long working hours affect their relationship with their partner and eat into the time they spend with their children. Seventy-seven percent said long hours had an adverse impact on their leisure activities, and 59 percent said long hours are damaging their health.
- Nearly one in five employed parents is single, 27 percent of single parents are men, and two-thirds of employed parents with pre-kindergarten children rely on partners and relatives as the primary childcare source. (In other words, childcare is one of the most pressing issues.)
- One out of six primary-age children and two out of five grade-school children arrive home after school to an empty house.

- The majority of babies born in the United States are placed in full-time daycare within a year, commonly within two or three months, so that both their parents can work.
- Nearly a third of the population suffers from a definable psychological problem; depression in particular appears to be growing. Many mental health professionals attribute this to a lack of deep friendships and personal time for reflection, compounded by a lack of time for healthy eating and de-stressing techniques such as exercise.

More than time

As the economy continues to speed up, the desire to add balance by devoting more time to pursuits outside of work grows accordingly. Balance is becoming increasingly critical to workers' mental and physical health. A company of one thousand employees loses $1 million per year in stress-induced absenteeism alone. If so much of workers' waking life must be spent at work, they yearn for work to take on some of the qualities of fun and community that they used to enjoy after hours. And if work no longer lays primary claim to their sense of identity, contribution, and self-esteem, commitment to it is easier to shrug off—unless the workplace deliberately offers synergy in this regard.

Employees of Amgen in Thousand Oaks, California can get free shuttle service to the airport, on-site car rentals, on-site childcare, and an on-site fitness center open seven days a week.

It's also true that an increasing number of men and women are finding themselves alternating between periods of underemployment and overly demanding employment—that is, they are either trying to find work or drowning in it. One of our clients, a senior vice-president at a large bank conglomerate, is fond of answering the question, "How are you?" with the quip, "Like drinking water from a fire hose." Today's workers spend half their time trying to find water and the other half with a sore mouth. Not surprisingly, this contributes to that searing desire for balance and relief from the stress that seeking it in a less-than-supportive environment inflicts. When companies respond to the worker's profound sense of frustration by offering tangible solutions, they impact engagement and retention in a powerful way.

Younger workers are particularly likely to speak of balance as a matter of harmony, not simply time. Again, workers define synergy as feeling free to be themselves, a sense that they need not pretend that the company is their life's work.

The other day John met a twenty-five-year-old woman at a large marketing agency in Washington, DC Although she enjoys her job, she is quick to admit that singing and acting are her first loves. What she appreciates most about her job, she told us, is that the owner understands this and allows her—indeed, encourages her—to talk about her aspirations. She likes the fact that her "real" job supports her outside-work passions. This is synergy.

> At Edward Jones, most brokers qualify for twice a year, expenses-paid jaunts for two to places like Alaska or Pebble Beach.

Workers want the company to take an interest in their personal lives. In a 1998 study, Gallup found that managers who were perceived to care about their staff enjoyed the highest employee engagement. Royal Bank of Canada found a similar rise in productivity when supervisors took an interest in employees' personal lives.

Canadian Pacific/Fairmont Hotels' new annual performance planning process asks employees to set goals for their lives outside of work and to share those goals with their bosses as part of the performance appraisal process. Why? Because the company realizes that younger workers appreciate companies that take an interest in the intersection between these two aspects of life. Contrast this with the senior executive of a bank who asked us in all seriousness, "Isn't it illegal to talk to people about their personal lives at work?" Clearly, he doesn't get it, and odds are, neither does his company.

What is it he and his company are supposed to "get"? They are supposed to get the fact that a powerful phenomenon is reshaping how workers see work and the rest of their lives.

What does the desire for balance mean for your business?

What, you may ask, has all this got to do with the work world? Can't society simply get on with sorting out the balance issues and childcare debate on someone else's time? Isn't how much one indulges in leisure or family time up to the individual in the long run? Work is work, social and family life are private, and it's illegal, impractical, and unprofitable to get involved in workers' private lives, right? Besides, hasn't the business world already responded admirably to the so-called work–family tug by introducing personal days, flex time, corporate daycare, job-sharing, and counseling services?

On the contrary, the bottom line is that workers' efforts to balance the work/life ratio is now part of the corporate landscape, whether we like it or not. Flex time may get great workers to turn their heads your way, but it won't entice them through the door or keep them in your company. And family problems are one of the top five reasons that relocations fail.

At credit card company Total Systems Services, every employee is made to feel an instant part of an extended family. To symbolize this, when the company built a new campus in Georgia, it designed a river walk of bricks, each inscribed with an employee's name.

Today's stars—the highly sought-after, self-reliant, high-tech workers—have come to *expect* flexibility as a *starting point*. They want much more. Where technology initially seemed to offer the freedom and flexibility for which many workers yearned, no one argues that it has also invaded the privacy of their homes. It has inflicted longer, less predictable hours on many. In collusion with fading international boundaries, work across time zones and speeded-up product cycles, work has evolved from a nine-to-five proposition to an "everywhere/anytime" scenario. Fanatical amounts of time spent on the computer now ranks No. 3 on the list of reasons for divorce.

The *Wall Street Journal* recently reported on an Internet search firm executive whose two children, ages nine and fourteen, presented him with a "Family Miles" program—a system of rewards for staying home more, resisting a ringing phone, and "getting home on holidays and breaks without being days late." He responded to the wake-up call by learning to let the phone ring during meals without breaking out in a cold sweat and by working fewer weekends. Today's offices are filled with workers who feel they were robbed of intimacy with their parents by unreasonable corporate demands and by their parents' misguided expectation that loyalty was a two-way street. Determined not to fall into the same mold, today's workers want to be "true to themselves" in each and every chosen role. The point that employers often miss is that this is no idle whimsy; it is a goal for which they'll leave a good job. As Claire Raines writes in *Beyond Generation X*, "Members of the X generation ... have witnessed firsthand a work ethic that eats people up and spits them out—and they want something different.... They believe that work should not be more important than their friends, families, and hobbies."

We're talking about at least two generations' worth of workers aware *at some level* that an all-new balance is required to begin healing hidden wounds and to prevent the next generation from a similar fate. And just as they know that tossing a few tin cans in a recycling box is not going to save an environment in distress, they know—at some level—that flex time in the workplace is less than a finger in the dike of family distress.

Their quiet revolution may even be reaping results already. In 1999, the Families and Work Institute reported that while the amount of time mothers spend with their children (3.2 hours each workday) has remained constant over the last twenty years, the time employed fathers spend with their children (2.3 hours each workday) has increased significantly, by one-half hour per workday. The result is that children are receiving somewhat more attention from their employed parents than they did in 1977. However, 70 percent of all parents still feel they do not spend enough time with their children and that they have less time for personal activities.

> Computer Associates International Inc. in Islandia, New York, is planning a child-development center for four hundred children.

Time is one issue. But as we can't overstate, today's workers want something else they can't quite define, and something many managers are far from willing to accept: balance on a very deep level. Synergy between work and what some euphemistically call their "real life." Acknowledgment, if you will, that their work and personal selves need not be chopped up and displayed selectively to different audiences. Support—physically and psychologically—of their goals and activities outside of work. Confirmation that if work can invade the rest of their lives, then the rest of their lives can do "field trips" to work.

Inc. magazine ran a cover story in 1998 about a worker's request for permission to bring his parrot to work with him. Initially, he received a chilly reception. Eventually, however, the company gave in and the proud employee ended up on the cover of a national magazine, where the parrot clearly symbolized a new fight to fill the world of work with matters previously reserved for the personal realm.

Classic Packaging, a packaging manufacturer based in Vancouver, Canada, pays for employees' music lessons because they believe that if people are learning they will come to work happier, willing to contribute and do their best for the firm. Their employees never hesitate to tell customers it's a great place to work.

Putting it all together

How does a company respond to this search for balance and synergy? As with so many of the shifts we have identified in this book, each organization must find its own best answer, but we have identified some of the trends and supplied examples of companies that have forged creative solutions. It all begins with helping people juggle work and personal life more effectively. For example, companies are taking increasing responsibility for helping their people with the day-to-day challenges of parenting. In 1984, when *Fortune* magazine first started publishing its list of the one hundred best companies to work for in America, only two of the hundred had on-site daycare. Fifteen years later, one-third of the top one hundred had such facilities.

Ninety-five percent of employees at WRQ in Seattle have flex time.

The same is true for things like flexible work schedules. In the early 1980s, only two of the top one hundred offered flex time. By the late 1990s, 87 percent of the top one hundred offered telecommuting, 72 percent offered job sharing, 89 percent boasted the option of a compressed work week, and 70 percent included flexible work schedules. Times have changed, big time. These figures demonstrate how balance has come to be identified with great places to work.

One of the greatest challenges facing company leaders today is ensuring that the desire to support balance and synergy runs deeper than a slogan of the month. That's why at Edward Jones, the brokerage house, managers are encouraged to handle flex-time requests with the following guidance: "Do what is right and human."

Offering flex time and support for people's lives inside and outside of work is not just a retention technique. It is a philosophy. Either a company accepts the need for this synergy or people will leave, even though the company's childcare center is full.

What happens when a company creates balance and synergy? At one manufacturing company, the simple act of changing a work shift to coincide with the end of the school day cut turnover in half and created a buzz in the community that working women should try to get a job at this particular plant. This company is now the employer of choice in its community.

As a young American entrepreneur has said, "The biggest challenge for our generation is providing our own children with what we didn't have: fathers, time, attention, and security."

Work today is filled with ironies. Here is one of the more profound and important ones: On the one hand, work is becoming less important to people. Work has eaten up so much of people's lives that many are saying, "Wait a minute. The rest of my life deserves attention, too." On the other hand—thanks to a lack of job security, more invasive technology, and the new empowerment of front-line workers—work is by necessity a greater obsession than ever. Younger workers, especially, must constantly groom new skills and networks in order to "make a living." Older workers must live with increasing age discrimination and a sense that they had better stay on guard lest they become expendable at work. All of this means that companies must deal with their employees' growing desire for balance and their obsessive compulsion about staying employed. Perhaps it is this paradox—the desire to work less and the need to focus on it obsessively—that drives today's workers to demand more synergy.

A mid-level manager in a large technology company said it best: "In this company, you get the feeling that they really care about your personal life. Whether it's a sick kid, a death in the family, volunteer work you believe in, or a course you want to take, there seems to be a core philosophy that these things are central to productivity. How do I know that? I think it's the little things they do and say every day, not the daycare center. If I can, I'll stay here forever!"

Tazeem Nathoo, Senior Vice President of Operations
VanCity Credit Union
Vancouver, Canada

When talking about VanCity, Tazeem Nathoo is quick to remind listeners of its modest beginnings as a small credit union in an underprivileged area of the city of Vancouver, Canada. Indeed, she credits those beginnings for a corporate culture that has never strayed from its determination to serve and respect people from all walks of life.

Since its early days, VanCity has grown into Canada's largest credit union, renowned for its leadership in corporate social responsibility. With 1,500 employees, it has been voted one of the top thirty-five companies to work for in Canada and one of the top ten companies for women. In 1998, it received the Distinguished Service to Families Award from the B.C. Council for Families.

In an industry where employee turnover averages 18.4 percent, VanCity currently maintains an 11 percent average – all the more astonishing when one considers that its employees are relatively young (the average age is thirty-seven) and 72 percent are women.

Typically, organizations heavily staffed by women suffer high turnover due to women's greater tendency to move for husbands' relocations and their more frequent entries and exits from the workforce for child-rearing. And yet the measures addressing these concerns that many firms consider progressive, Nathoo shrugs off as "the usual ones." VanCity has had flexible hours, four-day workweeks, an ability to work from home, and excellent maternity and paternity benefits for years. It's not always easy to grant these, given the demands of the customer base, but VanCity has never flinched in supplying whatever is needed to attract and keep good employees.

"We have a culture that is renowned for putting people first, and if you want to keep your members happy, you have to make sure your staff are looked after," Nathoo says, adding that retention is becoming ever more challenging in the age of the knowledge worker. Among VanCity's more generous policies is twelve "care days" per year that staff can put aside for their own relaxation needs or for family emergencies. Among the more unusual policies is free provision of a pager to pregnant staff and their partners.

VanCity also takes a strong position on contributing to the community. Not only does the credit union make funds available for community programs, but it encourages staff to get involved as volunteers. It leaves it up to the discretion of managers as to whether employees can do volunteer stints on company time.

One brand-new initiative grants points that lead to prizes for employees who are physically active, nutritionally conscientious, and environmentally sensitive. This Living Well program, which evolved from one that rewarded those who took part in physical fitness programs, was overhauled for a more strategic, preventative-health outlook and a more holistic definition of "living well." Whereas in the past, this program operated on an honor system and supplied participants with gifts like sweatshirts and running shoes, it now focuses on prevention and detection and encourages behavioral change.

As for diversity issues, Nathoo says that originally, the company brought in speakers to stimulate thought and conversation, had a diversity council check out the company for any inadvertent barriers, and ensured that all branches were accessible to the disabled. Eventually, however, the firm found that diversity was a non-issue. After all, this is a credit union that was one of the first to offer loans to women without requiring their father's or husband's signature, and that worked from the start to ensure employees of many different backgrounds excelled within the company. As Nathoo points out, VanCity draws staff from the highly multicultural city of Vancouver, which has inevitably resulted in "a myriad of people" throughout its branches.

"We reflect the diversity, and our staff feel comfortable in their backgrounds. The culture for this was already there."

She looks instead to tomorrow's diversity issues: ensuring that policies and programs for members reflect the reality that women have acquired tremendous purchasing and financial power. "Women are estimated to control more than 80 percent of consumer and household spending, and comprise 40 percent of all Internet users. The number and size of women-owned firms is also increasing. Women's more collaborative and consensus-building leadership style is needed in the new economy, alongside men's generally more controlling style. When you look at corporate senior management and corporate boardrooms, they're still so dominated by white males. The number of women on corporate boards, the number of women CEOs, is pitiful. Don't women make up 50 percent of the population? Where does it say that only one segment of our population should make up corporate boards? How can they claim to reflect the views of a diverse population? Due to globalization and the greater complexity of the world, we need all kinds of minds to come together, people with different perspectives. Those companies that understand and value diversity have the competitive edge."

Assessing your company for balance

Using the statements below, assess how your organization, division, and/or department is doing at responding to employees' search for balance and synergy. The assessment is meant to guide your thinking, not to provide a definitive quantitative assessment of your progress. For each question below, answer how true the statement is of your work environment using the scale provided:

_____ Our company encourages workers to discuss conflicts between personal and work commitments with the supervisor (if yes in general, give yourself 1 point; if managers have been given guidelines for how or why to do so, tally 3 points).

_____ Managers in our company take an interest in the personal, outside-of-work goals of employees (1 point if generally true; 2 points if they're actively encouraged or trained to do so; 3 points if a formal program addressing this is in place).

_____ Our company offers and/or pays for education and training even when it has no immediate, direct work application (1 point if company offers flex time to specifically accommodate this; 2 points if the company subsidizes it; 3 points if company pays in full).

_____ Our company offers flexible hours and/or job sharing (1 point if these are offered, 3 points if people don't lose status or opportunities by taking advantage of them).

_____ Our company offers services to ease the burden of personal chores or stress (on-site concierge or dry cleaning, free massages, subscription to e-mail services such as medical advice) (1 point if available to all permanent, full-time employees; total of 2 if also available to part-time and temporary workers).

_____ Our company offers flexible hours to all workers, not just managers (1 point if available to all permanent, full-time employees; total of 2 if also available to part-time and temporary workers).

_____ Workers who have personal commitments that make it difficult to work overtime are not penalized in terms of status and promotions (2 points).

_____ Both males and females at all levels discuss balance and family openly in our company as a legitimate concern (2 points).

_____ Workers in our organization are encouraged to take their vacation time (1 point).

_____ Our organization supports sabbaticals, where employees take a period of time off to achieve a personal goal (2 points).

_____ Our company actively monitors and attempts to prevent work burnout (1 point if applies to permanent, full-time employees; total of 2 if also applies to part-time and temporary workers).

_____ Our company has managerial guidelines in place to ensure that parents returning from maternity or paternity leave need not feel they have to "re-prove" their dedication. At the same time, we allow all employees the option of designing a less demanding schedule for a chosen period of time that need not lead to a loss in status or promotion (2 points).

_____ We sponsor many events to which workers' families are invited (1 point).

_____ We encourage/underwrite partner accompaniment on some business travel (1 point for encouragement, 2 for encouragement plus underwriting).

_____ We actively address childcare concerns by providing a referral service or on-site or subsidized childcare (2 points for referral; total of 3 if on-site facilities or subsidies are involved).

_____ Our company offers confidential counseling services and/or trains managers to proactively identify and supportively handle employees' "personal" situations (1 point).

_____ Managers in our company actively reward deserving employees with positive reinforcement delivered in creative ways (days off, surprise lunch, personal thank-you notes) (1 point).

_____ Our company organizes social, leisure, or sport clubs/teams (1 point if true for permanent, full-time employees; total of 2 if also open to workers' families and part-time and temporary employees).

_____ TOTAL

SCORE:

20 or under: Take a full week's management retreat for brainstorming policies that address these concerns.

21–25: You're beginning to look responsive.

26–30: You are above average in meeting today's workers' needs, but there is still room for improvement.

31–37: You are an inspiring example, and probably have the best workers and a strong bottom line to show for it. E-mail us: **izzoinc@aol.com**.

5

The expectation of work as a noble cause

"The experience of making a difference and the pleasure of giving something back to the local community pays huge dividends to the company in psychological, cultural, and therefore financial ways."

— CORPORATE CELEBRATION

At the Park Hotel in Charlotte, North Carolina, general manager Wayne Shusko runs a tight ship with a very clear mission: "To exceed the highest expectations of every customer and every colleague in every interaction." From the very first day of orientation, Shusko talks to staff about what these words mean and how to live them out. The first time John stayed at the hotel, he arrived late on a Thursday night for a Friday morning keynote speech. At midnight, he realized he had forgotten his contact lens solution and called down to the front desk in the faint hope that the gift shop might still be open. The front desk clerk said the store would not open until 8:30 a.m., half an hour after John's talk would begin.

"What is it you need, sir?" she pressed. After John explained, she placed him on hold long enough to get security to open up the shop and bring two brands of solution to her. Minutes after asking John if either of these would work, she had the correct one delivered to his room by an attendant who wished John a cheery good night and disappeared before John could even offer him a tip. Clearly, here was a staff that felt they were working for a cause greater than tips or filling rooms; they were inspired by the rewards of *truly* making people feel at home.

Workers today want their work to be about something deeper than the bottom line. They want a sense of sweating for more than a profit: making a meaningful difference in customers' lives or, if their work itself can have no such connection, a strong belief that their company takes its community and global citizenship seriously. If they're going to work longer hours at more complex jobs than previous generations, with less community-oriented time, they need more than a money motive to ignite their enthusiasm and loyalty. Sure, they know their company must make a profit to survive. But those lucky enough to work for companies that give them something else to latch onto—a more noble reason to pour their energies into daily tasks—offer so much more of themselves. This third shift in worker attitudes is about workers wanting to "do good" and make a living all at the same time. Call it multi-tasking in its most noble form, or the "ennobling" of the workforce!

At Lenscrafters, a leading optical chain, employees speak with pride about the company's "Gift of Sight" program to provide eyeglasses for children whose families can't afford them. The company also provides free eye exams and glasses annually to employees.

Companies are increasingly aware of this trend. Mary Kay Cosmetics says it exists to give "unlimited opportunity to women." Merck aims "to preserve and improve human life." Sony plugs the "joy of advancing and applying technology for the benefit of the public." Wal-Mart boasts of giving "ordinary folk the chance to buy the same things as rich people." 3M exists "to solve unsolved problems creatively." Hewlett-Packard is about "making technical contributions for the advancement and welfare of humanity." Walt Disney endeavors "to make people happy."

Then there are the actions beyond the words. Grand Metropolitan, the London-based food and drinks multinational, not only budgets thirteen million pounds annually on community involvement, but has developed a matrix to demonstrate why this tactic is worthwhile. Fannie Mae of Washington, DC, gives employees ten paid hours every month to do community work, and provides grants to nonprofit organizations where employees volunteer their time.

Workers flock to such companies and, all else being equal, stay longer. For companies, that means being "seen to do good" is no longer enough. Donating a hamper of food to the needy at Christmas is not sufficient. Most significantly, options about "doing good" have moved from "warm, fuzzy, and optional" to being key for attracting and keeping talent. Perhaps that is why Oxfam, the charity, receives a constant stream of résumés from high-powered executives looking for a change.

Although people have always appreciated working at companies with a deeper purpose beyond profits and money, we are arguing that a definable shift is occurring; employees now *expect* companies to state and live up to higher aspirations. When Gallup studied employee engagement in 1998, it found that a key predictor of engagement was poll respondents' agreement with the sentence, "The mission statement of the company makes me feel my job is important." This shift is most pronounced among younger workers. Three-quarters of college students say that making a difference in the lives of others is very important. More than half say that doing volunteer work is a worthy cause. And Gen X volunteers more than any other generation in America. Another driver of this shift is the aging of the workforce. Erich Fromm and other psychologists have clearly documented that as human beings age, they move from a focus on self, or what they will take from the world, to what they can leave behind. The combination of the aging baby boomers' focus on what they can contribute and the quiet activism of younger workers is having a marked impact on worker attitudes.

Seventy-two percent of corporate and human resources executives polled said their companies' values motivate them personally. Back in the days of tall hierarchies, that's where the influence may have ended: in the executive suite. Today, however, employees of all ranks are watching and waiting to translate corporate values into meaningful actions. As an employee of Bright Horizons, a worksite childcare center provider in Cambridge, Massachusetts, explained, "I love knowing children walk away from here better people."

> One company with a "founding purpose" is the Body Shop. Here, they do not simply sell products. The brand sells "hope" and calls customers to action for a higher cause. The Body Shop is successful precisely because it sells social relevancy and purpose. The Body Shop is also involved in programs to help children in poor areas of Britain, India, and Mexico.

The recent worldwide Millennium Poll on Social Responsibility by Environics International asked more than 25,000 people in twenty-three countries to name the factors that most influence their impressions of individual companies. The majority named labor practices, business ethics, responsibility to society at large, and environmental impact. Only one in three mentioned factors associated with the traditional role of business: financial issues, company size, business strategy, and management. The irony of this finding is that most corporate events and documents focus on the growth and size of the company as a major motivator for employees. Those polled—and in particular those in older Western economies—said they expect companies to become more active in social responsibilities, although those from countries just coming out of communism were less likely to say so. How both consumers and workers evaluate companies is changing. What we're saying is that individuals are becoming more assertive in their demands that corporations become good corporate citizens. Nearly half of the poll's respondents said they have recently "punished" a company they saw as not socially responsible!

And increasingly, corporations are striving to respond to that call — not always willingly, evenly, or for entirely altruistic reasons, but the operative word is "increasingly." Two things are driving this: One factor is a growing recognition on the part of forward-looking CEOs *and* workers that greater social responsibility is required, and that governments and individuals cannot achieve sufficient change alone. The other driving factor is the volatile new mix of democracy and demographics, in which highly educated workers employed in less-authoritarian work environments have the power and gumption to demand that corporate and individual values align. (The same can be said for more demanding consumers, of course.)

Associates III, a high-end interior design firm in Denver, has set aside funds to encourage employees' community service efforts. For example, the company pays entry fees in charity runs.

Although ours is a book about winning employee commitment, we can't help but remind the reader that the case for corporate citizenship has never been stronger:

- Every one hundred pounds of product manufactured in the US creates at least 3,200 pounds of waste.
- We are now producing almost five times per person what our ancestors produced in 1900.
- The world's population nearly quadrupled between 1900 and 2000.
- The world's income is now less evenly distributed than it was one hundred years ago.

When one thousand working adults were asked whether they would rather earn high salaries or earn "enough" doing work that makes the world a better place, 86 percent chose the latter. This is in sharp contrast to a decade or two ago, as confirmed by the results of a survey (previously mentioned in Chapter 2) of graduating MBAs taken ten years apart. The Class of 1989 defined their primary measures of success as power, prestige, and money. The Class of 1991 cited successful relationships, a balanced life, and leisure time. Even more recently, respondents responded marriage, health, and ethics! That's our point: Values are shifting in significant ways.

Reflecting these values, more than thirty college campuses operate what are called "pledge programs," through which graduates pledge to investigate the social and environmental responsibility of any employment they consider. These campaigns (an example is **www.manchester.edu/department/paceStudies/gpa.html**) help job applicants define the issues and stick with their goals.

The corporate manifestation of a noble cause can take many forms: a mission statement that reveals the deeper meaning of the work, a firm that trumpets its socially responsible policies, a policy that encourages workers to do volunteer work on company time, or a company that matches employees' charitable donations. Recognition for service above and beyond the call of duty is another staple of companies determined to show their noble side.

Velero Energy in San Antonio, the oil refining company, subsidizes up to twenty-four hours of community work a year. In 1999, employees donated over 28,000 hours of volunteer labor.

Although workers' desire to contribute is more intense today (thanks to less after-work time and organizational involvement), corporations making contributions to their communities is a longstanding tradition. When a devastating flood hit Dayton, Ohio, in the early 1900s, John Patterson, owner of a multimillion-dollar cash register industry, set his assembly line to work turning out rowboats and engaged his cafeteria in baking bread for refugees. Despised as a tyrant before this, he was feted with a massive parade afterwards. Of course, that was a one-off.

What is new and significant is this: Only recently have large numbers of employees come to work with the heady notion that they should be able to fulfill their desire to serve others meaningfully *at work, on an ongoing basis*. Workplaces that find a way to meet that desire sprint far ahead of their competitors, as was driven home to John when he paid two closely spaced visits to two very different firms in the same industry.

Medtronics, the medical device manufacturer famed for its pacemakers, is renowned for a loyal and engaged workforce. Is it coincidental, then, that the company holds an annual event attended by patients and physicians who tell workers how they and others have benefited from the devices they make? The event, open to all employees, reminds workers that they are not so much in the business of manufacturing mechanical devices, as in saving and changing lives.

The first was a world-renowned life insurance company holding its annual company-wide employee meeting. After providing the keynote speech, John took his seat and watched quietly as fifty PowerPoint slides were used to walk the audience through the financial results of the company's year. Although the figures themselves were impressive, at no point during the show did the presenters refer to how the insurance policies behind the numbers had benefited real people, the customers, in significant ways. The meeting ended with polite but subdued applause. Follow-up conversations with employees revealed to John a workforce barely committed to the enterprise.

The following week, John attended the annual sales meeting of another financial services company. Here, the requisite slide show of financial performance was kept short to make time for a viewing of custom-prepared videos. The first video featured widows and widowers talking about how much the company's products meant to them when their loved ones died. In the second video, recent retirees expressed thanks to company employees for helping them manage their lifetime savings for the exciting and daunting moment of retiring. Now the CEO rose to tell stories that drove home how various departments' work came together to positively impact people's lives. He ended his inspiring, "big picture" speech with the words, "When you serve people this way, people buy your stuff. Thanks for our best year ever."

The meeting ended in a five-minute standing ovation, and from subsequent conversations with employees, John could only marvel at how passionate they were about working for this company, how "on fire" they were about their jobs.

Take a moment and reflect on the last "big" meeting in your organization. Was the focus on "making the numbers" or on the service you provided that made for that success?

What business are you in? Mission statements that inspire loyalty

The search for a noble cause is fed or starved by the way a company celebrates its achievements and by how it presents its mission. And yet, a read through 301 corporate mission statements from America's top companies (*The Mission Statement Book* by Jeffrey Abrahams) revealed to us that only 10 percent of them put a noble cause *front and center*. Another 4 percent came close. The vast majority had no hesitation in telling it like it is—through chest-beating, shareholder-fawning, and self-promoting language. Reading through excruciatingly repetitive phrases such as "to enhance shareholder value," "to become world class" and "to be the most successful," one begins to yearn for anything with more noble content or a more original turn of phrase. Even the company that identified its mission as "to be the most efficient competitor" seemed a relief. Do sycophantic mission-statement writers envision only shareholders reading their statements? If so, why not provide a second set for workers—mission statements that will light a fire beneath them to deliver what shareholders want? Yes, workers read mission statements, as do prospective employees shopping around for the best corporate culture with which to align their souls. Potential applicants may eye the noble words with a healthy dose of skepticism but during the early winnowing process, they assume that mission statements, like the design of a front door, offer some clues as to what's inside.

To state the most crass goals of business up-front borders on insulting workers' intelligence and surely misses an opportunity to strike a chord with their values. Let's look at a few examples of companies with a more clever spin on their mission statements, if not a genuine commitment to noble goals:

Medtronic's mission is "to alleviate pain, restore health, and extend life." IKEA's driving purpose is "to provide a better everyday life for the majority of people." The aim of pharmaceutical/biotechnology firm ICN Pharmaceuticals Inc. is "to make health care products that improve the quality of life for mankind." (Note: Although the second and third lines promise to "provide a fair return to our investors" and "become one of the largest and most successful," at least the writers sensed what needed to come *first*.)

Here are some out-takes from the credo of Johnson Wax, one of the world's leading manufacturers of chemical specialty products for home, personal care, and insect control: "We must be mindful of ways to help our employees fulfill their family responsibilities. We are responsible to the communities in which we live and work and to the world community as well. We must be good citizens—support good works and charities and bear our fair share of taxes. We must encourage civic improvements and better health and education. We must maintain in good order the property we are privileged to use, protecting the environment and natural resources." (Note: The credo goes on to add, "The stockholders should realize a fair return," but how subtle to hold this off until near the end!)

Numerous companies these days are pledging pre-IPO stock to non-profit companies on the understanding that the money will go toward community causes.

The nation's largest security company writes, "[The] freedom to pursue economic goals is constrained by law and channelled by the forces of a free market.... For some companies, that is enough. It is not enough for Borg-Warner. We impose upon ourselves an obligation to reach beyond the minimal. We do so convinced that by making a larger contribution to the society that sustains us, we best assure not only its future vitality, but our own." The statement goes on to endorse "the dignity of the individual, our responsibility to the common good, the endless quest for excellence, continuous renewal and the commonwealth of Borg-Warner and its people."

Just a few more for good measure: Global pharmaceutical company Pfizer is "dedicated to helping humanity." AES, a world leader in power generation, exists to "meet the world's need for electricity in a socially responsible manner." Jostens Inc., the graduation-products company, desires to "help people celebrate achievement, reward performance, recognize service, and commemorate experiences." Shaklee US (consumer goods and services) "enables all people to own their own lives, make a positive difference in the world, and earn the respect of customers and communities." And finally, Tandy Corporation, known for its Radio Shack stores, "demystifies technology for the mass market"— surely a notion more likely to get a worker out of bed in the morning than enhancing shareholder value.

Semantics and spin, some will sniff. So what? A noble phrase doesn't prove these corporations will follow through with noble measures, nor does it prevent the companies with blunter, less eloquent mission statements from doing more for local communities than those who claim that's their orientation. True, but it's a start, a savvy recognition of this all-important shift in worker attitudes, a chance to make employees sit up, take notice, and grasp at the notion that they're doing more than serving their nine-to-five and paying off a mortgage. Of course, companies with a noble mission statement still have to prove that they're made of more than words. Our experience is that most are, and that far more than 10 percent of companies will soon "ennoble" their mission statements *and* their missions.

> Patagonia, the rugged outdoor wear maker, contributes 1 percent of sales or 10 percent of profits (whichever is higher) to environmental groups. The company also sponsors a three-day conference to teach environmentalists how to become effective activists.

As Steve Robertson at Catholic Healthcare West says, "Retention is as much about alignment of values as it is about having values. In our hiring process, we try to highlight our values—dignity, stewardship, excellence, collaboration and justice—and use selection processes that are tied to the values." If an organization hires people whose values align, those people are more likely to stay.

Some will say this makes sense if you sell pharmaceutical products, but what about those whose work lacks such a basic premise? Dennis Bakke, CEO of AES Corporation, told us, "Most companies do provide a deeper service, but it is not acknowledged or recognized." He went on to note that his company has conducted an exercise for many years in which people are asked to close their eyes, imagine a movie about their lifetime, and imagine the major themes of that movie. "Without exception," Bakke says, "one of the themes is, 'I want to make a difference.'"

Whatever business you are in, there is a noble cause at its root, and today's employees want you to talk about it.

Demonstrating the connection

Mission statements, videos of grateful customers, and carefully crafted awards programs are all effective tools for helping workers see a connection between their work and a higher cause. Yet even leaders who are intent on creating an engaged workforce may miss the importance of connecting words with a noble purpose.

A client of John's in the software consulting business designs systems to help government agencies manage finances. When the firm hired John to help increase employee retention, they were surprised at his finding that the software consultants—mostly under thirty and highly marketable—felt under-fulfilled in their service role. These consultants expressed the feeling that the product they provided made little real difference in people's lives. The leaders of the division were surprised because to them, the deeper impact of the work was evident.

Over the next year, through customer forums, the company's leadership team worked hard to illustrate the connection between the services the company provided and the positive experience of the end user. They talked about the importance of government agencies being more aware of where hard-earned tax dollars went, so that they could be held accountable. They even went out of their way to bid and win a contract to consult with a United Nations relief agency. By the time this project was complete, employees were telling us that they intended to stay at this particular firm because the company has a genuine commitment to their clients' success, not just to "selling products and services." Turnover dropped an impressive 35 percent in one year.

When Bell Canada installed computers and gave away hardware to students and teachers in troubled schools, those institutions blossomed into national role models. At the same time, the company enjoyed unexpected payback when it found itself in the new market of distance education.

In *The Hungry Spirit*, Charles Handy describes how a high-tech company in Silicon Valley, California, was growing so fast that it had no time for training new employees and could afford to fire any who made mistakes. The result was an increasingly tense atmosphere that choked initiative. As company leaders pondered how to turn this around, they focused on how the equipment they made saved lives, how it had helped to revolutionize education in poor countries, and the potential it had for bringing government closer to people everywhere. They decided this was the real purpose of their company, and that "the money bit was the scorecard." They decided to invest in the people who would be their future and put a stronger value on creating a trusting atmosphere. Employees were now encouraged to learn from (instead of fearing or hiding) their mistakes. In other words, the company decided to shift its focus from maximizing profit at all costs to longer-term thinking, while still ensuring a decent return on capital.

Why emphasize to workers the noble aspects of the company's endeavors? Because, says Handy, "a match of corporate and individual souls releases energy, enthusiasm, effort, excitement and excellence.... Without that match, work and life are dull." Words can facilitate or trip up companies that are endeavoring to respond to workers' desire for a noble cause. Empty platitudes served up to cynical employees will backfire on the leaders who parrot them. On the other hand, lofty words sincerely intended, if not perfectly practiced, will stimulate high levels of employee engagement.

Companies can begin to work with this shift when leaders reflect on the deeper ways in which their products and services make an impact on people. Perhaps, instead of managing money, they are "creating wealth." Surely "making people feel at home" is a better goal than selling hotel rooms. Are they selling insurance or "creating security"? Are they selling theme park tickets or "making memories"?

The Endangered Species Chocolate Company, which sells gourmet Belgian chocolate wrapped in packaging by world-class artists that depicts endangered species, gives over 10 percent of its pre-tax profits to environmental groups in the form of chocolate for resale. The founder also works the school speaking circuit, talking to teachers and students about making their lives count.

Of course, some corporate leaders look at others' efforts to insert noble cause into their agenda and say, "Well, that's a good idea, but the widgets we make can't be touted as saving the world or adding critical value to someone's life." Perhaps this was the line of thinking at the dog-food company that handed over the task of rewriting their mission statement to employees. The previous mission statement had read something like, "To kill the cornmeal competition!" The workers astonished management by kicking off the statement with the phrase, "Dogs contribute to human fulfillment…" The moral of this story? Even those who package dog food want to feel they are laboring for something deeper. Toss them a milk bone to gnaw on, or better yet, let *them* come up with something they can truly get their teeth into—then reorganize to help support them in more than words. Put bite into the bark.

The noble cause in a business does not always have to ring of Mother Teresa. Paul Hollands, executive vice-president of A&W Canada, when reflecting on people who serve hamburgers, told us, "Higher purpose on the front line is quick service, great food, and friendly, caring staff who take pride in their work and have the power to make choices." In other words, even the act of feeding people has appeal when people feel appreciated for doing so with care and dignity.

At Investorplus.com, a real estate investment firm in Calgary, employees work very hard in a busy, fast-paced environment. Ask them what they like about the company and they comment on how much they believe in the products they provide and how their services are creating wealth for their clients. We found the same scenario at a software-consulting firm in Virginia, where employees describe what a difference it makes working for a company that really cares about their clients' success, and not just about selling software.

Beneath all this lies a simple paradox. Companies spend millions of dollars on public relations aimed at *consumers*: They promote the fact that they're in the business of caring, of flying friendly skies, and so on. Yet how many extend this campaign to portray their best side to *workers* (or prospective employees, who are becoming ever more discerning shoppers), remembering that additional follow-through is required to drive home the communication and render the noble words into noble deeds?

A general manager for Placer Dome reports that university students come with tough questions about the company's business practices both nationally and abroad. "They want to know what our values, policies, and vision are."

At Southwest Airlines, known for its loyal and engaged employees, corporate values are supported by regular meetings at every level of the company. During these meetings, workers and managers are expected to identify ways they are currently not living these values, and ways they can take steps towards greater alignment. This illustrates that putting values on paper or a lobby plaque is not the sole ticket to the game. The allocation of time and resources to underscore commitment to values is what ensures employee participation, engagement, retention, and loyalty.

Perhaps the rise of ethics or compliance officers in major companies is proof that companies recognize a need for special measures to ensure mission statements' validity and vitality. Ethics officers act as in-house moral arbitrators, mediators, watchdogs, and receptive listeners to whistleblowers. Companies such as the CIBC, Canada Post, Magna International, the Royal Bank of Canada, Northern Telecom, and McDonald's Restaurants all retain ethics officers. Nearly 90 percent of Fortune 500 companies have formalized ethics codes, and 30 percent of those have ethics officers or specialists to support their ethics programs. Canada alone employed sixty ethics officers in 1998, while another sixty Canadian companies boasted corporate ombudspersons.

AES, one of the world's largest power companies, says it is "committed to meeting the world's needs for electricity in a socially responsible way." The company has backed up that statement in hundreds of ways, from planting a million trees in Latin America to pledging 5 percent of after-tax profits to socially responsible projects. (By 1999, the company had reached 3 percent.) Like every business, AES has faced daunting challenges made even tougher by its mission statement's promise. For example, when the company took over a power plant in Panama that employed three hundred people, and knew one hundred could operate it just as efficiently, it offered laid-off workers not only a generous severance package, but loans to help them start up new businesses. To date, this program has inspired sixty-seven entrepreneurial start-ups.

More importantly, every year AES issues a "principles survey," in which it asks employees to state how they are doing on their four goals—which are "to act with integrity, to be fair, to have fun, and to be socially responsible." In 1999, the survey elicited 28,000 responses, and CEO Dennis Bakke promised he would read each and every one personally.

When a *Fortune* magazine reporter worked for a week at a Container Store outlet to determine how the company managed to hit No. 1 on the *Fortune* 100 list in January 2000, he was told by a manager that when a customer comes in for one item, "You're cheating the customer if you're not offering them the opportunity to buy more."

DaimlerChrysler AG of Stuttgart, Germany, has joined forces with Mattel Inc. to help teach parents how to properly install child-safety seats.

"Hmmm," reflected the reporter in his follow-up article: "In other words, selling is good for the customer." Or, the company's six esoteric principles have been driven home so well, that they "allow you to be a pushy salesperson but feel as if you're a public servant—a useful sensation for a company that doesn't offer sales commissions." Argue that this organization's principles are strange and the employees suckers if you like, but remember, this was a relatively small company that hit No. 1 on the Fortune 100. Nor would customers return if they felt ill-served. This outfit is an example of a company that has learned to help employees make the connection between company principles and daily work, and "ennobled" them as a proud team.

Our favorite story of how a company gets its noble message across involves the Body Shop, which broadcasts inspirational messages such as the following to its delivery trucks as they go about their business: "If you think you're too small to make a difference, you've never been in bed with a mosquito," and "You think education's expensive? Try ignorance."

The new corporate citizen

"Until recently, the idea that a company should take on the additional responsibility of social and environmental degradation was anathema," acknowledges Paul Hawken, visionary businessman and author of *The Natural Step for Business*, which outlines a program that helps corporations adopt measures for sustainable development. And yet, not only is payback possible, but it can be twofold: financial and in the form of a fired-up workforce.

The four companies profiled in *The Natural Step for Business* all overhauled operations to be more environmentally sensitive and reported significant cost savings as a result of their initiatives. One company realized $75 million in savings in the first four years; another saved an estimated $500,000 to $750,000 in replacement costs for just one technical change, and $525,000 per year in raw material costs. IKEA North America expects annual savings of more than $500,000 from just one program. But as the authors of the book point out, "These cost savings are only part of the story. As employees become engaged in sustainability efforts, they become more conscientious, creative, aware and interested in how they use resources and there-

At Scandic Hotels in Sweden, employee teams have been involved for more than two years in environmental initiatives that aim to cut their operations' water and energy consumption by 20 percent, and unsorted waste by 30 percent. Through employee suggestions, the company has so far saved 17 percent of annual laundry costs by reducing their use of energy, water, and detergent—enough to achieve payback within a year on new equipment purchased to achieve this. As for employees, not long after this initiative was put into place, they voted the company into the top one hundred most desirable companies to work for in Sweden.

by contribute to reducing the aggregate impact of the company on the environment. This creates leaner production and operations and often leads to innovations that improve both operational and environmental performance."

Another organization promoting sustainable development on the part of businesses is the Coalition for Environmentally Responsible Economies (**www.ceres.org**), representing more than eighty businesses, nonprofits, and public agencies.

Two hundred years ago in Great Britain, George III's chancellor, Baron Turlow, asked, "How can you expect a corporation to have a conscience, when it has no soul to be damned and no body to be kicked?" But today, corporations without a soul and conscience risk being damned by the press and kicked by talent that has moved on to the competition.

David Packard, co-founder and inspiration of Hewlett-Packard, said, "I think people assume, wrongly, that a company exists solely to make money. Money is an important part of a company's existence, if the company is any good. But a result is not a cause. We have to go deeper and find the real reason for our being. As we investigate this, we inevitably come to the conclusion that a group of people get together and exist as an institution that we call a company, so that they are able to accomplish something collectively that they could not accomplish separately—they make a contribution to society, a phrase which sounds trite but is fundamental."

Nike Canada has a P.L.A.Y. (Participate in the Lives of All Youth) program, through which six inner-city basketball courts made of ground-up Nike running shoes have been built to give disadvantaged children a place to play. Altogether, Nike Canada has donated more than $1.8 million to Canadian communities.

Anita Roddick, CEO of the Body Shop, is renowned for advocating business as a powerful force for positive social change. In *Spirituality and Service*, she says corporations were invented to serve people and society, and business managers therefore have a moral obligation to designate a higher purpose and demonstrate good corporate citizenship.

The list of leaders who understand this is growing—and those leaders are at the head of the pack. Michael Dell, chairman and CEO of

Dell Computer Corp. in Round Rock, Texas, has said, "The best advice I have about giving back is this: Do it. If you're leading a company, or if you're in a management position of some stature or power, it's just as important to serve as a role model as it is for you to help a specific cause." (See Bakke's profile on p. 147.)

"Why does business exist? It's not to make profits or serve shareholders. It's to serve the world. That's why business is allowed to exist as a public entity, and that's what we should be focused on," Dennis Bakke, CEO of AES, told us. (See the profile of Bakke on page 147.)

Interestingly, a worldwide survey of managers' values found that focusing on profitability *without* an eye to social consequences is a heavily American perspective. Only 3 percent of Japanese managers share this criterion, and in Singapore, 89 percent of managers reject what a majority of US managers embrace. This is especially valuable to keep in mind when dealing with an ever more diverse and widely traveled workforce.

The impact of a noble cause on employee loyalty is often subtle but nonetheless profound. Fairmont Hotels, formerly Canadian Pacific Hotels, has had an extensive recycling program on their premises for some time. We vividly recall a maid in one of their hotels telling us how much extra time it took her to sort the recycling property. "But," she added proudly, "doing the recycling is the most important part of my job and makes me feel like I did something important in my day." Winning over today's workforce—or, better put, serving them—can happen in any of thousands of ways, many all too invisible to executives.

Corporations that attempt to be good corporate citizens may win better and more engaged employees, but they'll never be free of the trail of cynics who accuse them of making fraudulent, contradictory, or self-serving claims. When John's first book, *Awakening Corporate Soul*, was published, he received a scathing e-mail from one critic who said, "Now even the spiritual traditions have been called upon to support the corporations' lies."

While detractors inevitably help keep the game honest, we think many of them are missing a few points. First, why remove the incentive to try? Second, if noble initiatives make a company a more fulfilling place to work, and if the movement toward corporate citizenship is often inspired by and for the rank and file, who's hurting whom by joining an anti-corporate crusade? And finally, with authoritarian rule and hierarchical structure in natural decline and profit-sharing becoming available to the full spectrum of workers, how outdated and counterproductive are statements like the following by Murray Dobbin, in *The Myth of the Good Corporate Citizen*? "Inside the corporate culture, the more ruthless a CEO is in dealing with expendable employees, the higher the esteem in which he is held and the more he is paid.... The social madness inherent in the drive for ever greater growth and profits, and its parallel creation of crushing poverty worldwide, will have a fearsome backlash. [Chaos and violence] are a virtual certainty if real citizens don't consciously direct the response to the corporate destruction of civil society." The reality is that we have experienced firsthand an awakening amongst the rank and file, one increasingly shared by executives. We celebrate this cause.

Altruism on company time

If mission statements set the stage, communication rallies the crowd, and organizational acts of corporate citizenship counter skepticism, offering employees the chance to practice altruism during work time is the most powerful medium for driving home the message that a company cares about more than profits. The effect can be surprisingly powerful. Employees who were previously focused entirely on work discover new emotions, an unexpected release of tension, a flood of warmth or joy that spills over to co-workers and managers. Work-sponsored volunteerism can be especially beneficial to young, self-absorbed workers, helping to mature their outlook on the world.

H.B. Fuller in St. Paul, a specialty chemicals firm, allows employees twelve hours of paid time every quarter for volunteer work.

Business-culture psychotherapist Francis Hope writes, "People's maturity and happiness ultimately depends on their concern for others and a living sense of connection to their environment." As discussed in Chapter 4, the simple act of volunteering can begin to redistribute an individual's energy more holistically, which makes for a healthier, more alert and focused worker.

A *USA Today* survey found that eight out of ten workers would be more likely to volunteer if their companies recognized their volunteer work by providing time off to do it, and yet only 14 percent have that time off.

While it's difficult to measure the payback on this increasingly popular form of noble cause, the fact that many of the Fortune 100 companies have installed such programs, and that employees flock to those companies and their charitable programs, implies much. At TDIndustries, employees are encouraged to volunteer and their work schedules are adjusted accordingly.

Another company trying this tack is Homestead.com. Joe Davila, the twenty-six-year-old "cultural czar" of the company, chose that title when he got bored with his previous one, "vice president of finance." Evidently equally bored with bottom-line-fixated cultures, he claims to be creating one at Homestead that values hard work while also recognizing the need for balance. "One aspect of balance is service, so my challenge is to find service projects that each employee will be willing to work on for at least two hours a week. People tend to support a culture that they help create, so we have regular meetings to keep everyone excited. Also, managers make it easy for their staff to volunteer, and that helps a lot."

Toronto management consultants Bain & Co., concerned by the fierce competition for hiring newly minted MBAs, recently brainstormed a way to grab students' attention, distinguish the company as supporting noble causes, *and* get a close-up view of participants' leadership skills all at once. The company invites new recruits to volunteer anywhere in the world with Habitat for Humanity (the organization dedicated to building affordable housing for poor people worldwide) for two weeks before they start their full-time posts and provides up to $3,000 US per individual for airfare and other expenses. Susan Caraviello, a vice-president who oversees recruiting, declares the initiative a success. "Students get excited about it," she says.

For every dollar that an employee donates to charity at Computer Business Associates International Inc. in Islandia, New York, the company will donate two.

General Mills also likes to demonstrate its social conscience in a way that directly involves employees by encouraging them to get involved. "We believe we have a responsibility to reach out to others, to take what we know, and do what we can to make a difference," says Stephen W. Sanger, chairman and CEO of the Minneapolis-based company. In the past five years, the company has also donated 76 million pounds of food and $155 million in donations and contributions to help combat hunger, provide education, give start-up companies a boost, and make the neighborhoods in which it operates safer. The General Mills Foundation initiated a monthly meeting of local residents, business-people, and public officials in a troubled north Minneapolis neighborhood. This has led to a reduction in crime, the closing of crack houses, a 50 percent drop in vandalism, and the creation of youth programs. Eighty percent of General Mills' employees and 40 percent of its retirees are involved in volunteer activities, but is that a contributing factor to the company placing in *Industry Week*'s "best-managed companies" for four straight years?

> Marriott, through its Pathways to Independence program, offers life-skills and job skills training for welfare recipients, and guarantees them a position when they finish the program. We attended a Marriott event and personally saw the pride managers took in the program's impact on people.

Industry Week itself responds with a definitive *yes*: "All of *Industry Week*'s 100 Best-Managed Companies ... have qualities beyond just financial performance that put them among the elite. Some work to curb child abuse or domestic violence. Others go the extra mile to provide the best benefits packages for employees or to provide an environment conducive to balancing work and family issues. Some have a strong orientation to recycling materials and waste and keeping the environment clean.... They understand that their success is tied to their people and their willingness to be responsible corporate citizens."

It's important to remember that workers respond best to hands-on efforts. Giving to the United Way is nice, but employee loyalty grows from the touch and feel of work-associated volunteering. When a friend of ours took over the management of a retail outlet in Vancouver, Canada, she identified her first challenges as low morale and poor sales.

She could have kicked off with a motivational talk about increasing sales. Instead, she involved her young staff in sponsoring a local AIDS march; they raised money from customers and helped promote the walk. Within a month, the employees were super-motivated, and guess what? Sales started going up and absenteeism went down. It wasn't the donations that had built team spirit and commitment, but the warm feelings the employees had gained and had come to associate with their workplace.

Need a few more examples? How about Whole Goods Market in Austin, Texas, which offers up to twenty hours' annual paid time off for community service? Or Finova Group in Phoenix, which gives unlimited paid time off for charity work? At Timberland, the boot makers, employees get forty hours of paid time each year to do volunteer work. Timberland also contributes $5 million annually to City Year, an urban Peace Corps active in eight US cities. Northwest Airlines employees get involved with Habitat for Humanity, building affordable housing for needy people. As they hammer nails together, the good feelings generated by contributing to a noble cause also lift team and company spirit.

Why people are drawn to value-driven companies

Employees are attracted to businesses where corporate values are strong and respected. Put another way, highly sought-after workers wither within—or won't even join—a company without a noble cause. But why, skeptics wonder, do employees suddenly want work to have a higher meaning? What makes them think they should be able to practice altruism on work time? Why should companies suddenly have to "go noble" to retain prized workers?

Like so many of the shifts we outline, this one has historic roots, and there are observers who have seen it coming for some time. Essentially, the search for a noble cause at work is a belated and bottled-up reaction to what the Industrial Age did to workers. The re-engineering of the 1980s uncorked that resentment, and more recent worker empowerment has given full-throated volume to its whisper.

Michael Hammer, author of *Beyond Reengineering*, explains: "The Industrial Age forced us to strike a Faustian bargain. In return for higher wages and an improved standard of living, we largely sacrificed the benefits to the spirit that pre-industrial work provided. How could it be otherwise? By focusing on isolated and atomistic tasks, by disconnecting people from the end products and customers of their labours, modern work squeezed all sense of transcendent value out of people's lives. It is difficult to take spiritual nourishment from processing a piece of paper or tightening bolts day in and day out. Without a sense of where your product goes or why you are making it, it is hard for your work to mean anything. It is empty, a mechanical ritual performed for transitory reasons."

If modern-day video clips of gushing customers, carefully crafted corporate party speeches, smoothly polished mission statements, and newly triggered avalanches of corporate altruism provide workers with a sense of where the product goes and why they are making it, of course retention and engagement will soar. Certainly, companies looking to build a world-class employee base are beginning to "buy in" to this theory. If workers lost pieces of their soul during the Industrial Age and have only just decided that material plenty was not a sufficient trade—if they are trying to recoup their loss just as work has all but bumped off family and "soul time", make way. It's yield or get run over. Or, as the saying goes, never wound a tiger.

Are workers seeking to grow back some of their soul on work time (either because they blame work time for taking it away, or because there isn't a lot of other time)? If so, understand that the three parts of one's soul, according to Charles Handy, are a sense of making a difference, a feeling of responsibility for others, and the satisfaction of living a life that is true to one's real values. Not at all an impossible slate for employers to fill, as this book demonstrates.

During a visit to the offices of Synovus Financial, the bank and credit card processor in Columbus, Georgia (No. 5 on *Fortune's* 100 Best list in 2000), fiercely loyal front-line employees told John they hope their children will work there. Indeed, lifetime, multi-generational family employment is alive and well at this firm, as is in-house talk about "doing the right thing." This phrase may be part of the company directive, but unlike other organizations with noble-sounding mantras, Synovus and its subsidiaries demand a daily focus on making those words real. One employee told John how she turned down a project that a client requested, explaining to the customer that it was more than he needed. Following the company directive to "do the right thing," this employee knew she would not suffer negative repercussions for turning away the work. Undoubtedly, the sense that her company walks its talk is a cornerstone of her loyalty and motivation, while her honesty significantly raised the client's long-term loyalty to the company.

As the Synovus story attests, the three factors common to *Fortune* magazine's 100 best companies, which may contribute to good morale of employees, are these: visionary leadership, a positive work environment, and a desirable mission or purpose. These are values that a company must build slowly and consistently from the roots up, not assets that can be custom-ordered from a consultant and plugged in tomorrow.

Stephen Smith, CEO
WestJet
Calgary, Alberta

"Anyone can go out and buy a 747, charge the same fares, serve pretzels, and fly," quips Stephen, CEO, the western Canadian upstart fast gaining a reputation as a great place to work. "What's going to differentiate us from any other airline? The only thing is people: customer service."

And how does WestJet ensure leading-edge customer service? Not through complicated training, because all staff have flown somewhere before, explains Smith with his trademark sense of humor: "They can look in a mirror and ask what guests want, and get straight answers."

No, WestJet's edge is having neither employees nor management – only partners. "We don't believe in the word 'management'. We don't supervise or manage people here; we lead. And we don't have employees; we have people. We don't have human resources; we have a people department. Our emotional contract with people is to treat them with respect, allow them to have input into the company, and allow them to self-actualize within their jobs."

WestJet conducts an annual salary survey and pays its people 95 percent of the industry's median wage. In lieu of the other 5 percent, it offers a profit-sharing program paid out every six to seven months, which amounted to roughly 30 percent of workers' total salaries — or $7.4 million — in 1999. Why a profit-sharing program?

"This allows us not to have supervisors, because we know the decisions people are making are coming from the same place where Stephen would make them," says Smith. "They're motivated to make the right decisions. There are hundreds of thousands of decisions made every day at this company that I'm not part of. We want them to make the decisions that owners would make, and the best way to do that is to make them owners. They think like shareholders – completely differently than people coming for a paycheck."

Of course, when a company is growing at WestJet's current pace – hiring three hundred people per year – getting the right people to start with is critical. Smith says he ensures this by showing applicants the company's mission statement: "To enrich the lives of everyone in WestJet's world, by providing safe, friendly and affordable air travel."

"I say, 'We have a mission statement. If its words match what you feel, stay with us. If they don't, don't feel badly; it's not a matter of right or wrong.' Unlike at other companies I've worked at, our mission statement's words actually mean a lot. We refer to them all the time. And we try to work with our people so that they believe there is something beyond what they're contributing, that they're part of the team, that the company needs them – the team, the community, our guests need them. We're not trying to say that by working at WestJet, you're going to solve the hunger problems of the world, but there's a whole other gestalt of reasons that your expertise is needed at our company: not letting people down. There are people who need us to get them to children's events, weddings, and so on."

Smith smiles. "In a customer service business – and to me every company is a customer service business – if you don't support people to make their job easier, you're never going to succeed in the long-term."

Assessing your company for noble cause

The statements below allow for an initial assessment of how your organization, division, and/or department is doing at responding to the employee search for work as noble cause. The assessment is meant to guide your thinking, not to provide a definitive quantitative assessment of your progress. For each question below, answer how true the statement is of your work environment using the scale provided:

_____ Our company has a statement that describes the deeper meaning of our product or service – for instance, making people happy, making people feel at home, preserving and improving human life (If your answer is "Yes, but it rarely gets talked about," assign 1 point; if your company's statement is alive, talked about and considered "real," tally 3 points).

_____ Employees are involved in community service or volunteerism on behalf of the company (1 point if the company provides opportunities; 2 if they're actively encouraged or trained to do so; 3 if they can do so on company time with pay).

_____ Our company has a set of values that are meant to inspire people to higher ethics and doing the right thing (1 point if you have it but it rarely gets talked about; 3 points if you have methods for ensuring that employees stay focused on those values; lose 2 points if you have such a statement but employees joke about how much you don't live them).

_____ Our company has a reputation in the community for its commitment to the larger community (1 point).

_____ At large company meetings, results are often presented in terms of how our services have made an impact on people, not just profits (1 point if done at all, 3 points if there is a stronger focus on service than profits).

_____ TOTAL

SCORE:

5 or under: Take a full week's management retreat for brainstorming policies that address these concerns.

6–9: You're beginning to look responsive.

10–11: You are above average in meeting today's workers' needs, but there is still room for improvement.

12–13: You are an inspiring example, and probably have the best workers and a strong bottom line to show for it. E-mail us: **izzoinc@aol.com**.

6

The expectation of personal growth and development

"Learning organizations are able to respond to a rapidly changing environment because they embrace change as the norm."

— *THE NATURAL STEP FOR BUSINESS*

Shorn of any sense of job security, restless by nature, and living in the era of personal growth, today's workers seek both personal and professional nourishment. Career-building skills are the new security, and companies that fail to provide them lose out, especially given that the desire to leave the corporate hearth for an entrepreneurial venture has never been so strong. But as any observer can attest, the line between "personal" and "professional" development is fading in acknowledgement that skills such as leadership draw from a well so deep that more than one source feeds it.

In Japan, companies have traditionally recognized the need for ongoing education and have underwritten it. Until recently, fewer employers in the West have wanted to risk training and re-training employees who might disappear tomorrow. And yet, as the new economy takes over, leaders are looking beyond the risk that their investment may "walk," and realizing that *not* investing in workers will influence them to walk faster. The most successful information technology companies spend between 7 and 10 percent of their payroll on training, compared with the standard 2 to 3 percent.

How important is it to support career development? In a recent survey, new MBAs put

> When Kinko's Inc. of Ventura, California implemented a training program that gave co-workers a training path and sense of career, turnover tumbled from 78 to 50 percent.

"developing a career" first on their list of nine priorities. *Fortune* magazine's "100 Best Companies to Work for in America" responded by underwriting an average of forty-three hours of training for each employee in 1998, almost a full day more than the previous year. Meanwhile, a Gallup study on employee engagement found that opportunities to learn and grow are tightly linked with commitment, in sharp contrast with a 1968 study, which indicated that few employees associated these two.

More and more companies are advertising their learning labs in recruitment materials, mentoring has come back into favor, it's trendy to build corporate campuses for "continual learning," and human resources staff are finding themselves charged with helping employees of all ranks in career planning.

To reduce the chance of boredom on the job, 3M long ago introduced its "15 percent rule," which encourages technical people to spend up to 15 percent of their time on projects of their own choosing and initiative. The company also promotes a "dual ladder" career track that allows technical and professional people to move up without sacrificing their research or professional interests. They believe this stimulates innovation and allows people to "advance without having to switch to a managerial track."

It is not that the desire to learn and grow is new, but rather that employees are now expecting employers to make their learning and growth a top priority, and employers are willing go along with this in hopes of keeping turnover low. Three unrelated but powerful phenomena are fuelling employees' expectation of constant growth and development. First, job insecurity has made it necessary for them to become mercenary about their own skill development. Employability rather than employment is now the contract between worker and employer. That is, although companies can no longer guarantee jobs, they can guarantee skill development that will keep workers employable.

Second, younger workers—born and bred in the sound-byte era, joystick in one hand and channel surfer in the other—get bored more easily than their older counterparts. They grew up in a rapidly changing technological world where new games and toys were a constant, and they learned to press a button whenever they felt jaded. In fact, members of the Net generation get itchy feet and scout around for new job opportunities every two years. It's hardly surprising, then, that the two most successful retention strategies are offering exciting work and ensuring the chance to work on leading-edge technology. When it comes to attracting, engaging, and keeping talent, perhaps the new millennium take on the decades-old bumper sticker is, "He who offers the most toys and training, wins."

The third fuel for this shift is the personal growth movement, which has now adopted the workplace as a new forum. This movement, exemplified by rows and rows of bookstore self-help bestsellers, has accelerated exponentially, especially among baby boomers, who buy more self-help books per person than any other generation.

If job insecurity, boredom, and the personal growth movement are driving this fourth shift in worker attitudes, successful employers are meeting the challenge with three offers: the opportunity to learn new skills, assistance with career management, and opportunities for discovering oneself at work.

Learning new skills

Back in 1996, in *Boom, Bust & Echo*, David K. Foot described four kinds of career paths and predicted that the two fastest-growing of these would require a serious investment in employee training:

1. **Linear career path**: characterized by upward mobility, associated with tall corporate pyramids, and offering a reward system based on steady promotion up a career ladder.
2. **Steady-state career path**: characterized by one occupation for a lifetime (say, professor or doctor); the reward system based on autonomy, fringe benefits, and tenure.
3. **Spiral career path**: characterized by lateral moves mixed with promotions (each lateral move involving a change of occupation), some within the same organization and some between different organizations. Associated with a squat pyramid and involving a reward system based less on promotions than on the satisfaction employees get from mastering new challenges through re-education and lifelong learning.

4. **Transitory career path**: in which the worker adopts whatever occupation is necessary to get a job—from management consultant to bicycle courier.

Have you guessed yet which two were tipped as the career paths of the future? They are spiral and transitory, both a comfortable fit with flattened hierarchies—and both requiring such constant states of learning that the company might as well hook up an intravenous tube between employees and local institutions that offer continuing education.

> VanCity, one of British Columbia's leading financial institutions, developed a Career Futures program that offers employees training initiatives to consistently examine where they are going and how to stay employable.

"A lateral organization needs to know people's job preferences, help them plan their career paths, and give them the training they need.... Companies that invest in worker training are more profitable than those that don't," declares Foot.

Many argue that employability is the new deal in employer-employee relations. John Reyson, the president of MDS Metro in Vancouver, Canada, told us, "I may not be able to offer people a guarantee of employment anymore, but I can guarantee that while they are here, they will always be learning new skills that will help them stay employed here or elsewhere."

Training accomplishes several things, all of which add up to higher retention:

- It broadcasts confidence in the employee ("We're willing to invest in you because you're worth it, and we hope you'll stay for a while).
- It raises the value of that worker to the organization (hopefully translating directly to profits).
- It acknowledges employees' need to keep skills marketable and to continually challenge themselves.
- It counters boredom.

Creating opportunities for people to try new skills and tasks also protects against young workers' nightmare: Boredom is death!

If performing repetitive tasks dehumanized workers in the

Industrial Age, imagine how well mindless work goes down today, given a highly educated workforce raised to prize personal freedom. Enter the philosophies of James Dyson, founder and chairman of Dyson Appliances Ltd., the unconventional vacuum-cleaner company and fastest-growing manufacturing company in Great Britain. Dyson believes that anyone can become reasonably expert in virtually any field, and he proves it by having all new hires—no matter what their positions—build a vacuum

Sears has a career development program that ensures its information technology associates enjoy varied assignments and that provides training and career advice for them.

cleaner on their first day of work. (Once they're finished, they can buy the machine for a mere twenty-five pounds!) Dyson combats the prospect of worker restlessness by having all assembly line personnel change jobs every forty-five minutes. The result is that every employee knows how to assemble every model, creating maximum flexibility in a change-crazed economy. If Dyson is right about anyone being able to learn anything, it means that daunting amounts of talent are going untapped in companies around the world. It also means that boredom at work is unnecessary.

Responding to the desire for constant professional growth means creating opportunities for people to learn and contribute outside the confines of their present jobs. AES is a global power company that aims to be socially responsible and the employer of choice. Its mission to be a place where "people can maximize their gifts and skills" is exemplified in one of its coal mine operations, where miners serve on a rotating basis as members of a task group that manages the portfolio of their pension fund investments.

A diversity of job assignments may keep employees in place, but this retention strategy must be matched with training that offers skills prized on the current job market, as well. Even in the warmth of a hot economy, one in five employees worries about losing his or her job. As we mentioned in Chapter Two, two in five say their résumé is always up-to-date, and six in ten have taken a course in the past year to upgrade their skills or develop new ones. Four out of five are confident that they have the skills to find a comparable position if they are laid off. The studies behind these statistics underscore the fact that employees today are competitive to an almost mercenary degree.

Need some evidence?

- A recent national survey on job training concluded that employer-sponsored training attracts recruits and contributes significantly to retention. It also indicated that employees particularly want high-quality training in technology, communications, and management skills.
- A *ComputerWorld* survey found that 79 percent of respondents remained with their employers because of training opportunities.
- A 1999 Gallup poll named the *lack* of opportunities to learn and grow as one of the top three reasons for employee *dissatisfaction*.
- The authors of *Chips & Pop: Decoding the Nexus Generation* say that at least every three months, Netters reflect on their satisfaction with their current position according to five key factors: compensation and benefits; opportunities for mobility, learning, and skills development; regularity of feedback; peer and management support; and the meaningfulness of work. The same authors quote Canada Information Office research showing that one in four members of this generation strongly agrees with the statement, "My skills and knowledge could grow obsolete in five years."
- A June 1997 survey of workplace benefits valued by Netters placed paid training as No. 3 on the most desirable list, after basic dental/medical benefits and extended leaves, and above flexible work hours, up-to-date technology, and casual dress.

"Train to retain" has become a common mantra for good reason, and that training must be available right from the start. A common question from job candidates these days is what kind of ongoing training the employer will offer, and the younger the candidate, the more influential the response will be on job selection.

Intel recruits college students in their second year and matches them with a company mentor in hopes they will apply to join the company after graduation.

As a twenty-eight-year-old bank employee told us, "Things have changed in the corporate world; there simply aren't as many promotion opportunities as there once were. So, growing and learning is the replacement. I want to be learning new things constantly and becoming more valuable."

If great training serves as an inducement to young talent, it's increasingly essential for retaining boomers who may be wavering between early retirement and staying on. Seventy percent of companies believe that phased retirement may be the solution to the growing labor shortage, and three out of four older workers prefer to reduce hours gradually, but how many boomers slipping away early are feeling unnecessarily insecure due to a lack of training in the latest technology?

It is difficult to overemphasize how effective training is as a retention tool. A 1998 Watson Wyatt survey of employers revealed that training was their No. 1 tool of choice for employee attraction and retention. Ninety percent of employers responding said they used training and development to encourage applicants, and 94 percent used training to retain workers (flex time and compensation were the second and third choices for successful recruiting and retention). And yet, in another Watson Wyatt survey, respondents stressed that the critical factor was not training itself, but "the degree to which training is integrated into company culture and strategy." Companies that performed best had adopted a continuous learning culture using informal methods such as mentoring and job sharing. In fact, 75 percent of higher-performing companies had linked training programs with strategic goals, compared with only 67 percent of other organizations. This point is essential to comprehend: Meeting the development expectation is not simply about classes, but involves a philosophy that providing opportunities for learning is paramount.

Applied Materials Inc. of Santa Clara, California, has its own Applied Global University, which offers employees six hundred courses and training segments.

Globalization has upped the ante for systems to embrace change, and has made constant training a requirement for organizational success. For instance, contemplate the fact that employment in the information technology services sector is expected to nearly double between 1999 and 2005, from a current 1.1 million workers. It's demographically impossible for that kind of volume to suddenly burst forth from the halls of college campuses. So to raise a just-in-time army of information technology workers will involve a massive retooling of the current worker population, and it won't all happen on the worker's time and bill.

Fortunately, training existing workers is getting cheaper and less disruptive by the minute, thanks to technological advances and the potential of distance education. In fact, job-related training really took off when technology made it more cost-effective. Technology-delivered training—which can be integrated into a workday, thus both reducing costs and making the training more relevant—is being adopted so quickly that by 2002, it is expected to account for 55 percent of corporate training, up from 20 percent in 1999.

Getting a head start on this trend, Days Inn of America has introduced Web-based training via the corporate intranet to help stem an industry-standard 120 percent annual turnover. It's the company's way of coping with the limitations of eleven trainers serving 18,000 workers at 1,800 sites around the world. Compared with traditional classroom training, this technique has produced a 50 percent savings in time and cost, although it's difficult to factor in up-front costs of computer upgrades and content design.

Still, distance education will never entirely replace classroom settings. Critics note that intranets are not suitable for teaching "soft skills" such as listening and coaching, and programs always need modification to maximize effectiveness. Recognizing these issues, Days Inn has arranged for instructor-led components to constitute 80 percent of their Web training program.

Schwab's "Schwab University" offers courses in leadership and management skills, technology, communication, securities exam preparation, and more. Both classroom facilities and online courses are available, as well as desktop resources.

Other companies have acknowledged the need for continual training by establishing on-site centers, which utilize current employees and managers as teachers. Still others are partnering with suppliers, customers, and institutions of higher learning. What some of these programs miss are courses in languages other than English, or in a manner that acknowledges attendees' lack of fluency. Where once it was relatively easy to train non-English-speaking employees to operate a machine or provide a service, today the tools they need to cope in the workplace are more complex—for instance, identifying safety procedures or supporting cross-functional teams. To quickly bring a diverse workforce up to world-class levels of productivity, it's vital to design the training around the task, not the language, keeping in mind that the desired outcome is productivity, not fluency.

Training is a philosophy, not a class

To meet employees' expectation for learning, employers must focus not simply on providing opportunities, but on communicating that company's commitment and intention to develop people. New employees often come to the workplace with unrealistic expectations. A software client of John's found that promises of exciting projects and the chance to work on leading-edge technology right away had wooed many of its new recruits. Once on the job, the new hires discovered that initial projects used old technology. After noting these new employees' frustration, the company initiated conversations that helped the recruits modify their expectations and put a more realistic time frame on moving to the kind of work that they coveted. These conversations alone—all of which emphasized the company's intention of providing opportunities for growth—helped cut turnover by 30 percent.

A learning philosophy involves putting employees at the center of their own learning, thus meeting two expectations at once: partnership and growth. One mid-sized insurance company gives every employee a career development account amounting to 2.5 percent of their annual salary. Employees are allowed to accumulate funds in this account for up to three years and can use it at their own discretion for career-related courses, conferences (including travel), association dues, and PC hardware for home use. The clear message: "You're responsible for your own career development, but we support you in your endeavors."

Responding to this shift may require your organization to rethink its philosophy at a very deep level. For example, Mercer Management of Vancouver, Canada, a leading consulting firm, realized that many of its consultants are ambitious people with a need to try new things. So the company instituted an "externship" program, whereby employees could take a full-time job at another company for up to one year, with no obligation to return. Since implementing this program in November 1999, Mercer has enjoyed a soaring number of applicants. Why would Mercer Management try such a counterintuitive idea—losing people to keep them? Because, like many consulting firms, the company was losing people to start-ups and this was a way to give them a chance to try new things, spread the word about "Mercer flexibility," and feel welcomed back to the fold if they rejoin. Presumably, those who return are that much more experienced and committed.

Chick-fil-A, a company strongly committed to employees, has awarded $1,000 scholarships to more than 6,000 workers who have put in an average of twenty hours per week for at least two years. Employees can also qualify for a four-year, $10,000 scholarship.

This is the kind of radical focus on employee growth and development that will ultimately win today's worker. As the vice-president of human resources at Mercer Management says, "We are learning how to hold on with open arms. You have to hope you have built something attractive enough that your people will want to return and stay. If they don't, you were going to lose them anyway!"

- At TDIndustries in Texas, entry-level employees are given unlimited training and development. CEO Jack Lowe says, "Five years ago, we had a plumber who wanted to get his bachelor's degree. We paid for it. Then he wanted his Masters, and now he has his Ph.D., all paid for by TD. Mind you, there are not too many of those, but we support them. We expect a minimum of 32 hours per year of classroom time."
- Benefits at Johnson & Johnson of New Brunswick, New Jersey, include 100 percent tuition reimbursement with no cap on the amount.
- Fenwick and West of Palo Alto, California the only law firm on *Fortune*'s "100 Best Companies to Work for in America", provides law school tuition up to $10,000 per year for paralegals.
- The Competency Transformation project at Sears is designed to close the gap between skills the company requires and skills its current employees have. Nearly 80 percent of information technology staff will be retrained in "boot camps" where they will

focus on intranet and Internet technologies, e-commerce, Microsoft developments, and telecommunications and call-centre technologies.

- At Motorola in Schaumburg, Illinois, every employee, from CEO to janitor, is required to complete at least forty hours of training every year.

Helping people manage their careers

Flatten a pyramid, shrink a ladder, bust up a hierarchy, and what are you left with? A nimble system based on merit, perhaps, but one with fewer opportunities for advancement. Many a young worker will say that's okay because they don't buy into "advancement" so much as constant challenge and stimulation, anyway. Today's workers may understand the shrinking vertical ladder, but they want and expect plentiful opportunities for lateral moves that come with raises and a never-ending stream of stimulating projects.

Land's End of Dodgeville, Wisconsin, has introduced a scheme enabling employees to try out new jobs in the company.

Meeting this need for lateral career moves requires organizations to be very intentional about how people make moves within the organization. In conducting employee-retention assessments for companies, John frequently hears about the difficulty of changing assignments within companies. A software consultant at one large firm told him, "It's easier to quit around here and apply to another division as an unemployed person than to get transferred." Companies that want to retain talent must make it easier for employees to change projects or roles. Wiser still are the companies that proactively help people manage their careers, like American Express, which created workshops for their call-center staff to help them identify what they like to do, how that matches their present job, and how to plan for their future growth.

Now that the crumpled career ladder makes an employee's next step unclear, career management becomes critically important. Career moves—especially lateral ones—tend to be highly personal and stressful decisions. Some individuals have strong navigational instincts, but most workers appreciate direction. Hence, the highly popular new term, "career sculpting," and the rising tide of in-house or on-retainer career counselors and corporate mentoring programs.

SAS, the largest privately held software company in the world, has a turnover rate of less than 4 percent (compared with the industry average of 17 percent). This is surely in part because the company has told employees that they can expect to have three or four careers in their lifetime, and it hopes these will all be at SAS.

One of John's clients, GTE Northwest, is a large telecommunications operator in the Pacific Northwest. Once the bastion of job security and long-term employment, utilities are now being forced to acknowledge the need for more lateral career moves. Managers at GTE tell us that in the old days, technicians would learn a trade (for example, high-wire splicing) and stay in it for a lifetime. Now, when young employees master a trade, they ask their supervisor what the next step is. That is, as soon as they experience a level of mastery, they want more challenge. Part of this trend is a desire to expand skills, but much of it is that generational tendency to get bored quickly. Either way, older supervisors with an eye on retention are well-advised to respond to this new and growing reality in ways that help the company—as in proactively implementing opportunities for change, challenge, and career mentoring.

The benefits of such an action plan go three ways: Employees motivated by new challenges are more productive, the company benefits from longer-term and cross-trained employees, and workers tapped to act as mentors develop their leadership skills and experience new energy and commitment as a result of making a difference in someone else's life.

"People who move laterally to another department seldom carry any occupational burdens or past obligations with them. All of a sudden, new ideas come rushing to the surface," says David K. Foot in *Boom, Bust & Echo.*

> Fuller Company of Bethlehem, Pennsylvania, wrestled its 20 percent turnover in the early 1990s down to 2 percent three years later by introducing a program that included leadership and technical skills training, combined with a twelve-week orientation and two-year mentoring program for new employees. The company believes that its leaders-in-training benefit from being mentors, while everyone seems to be collaborating better.

Because professional development keeps them marketable, employees don't want things left to chance when it comes to learning. And because constantly acquired new skills and challenges have replaced promotions as a carrot stick, workers need feedback and guidance more than at any other point in history. A Royal Bank of Canada study of worker attitudes commissioned in 2000 concluded that "Canadian employees rate their workplace high in terms of fairness, flexibility and vacation allowance, but are significantly less pleased with communication, feedback, rewards and opportunity for advancement." Sadly, fewer than four in ten were satisfied with the degree of recognition they receive at work.

A Gallup study found that two of the top twelve predictors for employee engagement relate to learning and development: "Highly engaged" employees reported that someone in the company had spoken to them about their progress within the past six months, and they felt they'd had the opportunity to learn and grow within the past year. How would your employees answer those questions? How often do you sit down with people and talk about their progress, where they desire to go next, and what your plans are for them? If the answer is once per year or less, consider yourself vulnerable to unnecessarily high turnover.

A well-worn maxim in business is, "What gets measured gets done." In many organizations, managers and supervisors are not held accountable for developing their people. To improve in this area, organizations might begin measuring the extent to which employees feel their careers and development are being managed by supervisors and to make high scores on those measures a key part of managers' evaluations.

If their company doesn't work at giving them professional growth, employees have newfangled distractions to remind them to do so. An Internet site created by Information Access Co. offers online diagnostic tools regarding one's work situation and possibilities. For instance, LifeCenter (**library.iacnet.com/lifecenter**) asks, "Do you get choice assignments? Is there room for professional growth?" The site also provides articles and tips to ensure that your next gig works out better.

However much room employees feel there is for improvement, at least they think companies are gradually getting better at feedback.

According to Gallup, the percentage of employees "completely satisfied" with the recognition they receive for work accomplishments grew from 24 to 38 percent between 1991 and 1999.

One facet of professional growth we've only touched upon so far is *job sculpting,* the art of matching people to jobs that embrace their life interests and values, of forging a customized career path. Once fitting person to job was seen as the responsibility of the employee, but today it stands as one of the newest and most effective methods for drawing and retaining skilled workers. During a recruiting session in 1999, one employer—a Wall Street firm—snatched numerous recruits from competitors simply by emphasizing its commitment to their career development. Students confirmed this in a follow-up session, citing the firm's promises to help them manage their careers as key in their decision to join up.

"Make no mistake: job sculpting is challenging; it requires managers to play both detective and psychologist," notes *The Harvard Business Review,* which explored the concept in depth in its September/October 1999 issue.

Of course, managers in a position to help employees with career decisions could use some specialized training for the job. But the real skill is caring enough to listen to the employee's aspirations. And as we've mentioned, managers most inclined to take on this role have been encouraged to do so by forward-thinking organizations. Unfortunately, many managers and project leaders fail to consider career development as one of their responsibilities.

One fast-growing trend is peer mentoring, which involves like-minded individuals exchanging ideas, perspectives, and experiences through a deep level of exchange to gain new insight and clarity into the business, personal issues, and opportunities they face. Peer mentoring was developed around 1975, and many business people find it works better than other models because of the definitive shift in society away from authoritarianism. The concept of an older know-it-all matched with a sponge-like protégé doesn't apply in peer mentoring. Participants believe they can learn much from their peers, especially because it is likely these peers have battled the issues in question more recently than a semi-retired sage.

"We don't have a need to impress each other. We can be open and honest about what it is we're going through," explains one new convert.

Joan Mara, a Vancouver-based consultant who trains businesses around North America in this concept, helps entrepreneurs move from what they do best—help people solve problems—to what they do less well: come together in a peer context to discuss the most important issues they face, business or personal, with a high level of vulnerability.

"We create a non-judgmental, confidential, non-advice-giving environment that supports people to talk about what's keeping them up at night. These are often topics not easy to discuss even in a group of peers. The model moves away from trying to fix it, to one of storytelling and sharing from experience."

The Tandy Corp./RadioShack recently implemented some significant business strategies that included a mentoring program, revamped orientation, and enhanced benefits. The result: "Now people are contacting the corporation to ask to work for us, and although we don't release specific figures, I can say that from a year ago, we've seen an eleven percent to twenty-two percent reduction in turnover," reports the "vice president of people."

Mentoring is more personal and, perhaps in the end, more effective, than access to formal career counselors. And since up to 70 percent of employee knowledge is obtained informally on the job, it makes sense to assign workers problems that will expand their repertoire of skills and contacts (with or without the help of mentoring) than to over-rely on formal learning programs. At TDIndustries, a peer mentor is assigned to every new hire for six months.

Beyond mentoring, formal training, and problem-solving opportunities lies the overseas assignment. When *Fortune* asked employees who had resisted headhunters' offers why they stayed put, one of the most-cited reasons was the opportunity for an interesting overseas assignment. Global-minded workers want the opportunity to explore new places on company time. Perhaps that is why HSBC Bank of

Canada, known for its overseas assignments, is one of the favored employers in Western Canada.

Discovering oneself at work

Until the twentieth century, work was secondary to other parts of life, and certainly not a celebrated portion. The Spanish word for work—*trabajo*—comes from a Latin root for "torture." The Irish word for job has its roots in the words for "a temporary assignment" and "excrement"! Yet, since World War II, the status of work has risen steadily to the point where some have called it the "new religion," the place where people look for growth and development. This is in sharp contrast to a 1960s study in Great Britain, which found that even among the most affluent workers, work was seen purely as a means to an end, and "job satisfaction" translated as plenty of salary to spend on after-work social opportunities, the primary focus of life.

Today, 57 percent say work is more a "sense of identity" than a way to "make a living"—a major about-face that has taken *less than a generation* to occur. In evident agreement with this, a *Fortune* study in 1996 found that about 80 percent of Americans would continue to work even if they did not need to. Why? They wish to contribute, connect with others, and grow. In other words, work offers personal fulfillment.

Baldor Electric in Fort Smith, Arkansas—located in the Ozarks—has helped 1,150 employees upgrade reading and writing skills since 1991.

Since a growing number of workers are *rebelling* against the work-as-self-identity trend, today's employers need to walk a fine line between catering to that need for personal fulfillment on work time, and respecting those who wish to deny or back away from it. Remember Mark Metin, the manager of a mining software company described in Chapter 4? He promotes flex time, a social atmosphere, and in-house mentoring, while staying vigilant for burnout. He has been known to send over-dedicated workers home to get some rest, knowing that burnout only triggers employee turnover. Metin clearly understands the contemporary employee's often-conflicting needs.

What *is* personal fulfillment on work time? Countless studies boil it down to three variables: ability (the skills, experience, and knowledge that make a worker feel competent); values or preferred rewards (money, challenge, prestige, power, or influence); and life interests. The first, ability, is the weakest predictor of job satisfaction; one can be good at a job and not enjoy it. Matching personal and corporate values is much more important for keeping retention high. But matching life and work interests is the most important of the three for long-term career satisfaction, according to *The Harvard Business Review*. An employer can impact such a match best through a mentoring or career-sculpting program.

There are other, subtler ways of linking work and personal fulfillment, however. Skilful trainers can help workers make the connection between workplace communication skills and communication in the family. The six hundred people who went through a "spirit-at-work" program John designed for a client in Calgary told the trainers that an unexpected and valuable benefit of the program was how it applied to their lives outside of work.

Among the most popular life-management skills are leadership, financial planning, retirement planning, stress management, creating a work/family balance, and time management.

Since Silver Diner expanded its training program to include developmental life skills, the firm has been able to recruit 30 percent of its management from line employees, and promote 20 percent of operating partners from entry-level ranks.

Leading-edge companies are beginning to offer personal coaching in these areas, especially for high-level executives. Clearly, the next step would be to roll that out to the rank and file. Offering personal growth opportunities to employees has had some surprising effects. Employers who thought that employee loyalty was dead have learned that this is the hot button for reviving it.

In 1997, Arlie Hochschild wrote a controversial book entitled *The Time Bind: When Work Becomes Home and Home Becomes Work*, in which she suggested that dual-income couples were working long hours to escape their hectic home lives. If we extend her hypothesis, it implies that the complexity of modern family life—dual incomes, unclear roles, blended families—have produced less satisfaction outside of work and put even more pressure on the workplace to produce personal development.

Along those lines, *Fast Company* ran a cover story in 1999 with the headline, "Betrayed by Work," which focused on people whose lives were being ruined by negative work situations. Expert after expert talked about how people were letting work become too central to their lives, and how their stories of missed promotions and abusive bosses were symbols of a work-addicted culture.

This trend has even extended into attitudes about retirement. Although once work was a way to pay the bills and retirement was something for which people longed—with dreams of cruises, golf courses, recreational vehicles, and gold watches—the American Association of Retired Persons recently shed light on a major change in attitude. In 1999, for the first time ever, over half of people in their fifties had no plans to retire in the traditional sense; they wanted to keep working until they were unable to do so. Instead of retirement, they anticipated flexibility—the opportunity to work part-time or pursue a new career. The magnitude of this shift should not be underestimated. Today's workers see work in a whole new light, as a place where they find themselves and contribute. Although work often disappoints in this regard, the fact that people are coming to work today expecting to grow is beyond question.

Paula Lawlor, founder of Medi-Health Outsourcing (No. 87 on the 1999 *Inc.* 500 list) estimates she has spent at least $10,000 on course work and on-the-job training for one employee whose organizational skills she valued.

The impetus for personal development on work time is the assumption that it goes hand-in-hand with one's development as an employee, and promotes company loyalty. Does it work? Just look at the phenomenal popularity of Stephen Covey's *Seven Habits of Highly Effective People* to answer that. All over North America, employees are going through Covey courses on company time, and associating their growth as a person with the company for which they work.

Promote growth or pay the price

Whether today's employee is a workaholic or is simply taking work too seriously, the point for today's employer is that work has become a part of who we are, not just what we do. We may say that family and personal life is our real lifeblood, and it may well be, but the first question hurled at strangers in North American social gatherings is, "What do you do?" Work has become more than a means to make ends meet; it has become an end in itself.

Brenda Reed, Director of Employment Services

Total System Services, a division of Synovus Financial

Columbus, Georgia

A recent employee survey made Total System Services (TSYS) sit up and take more notice of employee development. "We already had a great place to work, but we thought we could do a better job on career-pathing," says Brenda Reed, Director of Employment Services, who has watched turnover at the 5,000-employee company drop from 15.5 per cent in 1998 to 11.4 per cent in 2000. (It was at 9.4 per cent last check.)

By career-pathing she means improving the company's performance evaluation system through a new process called "Right Steps," listening better to the career aspirations of "team members" (the TSYS word for employees) and offering them more feedback to help with career development and growth. Central to this aim was the parent company Synovus' implementation of three new initiatives: Foundations of Leadership, The Leadership Institute at Synovus and Right Steps, all administered through a restructured Center for People Development. (And these are separate from two more new facilities, one for on-site day-care, to be completed in summer 2001, and the other a new campus complete with library, fitness centre, dry cleaner, cafeteria, bank, travel agency, store and rental car service — accommodating 2,500 employees.)

Where once team members received feedback annually, they now sit down with their managers three times a year through the Right Steps process and review where they want to go, in addition to a year-end session. "That's a lot of constant feedback from the manager, which helps with career development and growth," says Reed.

All managers and team leaders are required to complete Foundations of Leadership, which teaches the company's "Leadership Expectations:" live the values, share the vision, make others successful and manage the business. Foundations of Leadership is a prerequisite for managers who might be chosen to attend the Leadership Institute, which "cultivates leaders who are going to take us into the next millennium," Reed says. Acceptance is competitive and selective, and applicants must be recommended. First there's a one-year "emerging leader" course for experienced, high-potential managers that includes two week-long retreats offsite focusing on individual development An 18-month course for more senior "executive leaders" includes three week-long offsite retreats for coaching on performance, and a two-year course for presidents, CEOs and other "organizational leaders" who attend four week-long offsite retreats with guest speakers and special attention on strategic planning and direction.

Besides these more formal programs, TSYS has introduced a "lunch and learn" program, allowing employees to attend free workshops during their lunch hours, on financial planning, purchasing a home, writing a will, and so on.

Why such emphasis on employee development and growth? "In my father's generation, people believed in taking a job and staying with that company until they died – forty years without missing a day's work," Reed says. "This generation sees that they have to grow in order to be successful and happy with what they're doing. And they have to feel they're growing personally as well as professionally. They're able to do a better job if they feel they're growing."

Employee surveys have also led TSYS to do away with traditional titles in a process the company calls "leadership titling," and introduce a "family education leave" program, which allows employees 20 hours' paid leave per year to participate in their children's school programs (to attend a play, help with a field trip or eat lunch with them). They're also entitled to leave for volunteer work, "because they want to be in a place through which they can contribute; they want to feel like they're giving back to the community, making a difference," Reed says.

"We're more like a family than co-workers," says Reed. "A lot of what we're doing is listening."

Assessing your company for development

The statements below allow for an initial assessment of how your organization, division, and/or department is doing at responding to the employee search for personal growth and development. The assessment is meant to guide your thinking, not to provide a definitive quantitative assessment of your progress. For each question below, answer how true the statement is of your work environment using the scale provided:

_____ Managers in our company sit down with employees and discuss their development and the organization's plans for their growth at least every six months (If the answer is yes, informally, 1 point; if managers have been given guidelines for how or why to do so and are held accountable for doing it, tally 3 points).

_____ Employees are often given the opportunity to be part of task groups and assignments outside their core job responsibilities (1 point if it happens informally; 3 if a formal program addressing this is in place).

_____ Our company has a career development program that helps people become more aware and responsible around their own career development (1 point if the company offers such a program to most people; 2 points if it is considered a priority and the program is a success).

_____ Employees in our company have learning plans that identify what skills they want to learn and they have input into those plans (1 point).

_____ The training programs in our company and the trainers who lead them focus on the application of the learning to personal as well as to professional life (1 point).

_____ Transferring to a new project, assignment, or division in our company is an open process with few barriers (1 point if generally true, 2 if this has been formalized so that "people" movement is a priority for leaders).

_____ During their first year, new recruits are often disappointed by the lack of opportunities for growth and/or opportunities to do interesting work. (lose 2 points).

_____ The annual performance appraisal is the primary if not the only opportunity to discuss development needs (lose 1 point).

_____ Our organization supports sabbaticals, when employees take a period of time off to achieve a personal goal (2 points).

_____ TOTAL

SCORE:

4 or under: Take a full week's management retreat for brainstorming policies that address employee development concerns.

5–7: You're beginning to look responsive.

8–10: You are above average in meeting today's workers' needs, but there is still room for improvement.

11–14: You are an inspiring example, and probably have the best workers and a strong bottom line to show for it. E-mail us: **izzoinc@aol.com**.

7

The expectation of partnership

"I sometimes miss the old days, when offices operated on the feudal system. There was the boss, or liege lord, who occasionally dispensed favors (raises, that is) but more often withheld them. For his gaze to fall upon you was supposed to be reward enough. There were the knights, in their three-piece armor of worsted and sharkskin, and beneath them were the courtiers—the toadies and rumor-mongers who pored over the entrails of the wastebasket, in hopes of clues to the lord's disposition...The whole system depended on everyone's knowing his or her place... [but] if you were patient and kept your nose clean, you could slowly, almost effortlessly, rise from serf to squire and maybe even all the way to knight, in which case you, too, would be entitled to quaff bowl-size martinis at midday."

— CHARLES MCGRATH, *NEW YORK TIMES MAGAZINE*

Time-traveling knights would have a hard time identifying "place" or status in today's work world. They'd be rattled by participants' total disregard for knowing it. And depending on which establishment they dropped by, they might even have a devil of a time identifying the boss. That's because everything from dress code to office architecture, paycheck to training, has been turned inside-out to accommodate the new economy's demand for speed and efficiency—which has resulted in an ongoing collapse of hierarchical structures.

By now, everyone knows that to survive in today's marketplace, work teams must be able to make key decisions at lightning speed. It's old news that the environment that best nurtures these qualities is short on rules and middle managers, and long on a solid understanding of core values that allow for greater freedom, flexibility, and experimentation. Intellectually, we accept the result: a squashed hierarchy and empowered workers. But "empowerment" was only a transitional stop on the new-economy express ride—and one through which many a passenger slept. We've long since moved on. The destination for which business-class travelers must now prepare is partnering with the employees they've only just backed off micromanaging.

The desire of today's workers to work on more equal terms with their bosses defines the fourth of the six shifts we've identified in workplace attitude. Although this desire is more prominent among younger workers, in the end it cuts across demographic categories. Never confuse partnership with empowerment. Partners command more "say," respect, and stake. Empowerment is passé, at best a half-measure that was hopelessly open to meaningless mantras. In fact, if your company is just beginning to work on empowerment, we suggest that you skip it and proceed directly to a partnering strategy. It won't be easy and it won't be comfortable. But done right, it might help increase employee retention and send profits soaring.

Among other things, the retreat of hierarchies means age is no longer equated with wisdom, nor youth with a need for deference. Boomers who can't handle reporting to supervisors who are half their age will find their own success at risk.

The signs of this desire for partnership can be found in a variety of places. In a study of employee engagement in 1998, Gallup discovered that workers who felt their opinion counted at work were most likely to contribute with full energy and dedication. While many executives believe that corporate hierarchies have already been busted, employees beg to differ. A 1999 Watson Wyatt Canada survey indicat-

At Kinko's Inc. in Ventura, California, turnover stood at 78 percent. The company brought it down to 50 percent through a number of measures, including issuing $300 worth of stock to all employees who had been there a year or more. They also offered a 100 percent matched 401(k) plan that put one-quarter of that match in company stock. They called these measures "trying to give co-workers a piece of the rock."

ed that 61 percent of senior managers feel they treat employees as valued business partners, while only 27 percent of employees share that opinion. The reality is that flattening a hierarchy is easier than creating a new system in which people feel they are truly a part of a decision-making process. This is the real shift we see happening: People are no longer satisfied with involvement; they want ownership. Toppled hierarchies are only the halfway point toward partnership, and most corporate hierarchies that think they have collapsed are still just swaying dangerously.

Earlier, we discussed demographic and sociological trends that have accelerated this shift toward boss/worker egalitarianism. Smaller families and a more permissive parenting style have produced young workers who feel that the right to debate is inherent. What's more, the very independence for which employees have longed—embodied in contract work and flex time—has given them a taste for freedom that leaves them wanting more. Add to this the democratizing effects of technology and the Internet, and the roots of this shift become apparent. What may be less apparent to business leaders is that we are not talking here about a minor shift in expectations. When we say people expect to be partners, we mean it in the most literal sense. What does that mean for a business? It means leaders who fail to take this expectation seriously will lose talent to others who do, or to the workers' own entrepreneurial pursuits.

To embrace the concept, companies need to understand that partnering entails five distinct traits:

> At the hugely successful Dyson Appliances in the U.K., each company has its own management, board, and budget, set by themselves in consultation with the founder/chairman, financial director, and group financial controller. "We try to avoid the idea of a formal head office and group directors, so each company feels that it stands on its own and makes its own decisions, independent of the holding company," says founder James Dyson.

1. **Communication above rank:** workers don't just want more say; they fully expect it.
2. **Open books:** workers desire a true stake in the game, which means employers must take a deep breath and provide them with a free flow of previously heavily guarded information.

3. **Performance-based pay:** a true stake also means devising profit-sharing plans of the generous variety. Options are getting more creative by the day as they shimmy down a melting ladder.

4. **Partnering leaders:** training more leaders in a less authoritarian style is emerging as the make-or-break factor in retention, engagement, and long-term survival.

5. **Vigilance and attention to symbolism:** younger workers in particular have no time or respect for false hierarchies, and they're as ready to read signs of them into day-to-day work processes as road-rage perpetrators are to imagine driving slights on the road. Here's where leaders must come squeaky clean, which is no simple task. Symbols such as titles and office layout become important clues to job applicants and employees who are looking for a collapsed versus structurally intact hierarchy.

Vanquishing centuries of hierarchical rule is difficult to accomplish in a day, especially when the alternatives are only vaguely understood. The truth is, we had a better grasp on the alternatives *before* the science of management appeared.

When Schwab, the high-tech financial company, abandoned a hierarchical structure, it quickly found that a flatter structure allowed them to move employees around more easily, thus building a broader base of skills in employees while preventing boredom. "Schwab challenges people to take on new assignments, join project teams, explore ideas, and set off down uncharted paths," its Web site proclaims.

Prior to the twentieth century, the only giant organizations in existence were religions and armies. Both glued their ranks together with a combination of authoritarian rule and shared values. Today, companies are striving to banish heavy-handed authority, which is incapable of responding to rapid-paced change and dehumanizing to a highly educated, democratic workforce.

As a twenty-six-year-old employee with a boomer supervisor remarked to us, "I am a competent professional. What drives me nuts is that so many managers make changes for change's sake. If the changes matter, fine, but don't micromanage me."

Salaries and benefits still count for something, and flexibility—which almost everyone is offering by now—is critical. But values represent the most powerful tool for engaging and retaining workers, assuming leaders know how to articulate those values that are common to the corporate culture. If being treated like a partner is one of the most universal and coveted values on workers' minds, a company need only meet that desire to achieve a high level of commitment.

Communication above rank

Ever heard the urban work legend about the office workers who continuously complained that their office was either too hot or too cold? A wisecrack executive arranged for a thermostat to be installed on the wall, after which employees stopped complaining, content instead to trot over to the device and alter it from time to time. The kicker, of course, was that the thermostat wasn't wired into heating controls. The workers were calmed by a mere *sense* of control.

We know a general manager of a small firm who, faced with requests for a bottled-water stand, purchased a model and refilled it with tap water each evening after hours. No one knew, so no one complained, and he smirked at the savings.

While neither of these stories speaks much for office integrity, both back up the Gallup finding mentioned earlier, that "having your own opinion count" is an important predictor of how engaged employees are. Most managers are afraid to ask workers what keeps them at the firm and what would entice them to leave. "They're afraid they will be asked for something they can't give," says Sharon Jordan-Evans, a Los Angeles leadership consultant and co-author of *Love 'Em or Lose 'Em: Getting Good People to Stay*. Just the act of asking them can make them feel valued.

At Donnelly, the glass company in Holland, Michigan, employees elect representatives to equity committees that have the power to address issues of policy and practice, including pay.

Yet clearly, asking employees for their opinions isn't enough. Employees must feel safe to respond and they must believe that their opinions may bring about change. Authors of a report on worker engagement found that while one-third of US organizations have employee involvement programs, only 10 percent of workers say they are part of a participatory environment. A cartoon of several years ago, depicting an employee suggestion box connected to a paper shredder on the other side of the wall, may have expressed it best. That is, sleight of hand and the pretence of wanting to hear from people enhance cynicism.

Another survey revealed that employees in the United States rate two-way communication and individual recognition as highly important to job satisfaction, second only to salaries and benefits. And yet fewer than 35 percent frequently share opinions with top management. This discrepancy points to shortcomings in corporate commitment to communication over rank and/or to a need for more and better leadership training.

Companies that wish to respond to this shift must make listening a form of religion. Getting out there and hearing what people have to say must be a priority for leaders. As often as not, the biggest obstacle to communication over rank is not so much poor communication as a lack of time set aside specifically for communication and the lack of an agenda for breaking down the remnants of deference by rank.

BC Hydro in Vancouver, Canada, has countered this problem by urging its executives to spend 15 percent of their time talking to employees. Without this kind of commitment, busy schedules and commitments fence out the very face-to-face communication that helps employees feel a sense of ownership.

At TDIndustries, a large mechanical engineering firm in Texas that has been on *Fortune*'s "Best Companies to Work For list" numerous times, CEO Jack Lowe has found a unique way to respond to this need. For several years, he has met with several dozen employees at a time, every three weeks for about three hours. "I randomly get to everybody every two years," Lowe says. "We have breakfast together, get to know each other a bit, and I talk some about what's happening in the company. But mostly it is an open forum; I answer questions and we talk about whatever is on their minds. The success of our company is a direct result of conversation. Our company was really influenced by the work of Robert Greenleaf on the concept of servant leadership. One of the ingredients of trust is

Microsoft's Bill Gates, who prefers that employees call him "Bill," is said to answer all e-mail from employees.

listening. Recently I asked a young man in our company what he liked most about working here. He said, 'I came here and you asked me what I think. It's the first place they have ever asked me that.'"

Employees at TDI are lucky; less than half of workers report regular communication with their supervisor regarding their work performance. A Montreal entrepreneur trying to profit from that communication gap has developed a Web site called the BrainBank (**www.brainbank.com**). Andre Laurin was frustrated by his own experience as an employee and believes that, too often, good ideas from the rank and file are not taken seriously by leaders who have the power to implement them. His site allows employees to submit suggestions capable of saving the company $5,000 or more per year. Laurin reviews incoming ideas, researches them, and when he deems one to have merit, endeavors to sell it back to the individual's employer, along with his supporting research. The employer must pay BrainBank half of the first year's savings, while BrainBank in turn pays the individual 75 percent of BrainBank's earnings.

> 3M introduced a "Golden Step" award to those responsible for successful new business ventures originated within 3M. Also, 3Mers who successfully push through a new product are allowed to run it as their own project, department, or division.

Management experts aren't thrilled with the idea, saying that the scheme will only exacerbate the communication problems so common in organizations. Certainly, companies vigilant about open communication and rewards are more likely to fill their suggestion boxes in-house. For instance, at Medi-Health Outsourcing, employees who pass on a lead that generates money can collect $500 to $1,000.

Free and open communication has always been a staple ingredient of true partnership. Employees who regard themselves as partners never hesitate to offer an opinion, on the assumption it might influence the course of things. Unfortunately, too many are inclined to agree with the young employee who confided, "We're not here to decide anything—just to create the illusion of support for what top management wants." Such employees see their role as guessing what the boss wants. They brainstorm to play along or they say nothing, convinced that their participation is token. Knowing their place in the hierarchy all too well, they also fail to take surveys seriously, so management is blind to its naked-emperor status. The best way to engage workers who have felt shut out for so long that they've grown a cynical shell is to ask them questions that cannot be answered with one word. Ask specifically what might go wrong with a project, what challenges they anticipate. Frame questions with an explanation of why you want the worker to respond and what you'll do with the information. Concentrate on questions of fact rather than fishing for opinions and attitudes—then act on the feedback. Effective leaders learn how to accept criticism because not doing so discourages employees from contributing.

Cruise through any popular Web site and you'll see that the opportunity to comment, complain, or "soapbox" has grown exponentially. The result is that younger workers in particular have come to feel that having a say is *their right* and *management's privilege*. They seek out work environments in which they need not have any qualms about speaking up, no old-world sense of "knowing their place." Wise leaders indulge or harness rather than quash this state of mind.

At Imagination, Britain's largest and most anti-hierarchical design firm, only four people have formal titles. Since no one is in charge, everyone feels responsible for the outcome of team projects and conventional power struggles are said to be rare.

"People who are difficult to supervise and free to leave, people who think for themselves, who question authority, are a leader's best source of information and only hope for achieving organizational goals," wrote the authors of *Megatrends 2000*.

BC Hydro created a president's page on the company intranet, where employees can grouse anonymously about issues that irk them.

It was Irshad Manji's outspokenness, lack of deference, and assumption that she had a contribution to make that got the Ugandan-born, twenty-three-year-old journalist the boot from the *Ottawa Citizen* in 1992. In her book, *Risking Utopia*, Manji recalls, "During one board meeting, I locked horns with the *Citizen*'s publisher, who advocated axing the country's deficit—and fast. Not at the expense of the unemployed, I piped up. His eyes fixed on mine, the veteran journalist snapped, 'Look, young lady. I'm saying this so people like you will have a future.'

"'People like me need a present before we can have a future,' I retorted."

Manji also relates "periodic comments from superiors that I should dress more delicately, and instructions...not to dispute the biases of older journalists."

Claire Raines, in *Beyond Generation X*, tells of a franchise company founder who, while visiting one of his outlets, asked a young employee how she was doing. "Well, a little hung-over this morning, but okay," she responded, clearly unaffected by his title. Generation X's "comfort with authority allows them to speak up with fresh ideas since they're not seeking approval from those in charge," Raines says. "This outspokenness is important to companies striving to stay on the cutting edge."

Noel Tichy, a professor at the University of Michigan Business School and author of *The Leadership Engine: How Winning Companies Build Leaders at Every Level*, masterminded the Business Leadership Initiative in 1997, by which leadership training and previously guarded company information filters quickly throughout an enterprise. Ford's CEO, Jacques Nasser, had realized that few of his executives, never mind employees in the lower ranks, understood the fundamentals of Ford's business. So, guided by Tichy, Nasser educated the first three hundred people who reported directly to him, and they were instructed to pass on what they had learned to another two thousand employees, who in turn were told to update subsequent layers. Within nine months, 55,000 Ford employees had learned about Ford's price–earnings ratio and why it mattered. Within another year, all 100,000 salaried workers worldwide had taken the message to heart. The next task was to extend the principles of this leadership method deep into the organization.

At Kinko's, which has very low turnover, the words "employees" and "boss" are never used. All employees, including the company president and branch manager, are known as "coworkers."

At Imagination Ltd. in London, England, employees are expected to come up with ideas outside of their own area. "People have roles, but rather than jealously guard those roles and say, 'You can't question me! I'm the subject matter expert,' they are willing to really listen," explains an account manager.

When communication crosses lines of rank and titles fade into the background, profound things can happen in a company, as demonstrated by Teknion Corporation in Toronto. After adopting a decentralized and non-hierarchical innovation process, the company found that it could identify a need and respond with a product within twelve months. The weekly steering meetings, which involve representatives from sales, marketing, and manufacturing, have been described as "messy, turbulent, and noisy," but with increased sales figures that outperform industry growth, who cares? Karen Anne Zien, author of *Innovation Explosion*, calls this approach "the fuzzy front end that, combined with strong senior leadership and support, creates the ideal microclimate of sustainable innovation."

We call it partnering, or dancing on the grave of hierarchy.

AES Corporation of Arlington, Virginia, set a goal of eliminating hierarchy in its operation to build "an engaged and accountable workforce." The company aimed for bottom-up, employee-led strategic, operational, and capital allocation planning processes. During a radical overhaul, the chairman of the board and CEO eliminated the majority of staff titles, including human resources, in favor of "employee generalists." The company reassigned decision-making to the team level, reduced the number of management "approvals" necessary for team decisions, and implemented team-based performance management that focuses on achieving results. As of 1999, the share value of AES has performed better than average by between 200 and 600 percent. But AES isn't finished yet. Its goals include eliminating all approval processes, integrating operations and maintenance, eliminating hourly work in favor of salaried positions, and handing over responsibility for setting compensation rates to the individual employee level.

At W.L. Gore in Newark, New Jersey, the words "boss" and "manager" have been replaced by the word "sponsor." Employees choose their own projects under what they call a "bossless" style of management.

"Sooner or later, executive leadership becomes crucial, especially in sustaining change that can have organization-wide impact. The real role of executive leadership is not in 'driving people to change,' but in creating organizational environments that inspire, support and leverage the imagination and initiative that exists at all levels," says Peter Senge, author of *Dance of Change*.

Need still more inspiring examples? Southwest Airlines turns its planes around in less than half the time of its competitors because employees' training emphasizes both individual and group discipline. Marriott's housekeepers and bellhops endeavor to accomplish their tasks with no delays or complaints because they're driven by a desire to make themselves and their organization proud. Instead of an executive-imposed, top-down system telling them what to do, there are only a strong commitment within a flattened hierarchy and conspicuous rewards for those who demonstrate self-discipline and teamwork.

"Working here is truly an unbelievable experience," one enthusiastic employee of Southwest Airlines in Dallas wrote in a *Fortune* survey. "They use your ideas to solve problems. They encourage you to be yourself. I love going to work!"

At Medi-Health Outsourcing, No. 87 on the 1999 *Inc.* 500 list, managers run their own divisions with maximum autonomy, hourly workers have the opportunity to become salaried consultants, and all employees have the freedom to move around the company until they find their niche, "often racking up training costs that some company owners might find excessive," notes *Inc* magazine. They're entitled because they're partners, and the investment is more likely to pay off because partners are less inclined to "walk."

Let's examine the Harley-Davidson Inc. saga. Shortly after Richard Teerlink joined as CFO in 1981, the company's market share dropped precipitously, and thanks to a 40 percent downsizing exercise, its workforce plummeted. Teerlink decided to invest in the people through massive training, an employee-driven performance-evaluation and effectiveness system, and workgroups made up of both blue- and white-collar employees. In other words, he collapsed the hierarchy, emphasized a lifelong learning environment, and "partnered" with workers. The result? By 1999, Harley-Davidson's market share had more than tripled, unit sales had more than quadrupled, and the employee count had nearly tripled.

"Managers can't manage by fear anymore. Long-term rewards, twelve-month reviews, and annual raises and bonuses are obsolete. So stop managing time and place, and start managing people and performance," says Bruce Tulgan, founder of New Haven, Connecticut-based consulting firm, Rainmaker Thinking.

Gordon Bethune, CEO of Continental Airlines, piloted a workplace turnaround through an innovative recognition program and by hobnobbing with the rank and file. The company placed twenty-third in the January 2000 Fortune 500.

Citrus Valley Health Partners, a multi-hospital organization in Los Angeles, opened communication by initiating what they called "what's-in-the-way meetings." Departmental leaders conducted monthly meetings for more than a year in which they asked employees the simple question, "What's in the way of you doing your job the way you want to?" All over the organization, the fire of commitment burned brightly because employees were given a say. They were made to feel their opinion counted.

One of John's first supervisors had a great way of welcoming new employees. At their first meeting, this manager said, "Look, you are new around here and will see lots of things we old-timers have let become habit. Many of these things make no sense, so in about six weeks, I want to sit down with you and hear all your ideas on what we need to re-think." He did have those follow-up meetings with new people and implemented some of their advice. The message from the start was simple: no false hierarchy around here. Everyone's ideas are welcome.

At Sun Microsystems, here's an early tradition that has stayed intact: No matter where you sit in the organization's pecking order, you can send an e-mail to anyone else in the company, including the CEO, with a question or idea. Of course, many companies *say* this is allowed, but without regular evidence that there will be no negative repercussions

Granite Rock, a Watsonville, California, construction firm that placed nineteenth on the Fortune 500 in January 2000, calls all workers "job owners." A title used back in 1998, which came with a raise, was "improvement champion."

and that the ideas submitted could change the way things are done, employees are usually loathe to go over the head of their immediate supervisor.

Dallas-based Texas Instruments is clearly a company determined to give the rank and file more say: Employees are actively encouraged to speak their minds, a quality that helped the company clinch the No. 77 spot on the Fortune 100 in January 1998.

"You can't build loyalty with just a paycheck," says Adrian Woodridge, a Washington-based correspondent for *The Economist.* "Building long-term commitment depends on four things: the nature of the work itself, the opportunity to grow, the chance to speak up and be listened to and the feeling of making a difference."

Partnership means eradicating many of the traditional barriers to communication. Today's employees, children of permissive parenting and the Internet, have little time for any other kind of system. What's more, baby boomers have had to pucker up for such a large portion of their careers, that they, too, are flocking to companies where partnership-style communication exists.

Open books

Responding to the desire for partnership also entails opening the books and sharing more strategic and financial information than many old-economy executives can fathom. Is it safe to share such details with the ranks? they wonder. What about confidentiality, potential leaks? And yet partners rarely worry about sharing these types of information with one another. Is not trust and confidence the basis of a high level of commitment? How can a partner see the big picture, execute his or her duties, or sustain all-out commitment if large chunks of information are withheld, signaling that the other partners do not trust his or her intelligence or integrity?

Dance of Change describes open-book management as training all employees in financial literacy, or de-mystifying the numbers. Every team tracks and interprets the numbers that reflect how their unit makes a profit and occasionally compares their results with those of teams with which they must interact, to make "mutual decisions."

"In an open book management system, people assume ownership for their actions—and are paid accordingly…not through bonuses or incentive pay, but through a genuine stake in the action…As workers become increasingly proficient at playing the game of business, they change the game. They set their aspirations higher."

In 1981, a group of International Harvester managers engineered a leveraged buyout of a truck engine remanufacturing plant, put every employee into an Employee Stock Ownership Plan, and taught them about the business. In 1983, a janitor in the company (who happened to be a burned-out former Wall Street broker) stopped a manager and suggested that although the company's industry was currently doing well, since it tended to experience a recession every six years, why not diversify to avoid layoffs. The astonished manager researched this plan and ended up doing precisely that, profiting richly from the move by 1988.

"A funny thing happens when you take the time to educate your employees, pay them well, and treat them as equals. You end up with extremely motivated and enthusiastic people," says Kip Tindell, president and co-founder of the Container Store, which placed No. 1 on *Fortune* magazine's list of the "100 Best Companies to Work for in America" in January 2000. Employee turnover at the Container Store registers between 15 and 25 percent, compared with an industry average of 100 percent. The company is big on partnering. Everything from daily sales and company goals to expansion plans are shared with everyone. Corporate leaders believe this approach adds up to a sense of ownership.

At AES Corporation, mentioned earlier, information is shared so freely that the US Securities and Exchange Commission considers all employees to be insiders for stock trading purposes.

The real point here is that employees today respond to the partnering model. Information is the lifeblood of partnerships, and when employees are aware of what the company is doing, they want to help. Examples abound at TDIndustries, where all stock is in the hands of employees and a monthly meeting fills them in on financial matters.

Open books lead workers to see and understand the big picture, contribute in a bigger sense, take more initiative, and improve things in their own area of responsibility, particularly if they are recognized for it.

We recommend the following four books on open-book management:

- *Open-Book Management: The Coming Business Revolution* by John Case (New York: HarperBusiness, 1995)
- *The Open-Book Experience: Lessons from Over 100 Companies Who Successfully Transformed Themselves* by John Case (Reading, Mass: Addison-Wesley, 1997)
- *Open-Book Management Bulletin: Resources for Companies of Businesspeople*, edited by John Case (Somerville, Mass. 02144)
- *Open-Book Management: Creating an Ownership Culture* by Thomas L. Barton, William G. Shenkir and Thomas N. Tyson (Morristown, New Jersey: Financial Executives Research Foundation, 1998, 800-680-FERF).

Performance-based pay

The old contract between employer and employee was simple: A worker traded time for a defined amount of income. Hourly wages and defined benefits were the norm. But today's increasingly entrepreneurial employee wants a greater stake in the game. Workers are interested in being paid based on the value they add rather than the time they put in. This represents a major shift in thinking, and according to a recent Royal Bank of Canada study, companies are not responding well to it. Forty percent of workers said that the average employee doesn't benefit from profitable periods, and 46 percent said they are finding it hard to make ends meet. Still, companies are beginning to change their tune.

Thirty-six of the fifty-eight publicly held companies on the *Fortune* 100 list in January 2000 offered stock options to all employees.

Partners have always received a bigger slice of the pie than run-of-the-mill employees, and as today's workforce becomes mass-deputized as partners, profit-sharing is being extended far beyond its original boundaries.

"The new economy is about unlimited opportunity, democracy in the workplace and a commitment to link financial rewards to individual contribution and effort," *Fast Company* has declared.

For almost as long as there have been CEOs and senior executives, their compensation pies have been sliced into four portions: salary (60 percent), short-term incentives or an annual bonus (15 percent), long-term incentives or stock options (15 percent) and benefits (10 percent). Pies for executives on lower rungs differed only in having smaller long-term incentive slices and proportionately larger base-salary portions. Workers, of course, received a sliver of benefits within their salary tarts. All that changed in the early 1990s, when global competition made shareholders more demanding and "pay for performance" entered the business lexicon. Suddenly, executives were pressured to put their money where their mouths were and, to a lesser extent, apply this formula right down the ladder. The result: Salary growth has slowed while incentives have grown. In other words, where salary once "defined the man," it now means relatively little. Instead, short-term (one-year) incentives like the annual bonus are shriveling relative to the fast-expanding, longer-term (three- to ten-year) incentives, which no longer consist solely of stock options.

During its first decade, pay for performance attracted controversy, but now that early loopholes that gave some poorly performing executives a windfall have been detected and clamped shut, trackers are more confident of the correlation they've found between an increase in bonuses and company profitability.

Wall Street kicked off the pay-for-performance trend in the late 1980s, according to the *New York Times*. Leveraged buyouts meant that companies ended up, via stock, in senior employees' hands. The theory was that with a greater stake in the business, they'd work harder and smarter (now a widely accepted maxim). But remember, these were senior executives, and after watching the risks they took for personal gain, lower-ranked employees were soon demanding their own stock packages. By the mid-1990s, the profit-sharing model had trickled down to the rank and file. In 1999, ten million held company stock. Today, in new-economy firms, even janitors and secretaries have become wealthy through stock options. Now *that's* partnership.

Somewhere along this journey, employees have become far more informed about their personal market value, their companies' performance and potential, how competitors are operating, and what benefits they offer. Since the Internet makes such research easy, profit-sharing programs that contribute to employee retention and boost profits are mimicked in a flash. Let's explore a few examples of companies with innovative pay programs.

- A growing number of companies, including AT&T, Blue Cross Blue Shield, and Owens Corning, have traded in the traditional pension plan for a cash-balance plan that pays employees for their current performance, not past performance or longevity of employment. They grant everyone the same annual credit (between 4 and 8 percent of salary) plus interest on eventual pension. Employees generally take their cash balance with them when they leave.
- One pharmaceutical manufacturer offers annual bonuses to information technology staff who have skills that are in particular demand. Staffers nominated at the beginning of the year get a bonus of up to 15 percent of their salary if they stay through year-end. The company also offers bonuses based on projects or for staying with the company for a predetermined amount of time.
- Austin-based Whole Foods Market came up with "elder grants," whereby for every six thousand hours (about three years full-time) an employee has been with the company, he or she is given two hundred stock options, which vest 25 percent every year.
- At Synovus, all employees find a share of stock waiting for them on their first day on the job, a powerful symbol that they are partners, not just employees. Coincidentally, Synovus's turnover rate

The millionaire clubs: Southwest Airlines in Dallas, No. 2 on the *Fortune* 100 in January 2000, has created dozens of millionaires through profit-sharing. At Abbott Laboratories in Abbott Park, Illinois, internal stock has made 650 employees millionaires. More than one thousand Charles Schwab employees have over one million dollars in their accounts from generous stock grants. At Intel in Santa Clara, California, more than one thousand employees have become millionaires through stock options. Then again, most of the professionals hired before 1992 at Microsoft have become millionaires, and six have become billionaires.

for tellers is 20 percent, compared with the industry average of 49 percent.

- No. 3, Cisco Systems in San Jose not only issues stock options to everyone, but also on-the-spot bonuses of up to $2,000 for exceptional performance.

Leaders need to catch up with workers' preferences on this issue, especially when addressing the best and brightest—the employees most challenging to keep. Pay for the value they add, even if this requires dealing with the headaches of developing variable pay based on individual and corporate performance. If paying for value means ripping out the roots of the old compensation system in favor of a system more tuned to the partnering desires of your people, hesitate no longer. To be sure, there are those in your ranks who still prefer the old fixed system, but their numbers are shrinking.

The practices of partnering leaders

Management guru Mary Parker Follett wrote that, "the person who influences me most is not he who does great deeds, but he who makes me feel I can do great deeds." Although she preached this philosophy in the 1920s, only recently have corporations begun to tune into this line of thinking.

Leadership, having shed its authoritarian image to cope with the new economy and the new worker, has never been more challenging or more in demand. Today's leaders face highly self-reliant workers whose primary motivation often is garnering enough experience to leave and start their own businesses. Until they reach that goal, today's workers can and will change jobs at the drop of a hat. Managing them and coping with the pace of change demands more, not fewer leaders.

"We are long past the time when leaders can do it all alone, or even by the dozen. It takes hundreds to lead," Harvard Business School professor John Kotter has said.

Leaders, defined as people who are willing to stick their necks out and grant others the rope to do the same, are "in." Managers, defined as people who enforce orders from above, are "out."

Blaine Lee, author of *The Power Principle,* says that true leaders inspire loyalty, trust, admiration, and honor, and they possess principle-centered power. Coercion and compromise have no place in the new leadership. Lee presents ten principles of power:

1. Persuasion
2. Patience
3. Gentleness
4. Teachability
5. Acceptance
6. Kindness
7. Knowledge
8. Discipline
9. Consistency
10. Integrity

"In our business, it used to be clear who had the financial muscle to be on top. Now we're facing a wide range of well-financed competitors. So it's more important than ever for us to draw upon our entire organization," explains Andrall E. Pearson, chairman and CEO of Tricon Global Restaurants in Louisville, Kentucky.

Today's most successful leaders are cut from a different cloth than last generation's, yet they must operate within the toppling confines of yesterday's corporate structure. Not surprisingly, all this has fueled phenomenal growth in the leadership industry: It generates $15 billion US annually across North America. Although Follett has long since passed away, her advice has never been so current. True business leaders, she said, lead from within a group, listening to different points of view and integrating different ideas into a workable solution. Follett saw this method as distinct from both domination and compromise. She called it "the third way." We call it partnering. Since partnering is precisely what today's workers are cut out for *and* what they hotly desire, it's a concept that—applied with commitment—works like no other.

Let's face it. Today's workers are the best-educated in history, extremely entrepreneurial, technologically savvy, and global-minded. This makes them "unmanageable" in the traditional sense, but ideal candidates for partners. Can a company "let go" its entire workforce and "rehire" them all as partners? Wouldn't such a move break the bank and cause mayhem? As we've pointed out, partnership doesn't promise employees a bigger pie, just one cut in a different fashion (although in fact, experience has shown that the pie does tend to expand). As for mayhem, look at the experience of Allegiance Healthcare Corporation's plant in El Paso, Texas. Sales per employee have risen 61 percent in the five years since production workers were given responsibility for making assembly-line, purchasing, and shipping decisions that formerly rested with supervisors. Workers are way ahead of management on this one. Senior-level acceptance of this concept couldn't come at a better time, or be applied to a more primed force. In any case, here is where all those leadership-training courses help. They train executives to deal with workers on a more egalitarian basis, and workers to relate to their mission and each other in a more team-oriented, disciplined, and responsible manner.

We'll say it again: Leadership has become the make-or-break factor in retention, engagement, and simply staying in business. Where once leadership was one of several tools in the toolbox—alongside salary, promotions, and a buyer's market (more qualified applicants than job openings)—now leadership must do the job almost single-handedly. Salary and benefits will still sway workers, but nine times out of ten it's a respected boss for whom employees get out of bed in the morning, and a despised one for whom they quit. Yes, this was always true. No, it was never as sharply true. The currency of leadership has skyrocketed in value, along with a demand for more leaders.

> Instead of a rulebook, employees of the Container Store (No. 1 in the January 2000 *Fortune* 500) are told to trust their instincts, as long as their actions follow the company's six principles. The company's turnover rate is roughly one-third the industry average.

So what, precisely, is the task of today's leaders? Identifying, articulating, and sustaining the organization's values. Treating employees more like partners, paying heed to shifting values, and coming up with inspiring solutions to meet these desires. Leadership no longer has any connection with rank—security guards can nurture and practice it as easily as CEOs, in the right business climate—and while some appear to be natural-born leaders, others, with training and mentoring, can learn to fill the role.

Strong leaders are good at spotting self-motivated people and figuring out what it takes to keep them. "Leaders who believe they must continuously scurry about motivating everyone are destined to a fatiguing, ulcerating career," says Robert Wright, a professor of organization theory at California's Pepperdine University.

Nokia, a Finnish company that is the world's leading maker of cellular phones, has been called the least hierarchical large company in the world. Divisions are encouraged to make as many decisions as they can for themselves without corporate permission. Nokia has always taken the time for deep listening through something the company calls the "Nokia Way." The process begins with groups of employees meeting worldwide to brainstorm what the priorities of the company should be. These discussions move up the ranks to the top managers, who use the information as the roots from which to grow strategy, which is then rolled back out to employees. Such a mechanism for listening is what creates an aura of partnership within even the largest of companies.

> There's only one rule at Nordstrom, the Seattle retailer: "Use good judgment."

Steve Robertson, corporate director of Catholic Healthcare West, says, "Today's employees want to have an experience of partnership, which means bring listened to, but also means a culture based on values rather than rules. Our values guide people's thinking and become internalized. When the values are internalized, the need for rules diminishes."

According to *Harvard Business Review*, the four qualities that characterize effective leadership are morality, courage, initiative, and respect for others. Initiative and respect amount to giving others recognition. Of course, recognition, or full appreciation for work done, is the No. 1 factor in retaining staff. It builds self-esteem, which inspires workers to do their best work. Unfortunately, compliments, recognition, and praise are not a natural part of our day-to-day culture. We could all learn a lot from Toastmasters International's technique of always sandwiching constructive criticism between two compliments.

Or we could learn from James Champy, co-author of *Reengineering the Corporation*: "Keep a sharp eye for bureaucracy disguised as discipline!" Indeed, the very popularity of the cartoon strip "Dilbert" is witness to the negative experiences most employees have with rules that seem irrelevant, if not demeaning.

When business consultants studied the US Marines to determine how to build a committed team, they returned with five recommendations: First, ensure that new recruits comprehend the organization's core values. Second, prepare every person to lead, including frontline supervisors. The traditional method of feeding an elite minority into management training keeps the hierarchical model alive and wreaks havoc with team loyalty. "The Marines believe every member of the Corps must be able to lead.... In a flash of gunfire, any Marine may find that he's the person responsible for giving orders. The policy of training every frontline person to lead has a powerful impact on morale. The organization's belief that everyone can and must be a leader creates enormous collective pride and builds mutual trust."

The 1998 annual report of Herman Miller in Zeeland, Michigan, carried the name of every employee.

Third, distinguish between teams and a gathering of individuals. As we've said in an earlier discussion, there is danger in using meetings to legitimize preconceived plans, or in assuming that the most vocal member of a team speaks for all.

Fourth, take the time to bolster anyone who is floundering. Such support reinforces the individual's sense of belonging and promotes an intense loyalty from everyone. "Loyalty and a sense of belonging are components of the mutual trust that is critical," the researchers concluded. This advice is particularly apt because, unlike in past decades, when it comes to knowledge workers there is no crush of applicants waiting to replace the unsalvaged underperformer.

Finally, the Marines use discipline to build pride, and their secret to applying discipline without seeming authoritative lies in the way they place equal emphasis on self- and group-discipline. The Marines also demand that everyone act with honor, courage, and commitment; when followers find themselves living up to these expectations, they experience a great surge of energy.

Vigilance and attention to symbolism

Although everyone from president to janitor can be a leader, in a business climate still stumbling out from under a top-down culture, it is the "top" that must begin the process and protect it until it has taken firm root.

Here are a few examples of organizations that have used symbolism to launch themselves down the path to partnership.

Applied Minerals of Santa Clara, California cut executive pay by 10 percent when it announced layoffs in 1998.

- At Ingram Micro in Santa Ana, California, employees can phone the CEO at an 800 number that only he answers, or they can go to his office—his glass door is always open.
- At Xantrex in Vancouver, Canada, only one person (the head of human resources) has an office with walls. Everyone else, including the CEO, sits egalitarian-style in cubicles sprinkled throughout a large, open office area.
- Ernst & Young, while arranging for new satellite offices recently, decided to base the space in each office on the particular job, rather than on a person's rank.
- At Whole Foods Market in Austin, Texas, and Worthington Industries in Columbus, Ohio, new hires must be voted in by a team of fellow employees to become permanent.

Maybe by now you've got it. Symbols matter, especially when they are rooted in a deeper commitment to treat people like partners. When it comes to vigilance and symbolism, the temptation to do a surface renovation is strong. Unfortunately, it's as tough to camouflage an iron-clad hierarchy as it is to disassemble it. Flattening an entrenched hierarchy is a Herculean task. Keeping it flat after centuries of conditioning is an ongoing challenge that requires constant vigilance and effort. But taking on these challenges pays more than dividends; it ensures survival in the current environment.

Vigilance requires exerting a sense of caring, as in having no executive parking areas, special executive benefits packages, separate executive eating facilities, or more expensively decorated executive offices.

Dyson Appliances Ltd. of the UK captured more than half of the UK's vacuum-cleaner market in just five years by turning against the grain of hierarchy. There are no reserved parking spots or separate entrances for management, everyone eats healthy meals at modest prices in the same cafeteria, and an open-space floor plan encourages interaction. Founder and chairman James Dyson is known by everyone as "James," and his small, unpretentious, glass-walled office always has an open door. Line employees change jobs every forty-five minutes to ensure cross-training and flexibility and to eliminate boredom.

Similarly, a corporation that located the company cafeteria in an area with a "prime view" that the architects had originally assumed would accommodate the executive suite, is just one of many organizations leading the charge for a more democratized office.

Every employee of New York-based Pfizer got one hundred and fifty shares in 1999 to celebrate the company's one hundred and fiftieth birthday. (They can also get a Viagra prescription for free.) The turnover rate for the manufacturing workers at Pfizer is 1 percent, compared with 10 percent for the industry.

A joke about automation is currently making the rounds: The factory of the future will have only two employees—a person and a dog. The person will be there to press a button that activates the factory in the morning, and the dog will be there to make sure that his master doesn't touch anything else until the end of the day. Although work has become more automated, and top-down companies can make today's highly educated employees feel useless, the truth is that companies are becoming more dependent than ever on the innovation and creativity of their people. What is the ideal company in terms of the shift toward partnership? One where the CEO goes by his or her first name, where titles are employee-chosen (if titles exist at all), where pay is based on success rather than seniority, where listening is a religion, and where truth is spoken in the scheduled meetings, not just in the bathrooms. It will all seem natural once you've turned the tide.

Dennis Bakke, CEO

AES

Arlington, Virginia

Dennis Bakke doesn't believe in responding to shifting employee values to boost retention, for two good reasons. First, he doesn't believe in employees. At AES, all workers are called "AES people." Second, he believes we've got it the wrong way around: Rather than respecting employees' values in order to boost retention, company leaders should respect employees because it's the right thing to do. If retention follows, so be it, but stop going about it the wrong way around, he urges.

"I want these [values] to be lived with in good times or bad. That linkage is very dangerous, filled with hypocrisy. The most radical thing about AES is its purpose, not its values. Why does business exist? It's not to make profits or [serve] shareholders. It's to serve the world. That's why business is allowed to exist as a public entity and that's what we should be focused on."

We applaud his point but live in the real world, where most CEOs crave a bottom-line incentive for doing the right thing, and most companies are not as super-successful as AES, whether due to that craving or not.

What does impress many a corporate observer is the stage of Bakke's hierarchical crash. At AES, acres of rubble lie where most companies have intact or slightly flattened pyramids. And "AES people" appear to move about the ruins unconcernedly, if not downright contentedly. After setting a goal of replacing hierarchy with accountability, the company eliminated most titles, moved decision-making to teams, and began replacing management approval processes with team-based performance management.

"Every person is a thinking, creative person capable of making decisions," Bakke declares. He also believes that AES is one of the few companies that lives its declared intention of serving the world before shareholders. People, he says, "want to serve the world, deep down....Overwhelmingly at AES, you can go to a higher calling, make a difference in the world, do something useful, and be somebody—not with a title, but making a contribution to the world. To have a whole company like that, it has awakened what was already in people. We don't motivate. We make it possible for people to live out their dreams."

As for people development, Bakke proudly declares, "We don't do any training, none whatsoever. We started off back when it was popular, when everyone had their own university and all that garbage. We realized that was a throwback to the 'we take care of you' [philosophy]. We don't want to have anyone dependent. Everyone wants to grow and learn, but the best way to do it is to actually make decisions and be responsible for stuff. When you're put in a decision-making role, something magic happens. What we do here is put people in decision-making roles day one. All decisions are made by people on the front line. The learning process is unbelievable. The only rule we have is that before you make a decision, you have to get advice. The first thing that happens when someone asks advice, is they inform a community about what they're doing and they draw that community to them. But we don't have communities making decisions. The individual, by humbling himself or herself before the group and asking advice, ties themselves into the community, and it's very difficult to find a person Lone-Rangering then. They get the best education on the history of the world from people who love them and the world. The role of educating and training in this company is all at the instigation of the individual. Groups can get together and hire a teacher, can go to courses. You're not in training, ever. You're always working. Our people learn faster than any school I've ever seen. All of us, every one of us, all the time, are in an educational process. The whole company is an educational institute."

Nor does AES believe in sick leave, vacation days, or career counseling. "It's all unlimited. It's whatever you decide in conjunction with your colleagues. When you need a vacation, you take a vacation. You're a responsible adult. If you need to see your kids play lacrosse at four o'clock in the afternoon, you make arrangements with your colleagues, not with your manager.... Since we don't have a human resources department to tell you where to go, everyone chooses where they want to move to. There are no rules. There are no constraints."

And is the AES philosophy catching on elsewhere? Bakke has an opinion on that, too: "Everyone says, 'That's really interesting, but it won't work here. People here really want....'" He scoffs. "It's always the leaders that say that. You don't hear it very often from the persons themselves.... You have to be really suspicious that people want to be treated like babies or children and be told what to do and taken care of. I know, or at least I think I know, that that is not how we were made. Henry Ford once said, 'All I want is a pair of hands, and every time I get a brain it messes things up.' You don't have to force managers to go to work, because they're having a great time, being responsible. I reject the hypothesis that a lot of people just want to be told what to do." Bakke goes right to the point of partnership when he adds, "Being treated like an adult and making choices is the core of making a workplace fun.

"I'm not at all an anarchist or someone who says there is no such thing as authority. We have leaders, and they have authority. What holds us together is integrity, purpose, fairness, justice, and fun. Those things are in fact very much the province of leadership."

Assessing your company for partnership

The statements below allow for an initial assessment of how your organization, division, and/or department is doing at responding to the employee search for partnership. The assessment is meant to guide your thinking, not provide a definitive quantitative assessment of your progress. For each question below, answer how true the statement is of your work environment using the scale provided:

_____ Managers and leaders in our company spend a good deal of time listening to employees' ideas, formally and informally (in general, 1 point; structured, consistent and pervasive, tally 3 points).

_____ Pay is variable and rewards both team and corporate performance (1 point if you are moving in this direction; 2 if your pay system has been re-vamped based on the core principle of pay for performance).

_____ Our company is governed more by principles and values than by policies (1 point if you have values that often let one break the formal rules; 3 points if the policy manual is thin to nonexistent and the values strong; lose 2 points if you have a policy manual thicker than the Bible).

_____ Hierarchy is not important in your company. For example, anyone can e-mail anyone, people are called by their first names, and challenging those in formal leadership is common (3 points).

_____ The books are pretty open, and strategic information on company and team performance is shared regularly (1 point).

_____ Workers have a "stake" in the game via profit-sharing or stock ownership (1 point if limited to a few people, 3 points if pervasive, open to all, and financially meaningful as a percentage of salary).

_____ Leaders and managers have a style that encourages people to take responsibility and authority with little micromanaging (3 points; micromanaging is common and pervasive, lose 5 points!).

_____ TOTAL

SCORE:

5 or under: Take a full week's management retreat for brainstorming policies that address these concerns.

6–10: You're beginning to look responsive.

11–14: You are above average in meeting today's workers' needs, but there is still room for improvement.

15–18: You are an inspiring example, and probably have the best workers and a strong bottom line to show for it. E-mail us: **izzoinc@aol.com**.

8

The expectation of community at work

"I believe that the ultimate in self-actualization is when a person is confused about the difference between employment and recreation."

— KEN BLANCHARD

"Welcome, recruits, and right this way please. Hope you had no problem finding our corporate headquarters. To our right, folks, just past the concierge's desk, is one of our fitness centers, and adjacent to it are courts for basketball, tennis, and volleyball. Out back is a driving range and horseshoe pits. Elsewhere on our acreage, we sponsor summer camps for employees' children, and employees can harvest herbs or relax on hammocks in our garden. The west wing holds a garage that offers free tune-ups and minor repairs to employees' cars. Upstairs, just beyond the hairdresser and nail salon, is our award-winning cafeteria, where a pianist serenades us as we eat our gourmet lunches. Between meals, of course, pastries, bananas, bagels, soup, and gourmet coffee are free—as is ice cream when the local baseball team is doing well.

"Speaking of food, we have barbecues and beer nights every Friday, as well as holiday parties for employees' children almost monthly. Last year, as you may have heard, we invited the entire town for a pancake breakfast and 20,000 showed up. We love celebrations, which is why we sponsor numerous parade floats and cookouts, too. Every employee's birthday is celebrated with teammates writing a personalized poem for the lunchtime party.

"Needless to say, we have relaxation rooms with pool tables and video games, one room is dedicated to laser tag, and the art and sculpture room comes complete with teacher. Up on level three is our massage therapist, the company physiotherapist, dentist, and in-house counselors—all free to employees. There's also a twenty-four-hour hot-line for those with personal or family problems. Mind you, when some-one is having a crisis, it's common for fellow employees to donate time off to them."

Which workplace offers all this, you may well ask. Are you sure it's a corporation, not an exotic country club and community center rolled into one? Does anyone truly work there in between all the distractions?

The "full Monty" we've just described may be fictional, but every component of it duplicates a real-life perk in an existing corporation. The point, of course, is to illustrate that businesses determined to woo the best talent today are metamorphosing into community centers, with both the recreational facilities *and* aspects of community spirit. An employee of one such enterprise, Wegman's Food Markets in Rochester, New York, said, "I feel as though it's my second family."

Family? In this day and age of revolving-door employment, shat-tered families, and prolonged adolescence? Aren't we all free-agent robots, wired and workaholic, coming and going so fast that we hard-ly know ourselves, let alone one another? Precisely. Which is why an organization interested in winning today's workers needs to build a sense of unparalleled community and fun. When the hunter becomes the hunted—when skilled employees become so scarce that employers begin scurrying around to find new and better bait—the lay of the land changes. Workhouses become fun houses—specifically for the benefit of stars so inclined to work hard that they must be enticed to play. Twenty-six of *Fortune*'s 100 Best Companies offer personal concierge servic-es, up from fifteen just two years ago. LesConcierges in San Francisco estimates that each dollar spent to provide its services yields $1.75 in gained employee productivity. We're not talking the entire work world, here—at least, not yet. But we are peering at a trend that the retention issue will help roll out far beyond the elite quarters of high-tech stars faster than most expect.

In Tampa Bay, a financial services firm called Capital One Services actually calls its leisure facility a community center. It includes a food court; a gym; an Internet café; basketball, volleyball, and racquetball courts; and a library.

The fifth shift in expectations is toward a proactive sense of community at work. Of course, work has always served a limited function in this respect, and organizational theorists have long suggested that when people have a sense of community, they work harder and are more committed. But we are suggesting that there is now a definable shift in the magnitude of this expectation. Work is now seen as a major source of friendships, fun, mentoring, and connection—all matters once sought after hours. What has driven this change in expectation? As always, there are a series of influences. First, we spend a lot more time at work than we used to (on average, about a month more per year than we did fifteen years ago). With work taking up so much of people's psychic energy, there is simply far less time for finding friendship and community outside of work.

Second, younger workers often have "unfinished business" when it comes to community. Many of them spent a good deal of time alone (the latchkey experience) and with much less focused one-on-one time with their parents than previous generations. Hence, the hunger for mentoring and recognition are much stronger. Younger workers, the X and Net Generations, are also marrying later, thus making friendship the focus of their community in the same way family serves this function for older workers. Fun, a sense of belonging, social life, leisure, and community-style caring are high on workers' "want" lists, and savvy business leaders are responding by sculpting the workplace to do double duty.

The workplace is demanding greater self-sufficiency of its workers, modern mobility is diminishing the traditional neighborhood and extended family, the new need for networking promotes shallow relationships rather than fulfilling friendships, and compressed production cycles leave little time for sports clubs or community work. Meanwhile, flexible work schedules, technology, and contract work disconnect the crowd once linked by water-cooler gossip. All of these trends have intensified the need for community. Bottom line: people expect work today to serve as a primary community center. Or as one CEO put it, to be "something between a college campus and a family."

Is the expectation of community new?

One fair question is whether the expectation of community represents a shift at all. Haven't people always wanted to experience community at work? The answer is that while we may always have appreciated camaraderie at work, the focus on work as one of the primary sources of social fulfillment is new and represents an important and fundamental shift in how we see work.

In Chapter 6, we mentioned Arlie Hochschild's 1997 book (*The Time Bind: When Work Becomes Home and Home Becomes Work*) about dual-income couples seeking refuge from hectic home lives in longer hours at work. We postulated that workers enter into these long hours hoping work will provide a sense of connectedness. Individuals with stressful home lives are not the only workers looking for community between nine and five. A *Fortune* poll found that one of the main reasons people continue to work even when they don't need to financially is for social reasons—to connect with other people. A US Bureau of Labor study in 1996 found that relationships were the No. 1 source of job satisfaction for women who work.

How's this for a social schedule? Annual company picnic, annual employee barbecue and oyster roast, annual employee golf tournament, annual holiday party for employees' children, and annual holiday luncheon for retirees. Organizing all this is McCormick in Sparks, Maryland.

Ironically, friendships at work were unusual, and certainly not a common expectation, from the dawn of the Industrial Age right through to a few decades ago. A British study in the early 1960s (also referred to in Chapter 6) found that unskilled workers rarely discussed problems with their work peers, although some skilled workers did. Few workers felt involvement or ownership with their work, the company, or their colleagues. Even among the most affluent workers, a job was principally a means to an end—a salary to support leisure time spent with family and non-work friends. That is why membership in workplace social clubs was low and social networks tended to come from outside work—from the neighborhood, church, family, and so on.

Even today, most full- and part-time employees—77 percent—say they get more satisfaction from time they spend away from their jobs than from work hours. This is particularly true among high-income earners who presumably have greater financial means to pursue favorite after-work pastimes. And yet there is ample evidence that expectations of social benefit on work time have grown. For instance, where once employees eagerly anticipated retirement, today, fully 85 percent expect to continue with some kind of work and 69 percent say they will work only because they want something to do, not because they will need the money. (A separate poll reports that 47 percent of senior citizens work because they need the money, 86 percent work because they like being with other people, and 82 percent work because they need to be productive.) The twin towers of learning and connecting with others stand out as primary supports of the "never plan to really retire" trend.

Somewhere between the post-war period and today, employees began to draw more on work for friendships and socializing, giving rise to 1950s- and '60s-style company picnics and bowling leagues. In the 1980s and early 1990s, amidst the re-engineering and downsizing craze, many companies deserted the company picnics and gatherings. While some, like Proctor and Gamble, kept to old forms of building community, a counter trend has developed, with leading-edge companies sensing that a more intense style of community and friendship has become a major source of employee satisfaction.

It is often during the hiring process that a company begins to focus on the need for community. At Stockgroup.com, a technology business in Vancouver, Canada, Cindy Donovan, head of human resources, encourages new hires to meet the team with which they'll be working *before* they accept a job offer. "I tell them that they will spend more time with these folks than they will with their families or friends, so they had better like them. We know that friendship drives loyalty, so it's more important that people figure out if these are the kind of people they want to spend time with." Today's successful recruiter must be at least one-part matchmaker.

> Free beer and refreshments flow every Friday night at Amgen in Thousand Oaks, California—as well as at quarterly parties.

Pete Makowski, CEO of Citrus Valley Health Partners outside of Los Angeles, says, "The biggest shift I have seen has been in corporate spirituality or soul. People are reaching out more so now for a sense that the organization is a caring place that provides a sense of deep community. They want to know they are loved because of the hectic pace of their lives. They need a 'warm embrace.'"

Does an experience of community contribute to an engaged employee and bottom line profits? When Gallup studied employee engagement in 1998, the organization found that the top 25 percent of businesses (measured according to employee engagement) produced stellar results in profitability and customer loyalty compared with others. It also found that two of the best predictors of fully committed employees are best friends at work and having someone at work they felt truly cared about them.

> Valassis Communications of Livonia, Michigan, throws parties to celebrate every company milestone it can think of.

In the sections that follow, we'll write a prescription for responding to this expectation for community.

It all begins with values: The new company town

In a bygone era, there were company towns. For better or worse, the company and community were one, and the company provided everything from picnics to parades. The company was at the center of the experience of community. Some companies, like Proctor and Gamble, have held onto that ethic. Let's explore P&G's successful, although some would say 1950s-retro, corporate culture, as described in *Built to Last*:

New hires—especially those in brand management (the central function of the company)—immediately find nearly all of their time occupied by working or socializing with other members of "the family," from whom they further learn about the values and practices of P&G. The company's relatively isolated location in a P&G-dominated city (Cincinnati) further reinforces the sense of complete immersion into the company. "You go into a strange town, work together all day, write memos all night, and see each other on weekends," described one P&G alum. P&Gers are expected to socialize primarily with other P&Gers, belong to the same clubs, attend similar churches, and live in the same neighborhoods.

Now let's dance briefly back to the '50s ourselves: A 1958 *Mill & Factory* magazine survey of close to three hundred organizations found that 68 percent had organized off-the-job activities to help bond co-workers. More than half of employers said such programs helped cut turnover, while 22 percent of them said it helped cut absenteeism. Other benefits cited: better morale (34 percent), easier recruitment (32 percent) and increased productivity (17 percent). Only 9 percent of the respondents reported that their off-duty programs had no discernible effects.

What goes around comes around. As we've already said, an increasing number of companies are now replicating these efforts, albeit in a less traditional manner than P&G. In fact, so many are beginning to resemble the facility described at the beginning of this chapter that the concept has been dubbed "the new company town." Here's *Fortune* magazine's comment:

This new workplace is not just a place to work. It's a place to live. It's where you can eat, nap, swim, shop, pray, kick-box, drink beer, run your errands, start a romance, get your dental work done, wield plastic light sabers, and sculpt nude models. It's where you can bring your whole self— mind, body, and spirit—to work each day. Which is a good thing, because you'll be here, if not from cradle to grave like the old company towns, then certainly from dawn to dusk.

The "Cat Lounge" of Catapult Systems Corp. features a pool table, pinball machines, a foosball table, darts, a television, and a wet bar. More importantly, employees volunteer for the company's Fun Committee, which has a generous annual budget.

Community and fun have become critical to worker loyalty. Certainly, as our profile of GTE Northwest's Craig Ritchie on page 168 shows, workers are openly bemoaning the loss of opportunities for work socializing while simultaneously rejecting traditional means of reintroducing it.

How do you put community at the center of the enterprise? AES boldly set a public goal of "creating the most fun workplace since the beginning of the Industrial Revolution." Southwest Airlines, the crown prince of companies with a reputation for fun, has declared fun to be a "serious management issue."

PeopleSoft of Pleasanton, California, has three core principles: "Make customers happy. Have fun. Be profitable." David Duffield, president, chairman, and CEO, says, "Having fun at PeopleSoft is mandatory. People who are having fun are more productive, they are nice to the other people in the organization, they become evangelists for the company, and they deliver fantastic customer service." The company sponsors a "Take your parents to work day," and employees have voted their company "the best place to have a bad day."

Employees of the Container Store are well-known for their over-the-top loyalty. One responding to a *Fortune* survey wrote, "We grew up with family values, and it's rare to find a company with the same values, philosophy, and foundation principles. Going to work is like going to a family reunion every day."

Is having fun, building community, and encouraging camaraderie a central part of your company's strategic landscape?

Creating a place where people feel connected

So how does an organization respond to this need for community? One way is to create the leisure-style atmosphere we discussed earlier: pool tables, volleyball courts, piano playing in the cafeteria, and so on. Whether lavish or subtle, such amenities create inside the workplace the facilities and ambience that people traditionally sought outside the workplace (when they had the time!).

At DeMarini Sports in Hillsboro, Oregon, there's a gym, an indoor go-cart for racing, a batting cage, a basketball court, and a ping-pong room. Oh yes, and free balls for the company's golf range.

Roy Wilson, chief of human resources for BMC Software in Houston (with facilities that resemble an exotic resort), has said, "I know this is hard to believe, but you do feel like you can get away while you're here. It gives you a balanced life without having to leave."

Of course, even companies without the resources to build country-club-style premises can work toward promoting community. They can do this through newsletters, celebrations of personal events (such as birthdays of staff members), and an onslaught of optional company events that, if offered frequently enough and made inclusive of employees' families, can't help but draw some of the people some of the time.

"Work feels a lot more like hanging out with your friends than going to work," an employee of Great Plains Software of Fargo, North Dakota, has said.

Although workers' aspirations for community at work crosses generational lines, the companies quickest to respond tend to be those catering to younger workers. There are four dimensions of community as the Net generation sees things:

1. Create plenty of opportunities for co-workers to interact both intellectually and socially.
2. Tinker with the workplace design to ensure more social interaction. Executive floors, long hallways, and the lack of natural gathering points work against this aim.
3. Get creative about initiating opportunities for *quality* interaction, such as barbecues where workers of all rank mix casually.
4. Emphasize an open community by welcoming new members with vigor, and allowing "alumni" to come and go with ease, too. (Don't make them feel like turncoats; they remain useful industry contacts for your employees, and may even be persuaded to return.)

A community is also a place where people genuinely care for one another. Now that neighborhoods and extended families are less central, work can help fill in. In one company, maintenance staff came up with the idea of setting up an emergency fund for people who run out of workers' compensation. After they encouraged employees to donate one hour's pay per week into this fund, executives joined in by setting up a system that allowed employees to make their donations through payroll deductions. Those who did not contribute were still allowed to collect, which quickly converted them into the

The Seattle headquarters of WRQ, the software company, boasts a nap room with futons, on-site massages, and dock space for kayaking commuters.

most enthusiastic proponents. Imagine the emotions at a Christmas party when one man who felt his life had been saved by this fund stood up to thank everyone.

Following are more examples of compassion alive and well in the corporate sector:

- In 1997, forty employees of Baptist Health Systems in Miami who were confronted with personal crises received donations of paid time off from fellow employees—coordinated, of course, by the company.
- Marriott International has set up a twenty-four-hour hotline to help employees with family and personal problems.
- At BE&K, the construction company in Birmingham, Alabama, employees who undergo a personal crisis can use the company plane to get to another city quickly. In fact, stories abound of employees who have been supported by this company during periods of personal trauma.

Michael Hammer, author of *Beyond Reengineering*, foresaw the need for new workplace values to take the edge off increasing work stress: "Will a hunger for change produce a permanent condition of future shock? Will we face spiritual poverty even as we enjoy material plenty? Will never-ending organizational improvements inevitably produce a culture of tension and stress? Will it destroy our very humanity? Will intense concentration on customer demands usurp attention to family and community?"

As corporate leaders ponder these questions and open their hearts and facilities to help soften the edges of new-economy stress, grateful workers stay put long enough to contribute to and enjoy the fruits of community at work. Of course, the key to building community is found not just in amenities, but in the day-to-day actions of leaders.

At Lawrence Management Services Inc. of Sweetwater, Texas, the CEO has managers continually forward personal information about employees to the main office: anniversaries, deaths in the family, and so on. This helps the partners offer a more personal touch during conversations with employees, even those far afield.

Years ago, an executive sent a personal note to a low-ranked employee whose name had appeared in the local paper for winning the lottery, saying, "Warmest congratulations, but I sincerely hope this won't influence you to leave us, because we need you." She recalled this note with tears in her eyes many years later at his retirement party.

Scott Gassman, a director with Empire Blue Cross and Blue Shield, says a small change such as asking employees to share something about themselves prior to kicking off a meeting or other work-related activity changes the whole business environment.

> Four Seasons employees say they like working at the company for its great food, access to showers (and soap and lockers), and the chance to stay free at any Four Seasons hotel in the world.

Naturally, a more personal style is easier to achieve in a small corporation than a large one, which may be why surveys show that employees in companies with five or fewer workers are more satisfied than other employees (although the most-satisfied are self-employed). If community is harder to build in large places, all the more reason to have an intentional strategy for it. Little things can make a world of difference in helping to allay employees' suspicions that a company is all work and no community. A Petro-Canada franchise operator who can spend only thirty minutes per visit with service attendants recently changed tack from "How are things going?" to "Tell me one thing you did that was exceptional that I don't know about." This approach established a new kind of relationship and gave the franchisee a new outlook. When the operator learned, during the course of the more personalized conversations that ensued, that one attendant hosted a late-night talk show in his spare time, he made a point of listening in to that show and commenting on it during the next visit, a pleasant surprise to the employee.

This kind of personal community-building also builds trust. A thirty-four-year-old hotel worker told us: "Trust with my boss means him actually listening to me. Maybe once upon a time you could get by with an empty fly-by 'How are you doing?' without waiting for an answer. These days people see right through that!"

Charles Handy explains the need for this more personalized approach: "The more virtual an organization becomes, the more its people need to meet in person. The meetings, however, are different. They are more to do with process than task, more concerned that the people get to know each other than that they deliver. Video conferences are more task-focused, but they are easier and more productive if the individuals already know each other as persons, not just as images on the screen. Work and play, therefore, alternate in many of the corporate get-togethers which now fill the conference resorts out of season."

Mountain Equipment Co-op, a nonprofit organization based in Vancouver, Canada, lets employees borrow its rental equipment for free. Pay raises here are based not on seniority or performance but upon completion of wilderness experience modules.

A great example of the personalized approach can be found in North Carolina-based Clarkston & Potomac, a fast-growing computer software consulting company. The majority of their three hundred staff works out of their own homes across North America. That's why the tradition of quarterly meetings involving the entire company has remained a priority even as the company has grown. At the one we attended, thirty new staff members took the time to tell their life stories to the gathered workers. And the four company founders have set a goal of every employee being on a first-name basis with at least one of the founders, no matter how large the company becomes.

Although leaders set the tone, it is the sense of community among co-workers that drives retention. Once inducted into a community, employees who value the warmth of that connection can find it difficult to leave. At a mid-sized information technology company, one professional cited co-workers' thoughtfulness and his manager's respect during the difficult birth of his child as the reason for remaining with the company.

PeopleSoft not only provides free bagels, pastries, and gourmet coffee to employees; it sponsors a rock band that plays at pep rallies.

As journalist Thomas L. Friedman has said, "There is still a deep hunger out there for that old-style, Main Street feeling, built on human contact.... The really successful [employers] in the Internet Age will be those who can combine the efficiency of cyberspace with the intimacy of the backyard barbecue." Okay, he actually said "retailers" where we've boldly substituted "employers," but you get the idea.

So, community-building doesn't necessarily entail massive restructuring or expensive new initiatives. A more personal, community-oriented approach wields considerable influence, including the use of symbols. A software company in Silicon Valley that was losing more than half its people when projects ended decided to institute a BMW lease program. Any employee moving to a new project while remaining with the company received a leased BMW, which they could keep as long as they stayed at the company. Retention suddenly skyrocketed, even though the value of the BMW leases amounted to less than pay raises being offered by competitors. Why did this program stem turnover? We believe that the employees suddenly felt part of a BMW "club," a community that had until then been merely a workplace.

Here are some more examples of community-building practices:

- Jack Harnett, the president of DL Rogers Corp. in Bedford, Texas, not only makes a point of playing golf with his managers and supervisors, he sends them birthday cards and drops by their homes to take them to dinner. He has even been known to help employees with marital or financial problems. "I don't think you can be totally focused on making money if you're worried about what's happening at home or at school with your kids. I want to help you," he declares. Harnett's managers stay an average of nine years, compared with the industry average of two.

- Total Systems Services, the world's second-largest credit card processors and a subsidiary of Synovus Financial, came up with an interesting way to help employees feel like part of a community. As mentioned previously, when the company built a new campus in Columbus, Georgia, it designed a river walk comprised of several thousand bricks, each of which bore the name of an employee. The message: When you work here, we create a permanent place for you, and your role in the community begins the first day you show up.

- It must be a Georgia thing, because Atlanta-based RTM, the world's tenth-largest restaurant company, puts your name on a brick when you become a member of the 2001 Club. That's a leadership organization into which employees and managers must be nominated, and through which one gets invited to an annual conference on strategy.

- HRH Prince Philip, CEO of Liechtenstein Global Trust, was recently asked why he underwrote a three-day gathering of 120 executives plus their spouses in Whistler, British Columbia. "It worked," he responded with a smile. "It started the process of bringing the company together."
- MTW Corp., the software and Internet-applications company near Kansas City, has taken steps to ensure that its employees endure less time on the road and more in regional centers, where they can interact. "We thought that if we started by creating a place where people like to work, we'd achieve our financial goals," says Richard Mueller, founder and CEO.
- A&W Canada has formalized one of its values in the motto, "Treat each other as friends." Lofty words, but when applied to a performance problem, they become more than corporate rant by ensuring the kind of tough love that pushes people to excel.

Building community across rank

Just as true community at work cannot be achieved in an "us and them" atmosphere, joining hands across rank has proven to be a highly effective retention strategy. All the dimensions of community mentioned earlier must bear this hallmark: Opportunities for executives and staff to interact informally must become more commonplace, and workplace design must support this.

You thought we were making up the bit at the beginning of the chapter about a corporation holding a pancake breakfast for 20,000 residents in the headquarters' small town? It actually happened at JM Smucker.

Getting rid of functional and hierarchical barriers is key to responding to this shift. Some companies tackle the challenge of breaking down the "us–they" feeling by having executives walk for a day in front-line workers' shoes. When Eileen Odum was CEO of GTE Northwest, she was known for riding along with telephone repair personnel. Images of this diminutive woman in a hard hat, and her decision to be accessible, built her reputation as someone who cared and was willing to listen to ideas. BC Hydro, also known as a progressive employer, went further. Company executives set a target for spending 15 percent of their time talking to employees—an ambitious goal in any enterprise, but an effective one for companies endeavoring to respond to employees' heightened desire for community.

Labatt outfitted its head-office marketing division with a neighborhood-style pub as a main meeting space and attributes a greater sense of staff cohesiveness to this move. Similarly, McKinsey and Company's Toronto office underwent a redesign to include brainstorming dens, video-conferencing rooms, team problem-solving spaces, and a three-story atrium for company-wide social events and announcements. "The old architecture was in conflict with what we wanted to be," explains a manager.

Then there's ObjecTime's president, who set up a "Pool with the President" time on Friday afternoons so he could interact informally with younger staff around the billiard table.

Following are more examples of building community across rank:

- In a move that emphasizes how highly they value their employees, the 1999 annual report of AES lists every staff member by name, even though this expanded the report by one-third, to ninety pages. Talk about meeting people's need to feel a part of something bigger than themselves!
- At Electronic Arts in Vancouver, Canada, President Glenn Wong wanders the company's offices so often that he is on a first-name basis with most of nearly six hundred employees.
- Similarly, Synovus Financial CEO Jimmy Blanchard is known for being more likely to ask employees about family matters than about departmental goals.
- At Total Systems Services, supervisors are encouraged to set up a "purely social" dinner with new employees on the first week of their job. Why? Just to get to know them, and help induct them into the community.
- Once a year, the employees of San Jose-based Cisco receive an e-mail inviting them to have breakfast with their president and

CEO, John T. Chambers. Several dozen of the corporation's seven thousand employees take up the offer. During the breakfast, Chambers chats with employees and gathers twenty to fifty questions. He calls it "the most effective vehicle for getting candid feedback from employees and discovering potential problems," as well as an opportunity for him to check on operations from the worker's point of view.

Making fun a priority

If there is less time these days for leisure, it certainly has not eliminated the *need* for fun and relaxation. The time and work crunch has simply forced individuals to find moments of leisure when and where they can. If "taking five" or having fun at work fulfills their leisure-time quotient without detracting from the quality of their work, all the better. Communal high spirits can only enhance productivity.

Kingston Technology of Fountain Valley, California, has a driving range behind its plant.

As mentioned earlier, studies have shown that until recently, a strong division existed between work and play. Employees worked in order to afford play and sought friendships elsewhere. More recent studies show that not only are workers increasingly inclined to blur these lines but North Americans with higher socioeconomic status and optimism about their personal finances are now *least* satisfied with the availability of leisure time. Could it be that the elite skilled workers so heavily in demand right now have forgotten how to play, and must be nudged in that direction by employers for the sake of retention?

Contemplate this: An in-depth Gallup study has tracked eight dimensions of satisfaction across time, asking the same questions forty-three times over two decades. According to the 1999 results of this survey, Americans have never been more satisfied with their lives—with the exception of two readings, which show growing *dissatisfaction*. One is contentment with work and the other is "the amount of leisure time you have." These two criteria are now 15 and 12 percentage points below their highest levels, recorded in 1969. And leisure time is the only dimension negatively related to income, education, and the shape of one's personal finances. (In other words, star performers are likely the most distressed by their lack of leisure time.) This insight makes the solution clear: Provide more relaxation opportunities through work facilities and the approaches we've discussed.

Companies have traditionally provided social events but most executives have not sensed how drastically the number of such social gatherings needs to be increased. In a recent survey, 62 percent of employees said their companies hold holiday parties and 61 percent said their firms hold occasional company picnics. Twenty-five percent named the odd dinner and theater event, 16 percent boasted of lunchtime seminars. These are fine as far as they go, but when it comes to company socials, guard against tokenism at all costs.

Community: It can't be left to chance

When employees saw work as a way to make a living, and when leisure time allowed for more sense of community outside of work, organizations could afford to leave most of the concerns expressed in this chapter to chance. But times have changed.

At VanCity, a leading credit union in British Columbia, fun is not left to chance. The company has a four-person "corporate spirit department" that spends lots of time planning community-building events. Other companies have ongoing task groups whose responsibility is to create community events. Yet being intentional about community ideally involves more than committees to plan social activities; it is also about focusing leadership attention on this dimension of work.

At Synovus Financial, leaders speak openly about having a "culture of the heart" and the "power of love." Talk to Synovus people and they will tell you about numerous acts of love and kindness, from helping people in a crisis to the day-to-day expressions of genuine caring that make employees fiercely loyal to this company. Where does such a strong focus on commu-

At the SAS Institute in Cary, North Carolina, a pianist plays during lunch at the company's stunning cafeteria. SAS also offers superb on-site childcare and an on-site clinic offering free primary medical care. Turnover, at 4 percent, is among the lowest in the software industry.

nity come from? First and foremost from its CEO, who was chosen over thirty years ago because "lots of people could run a bank, but not too many could make people feel loved." Almost four decades after he came on board, the company's financial success and reputation for high employee loyalty has earned it much praise, but few Synovus people even know that a decision to focus on building community was at the genesis of their firm's success.

Craig Ritchie, Director of Human Resources
Verizon Northwest
Everett, Washington

Craig Ritchie is old enough to recall a time when employee surveys were administered annually, and young enough to be held accountable for the results of Verizon Northwest's (formerly GTE Northwest) now monthly surveys. As director of human resources for the three-state, 3,800-employee telephone service provider, Ritchie helps set new policy in response to employee input.

What has he learned from recent samplings, now taken by Internet and telephone as well as in written form? First, that maintaining and improving morale is a constant challenge due to increasing industry competition, and internal reorganizations. "Employees have expressed a lower degree of trust and faith in senior management to represent their major interests. And people in our work environment are less apt to share positive stories and experiences with one another because a lot of radical changes, not all of them viewed positively, have transpired over the past ten years," Ritchie said, noting that Verizon Northwest workers tend to be mature and of long tenure.

The surveys have led to initiatives aimed at boosting morale and retention—turnover being of special concern given that approximately 25 percent of Verizon Northwest's technician workforce is eligible for retirement now. To promote better communication, the regional president recently conducted fifty visits with employee groups, answering their questions on the spot. "It really meant a lot to see the leader of our region not afraid to address tough issues, tough questions, and present herself as the honest and very integrity-bound person she is," Ritchie says.

To boost morale, Verizon Northwest reinforced and expanded its rewards and recognition program. Each major department surveyed its employees to gain a better understanding of what type of recognition was desired. Then, based on this feedback, each department designed several recognition programs and events. In addition, the region introduced the "herogram," cards with a fill-in blank for someone's name and deed worthy of recognition, which all employees are empowered and encouraged to pass out freely, whenever and wherever merited.

One of Verizon Northwest's biggest issues, however, remains employee development. First, past downsizing combined with a sudden, multi-industry demand for individuals with specialized telecommunications training has led to a dearth of well-trained, experienced people. "Traditionally, that has never been the case. We've always been the best. We're no longer the only game in town," Ritchie explains. He's responding with both expanded in-house training and overtures to outside community interests to partner in education and training.

But the challenge in no way ends there, he adds. Today's greater need for information-sharing has erased the line between "soft" people skills and "hard" technical skills, thereby changing the style and scope of training required. "Even people who have traditionally been in technical fields now must have good communication, people, and leadership skills. The bottom line is, if you're designing an application for a customer, you'd better be able to communicate effectively with that customer."

Yet another shift Verizon Northwest finds itself addressing is employees' need for community. Where once technicians drove to a facility and chatted with supervisors and workmates while picking up their day's assignment, today, technology allows some employees to check their schedule before leaving home and report directly to the job site. The result is more efficiency—at the price of less information-sharing with fellow field technicians, which adds up to less time for workplace camaraderie. The irony, as Ritchie sees it, is that on top of that, today's employees mostly reject traditional opportunities for socializing before and after work hours, due to longer working hours and correspondingly diminished family and free time. "We have people who bemoan the loss of the good old days, where people used to go out after work and bowl with one another and meet at the local pub and talk about the work day ... and yet employee-association membership has been dwindling."

Fortunately, the company understands the dilemma, and is making efforts to help employees achieve an acceptable work/life balance. To this end, the company has policies that allow for flex-time, telecommuting, part-time work, and job-sharing.

"Telecommunications is one of the fastest-growing industries out there. That means we're going to be continually challenged in recruiting, attracting, hiring, and training quality employees." The key, Ritchie adds, is administering and reading those monthly surveys—or keeping his finger on the pulse of what employees really want.

Assessing your company for community

The statements below allow for an initial assessment of how your organization, division, and/or department is doing at responding to the employee search for building community at work. The assessment is meant to guide your thinking, not provide a definitive quantitative assessment of your progress. For each question below, answer how true the statement is of your work environment using the scale provided:

_____ Building community and having fun is a stated goal of our company ("Yes, it's on the books" scores 1 point; for "Yes, and this is a living, breathing mantra of our top people," tally 3 points).

_____ We have facilities on site that allow for social mixing and "fun" activities to occur while at work (1 point if you have social gathering places that people use; 2 if facilities for fun activities exist and are used—e.g., volleyball, games room, aerobics, etc.).

_____ Our company uses "symbols" in a number of ways to make people feel a part of a community—e.g., bricks with employees' names on them, names in the annual report, pictures on the wall of people who have achieved a certain tenure, and so on (1 point if these things are considered "real" by your people. Sorry, no points for empty symbols!).

_____ Acts of kindness in times of crisis are frequent and leaders are role models in this regard (1 point).

_____ Leaders walk around a great deal and take time to get to know people on a personal basis (1 point if a fair number of leaders do this, 3 if it is so intentional that managers allocate time for it in their schedule).

_____ We get people from remote locations together on a regular basis for "face time" (1 point).

_____ We have a "no dating" and/or "no nepotism" policy in place (Lose 2 points).

_____ Most people in our company or department are personal friends with several co-workers outside of work (2 points).

_____ TOTAL

SCORE:

4 or under: Take a full week's management retreat for brainstorming policies that address these concerns.

5–7: You're beginning to look responsive.

8–10: You are above average in meeting today's workers' needs, but there is still room for improvement.

11–13: You are an inspiring example, and probably have the best workers and a strong bottom line to show for it. E-mail us: **izzoinc@aol.com**.

9

The expectation of trust

"Honesty is such a lonely word, but mostly what I need from you."

— BILLY JOEL

Once upon a time, security, loyalty, and trust were considered close cousins, a triad essential to building a long-term, profitable company. Job security built loyalty, which over time—and given good leadership—built trust. Trust, which could only be built over time, in turn nurtured loyalty and made security a two-way street. Inevitably, then, this threesome led to greater employee commitment and retention, an essential foundation for higher productivity and profits. Or so the theory went.

Then along came downsizing, rightsizing, re-engineering, and restructuring, all euphemisms for layoffs that were supposed to help firms survive the global marketplace (or, as detractors claim, cover up for decades of mismanagement), simultaneously inflating short-term profits for demanding shareholders. The jury may still be out on the long-term success of downsizing, but no one argues with the fact that the unprecedented rate of layoffs severely wounded a sense of trust between employer and employee, shredded unwritten contracts about lifetime employment and two-way loyalty, and permanently altered perceptions of job security.

Since there is plenty of evidence that neither employer nor employee favors a full-scale return to security and loyalty (for reasons we'll discuss momentarily), attention to trust has suddenly intensified. Without trust, companies experience increased turnover, absenteeism, and internal theft—never mind the possibility of decreased employee commitment, productivity, and profits. Can trust, the last, battered leg of a three-legged stool, learn to support productivity all on its own?

Why do employees crave trust even more now than before the rampage of downsizing? And how can today's leaders regain the workforce's trust?

They must and they can, as this chapter will prove, for trust is the workforce's sixth shift in expectations. But in this case, part of the challenge is that trust is far easier to build than rebuild, and unlike the other five shifts we've already explored, building trust is a reconstruction—as opposed to a new construction—for many companies. If security and loyalty are old-fashioned decorative pillars, trust is the retaining wall.

> "Our company culture places an emphasis on trust and respect, and we try to follow the golden rule," says Joe Demarte, vice-president of human resources, Nordstrom Inc., Seattle's upscale retailer, explaining the company's high retention rate.

This last of our shifts may seem a bit retro. After all, this is the new century, "job security" has become a term belonging to stand-up comics, and most people have long since accepted that corporate loyalty is dead. Faith in institutions, from government and church to corporations, is lower than it has been at any time since North Americans began measuring such things. In many circles, a Dilbertized view of work has become the accepted vantage point: idiot bosses who care little for the masses of drones that work for them. And yet, in the midst of this cynicism, we suggest that while the expectation of security and loyalty is dying, the expectation of trustworthiness is actually growing. Why? Because senior management and employees operate more as partners now. When young women were first allowed to decline those who came courting, they gained new expectations of marriage: They wanted not just financial support but a trusting partnership. Now that the power balance of the employer/employee relationship likewise has turned more egalitarian, workers have gone beyond *hoping* for a trustworthy employer to *demanding* one, and leaving of their own free accord when such values are not there. The buyer's market allows this demand, and even encourages it; recent history lends it urgency. Employers have been slow to see the trust issue from this partnership perspective.

From those on the brink of retirement to those just stepping out of college, workers long for the very thing they feel they have lost: to work for an honest firm that will tell them the truth and live by an admirable code of ethics. Daniel Yankelovich, a leading pollster of North American attitudes for the past twenty-five years, confirms this new paradox: While people are more skeptical and distrustful of institutions than at any time in the last half century, underneath that skepticism resides a longing, a desire to believe. Any organization that bucks recent trends and gives employees a reason to trust again will win loyalty big-time from its people.

To understand this last shift, it is necessary to revisit our basic view of the workforce. For almost one hundred years, workers have been depicted (perhaps rightly so) as an insecure mass, dependent on relatively few wealthy business owners and companies for meeting their basic needs. People traded their lives, literally, for at least the possibility of economic security. When the downsizing craze hit in the 1980s, that image of themselves as groveling dependants was driven home. Workers who lived through the beginning of the downsizing era, whether laid off or survivors, didn't like what they saw in the mirror. As luck would have it, shortly thereafter an unexpected power shift occurred. The new economy made small businesses the fastest-growing sector of the economy, and technology enabled small operations to compete with much larger enterprises in new ways. These changes allowed some of the downsized to sprout entrepreneurial wings, or work for those who did, which both nurtured their big-business resentment and channeled it into positive action. As we've mentioned before, 80 percent of workers are now confident they can find at least as good a job if they get laid off, and two-thirds feel quite confident that they have what it takes to be successful in the new economy. These events have broken downsized workers' sense of dependency, and with the help of demographics and a steaming economy, allow them to make their own demands. So what is it they want, anyway? We'll say it again: real trust, partnership-style.

"It's such a generous place, a high-trust place, that employees love it. They hire people with the same values as the leaders. That's the cornerstone," observes Leonard Berry, speaking of the Container Store after studying the company for his book, *Discovering the Soul of Service*.

The aftermath of downsizing

By now, the sad march of statistics and heart-wrenching human stories of the period from the early 1980s to the mid-1990s are old news. We skim their surface and strum some of the numbers only to set the mood or remind readers of the scene from which workers have just emerged. We'd also like to remind readers that downsizing activity may have decreased, but it has neither finished nor reversed. What has tapered off is the shock value of layoffs, especially given that, by now, some workers have been laid off a second or third time. Below is a distillation of the brutal history of this era:

- Eighty-seven percent of North American organizations and 86 percent of companies abroad (especially in the UK, Germany, and Japan) downsized between 1986 and 1993.
- Between 1987 and 1993—the peak of the downsizing era—large companies like IBM, Sears Roebuck, and GE shed a quarter or more of their workforces.
- One-third of households contained someone who lost a job, and nearly 75 percent of all households experienced a close encounter with layoffs between 1980 and the late 1990s.
- On average, workers who lost their jobs but found work elsewhere earned 15 percent less, and 25 percent lost their health coverage as a result of job dislocation.

In their book *Revitalizing the Workplace after Downsizing, Mergers and Reengineering*, Terence E. Deal and Allan A. Kennedy describe the process starkly:

The shock of permanent adjustments in workforce levels was further aggravated by the way most companies went about achieving the reductions. More often than not, reductions were orchestrated by teams of outside consultants hired by management under some popular rubric of the day, "reengineering" being a classic. Slogans about building a more productive future, eliminating waste, and "rightsizing" the organization rubbed salt into employee wounds. In effect, it blamed them for the company's underperformance. Ignoring the fact that most employees were working very hard indeed doing their assigned jobs, consultants, most of them young, had a field day. Without blanching at the levels of pay they themselves were earning, they produced charts and graphs and presentations that showed how most of the work being done was not only futile but was actually destructive to the company's competitiveness. Top management ate this up because it offered a quick and relatively easy way to solve problems they faced. Ordinary employees felt victimized because they had never been asked their opinions about what should be done, the rhetoric that accompanied the formal announcement of the consulting project notwithstanding.

Then the outplacement lists were drawn up, department by department. Despite claims that everything was going to be done analytically and based on reason, somehow the names on the lists did not seem to make sense. Too many of those tapped for outplacement were older. Too many of the bosses' favorites found jobs in the redesigned organization. This fuelled the perception that finger pointing was the primary basis for making decisions. Before long, the realization set in: The downsizing was arbitrary. It was mainly the luck of the draw as to whether you were picked to stay or put on a list to go. The end result: Trust was the first victim of the downsizing.

To be fair, however, most executives were good people striving to do a painful task demanded of them from many different fronts.

Let's take a magnifying glass to the shrinking levels of trust that resulted:

- Between 1988 and 1996, the number of employees who said that they often did not believe what management said rose from 33 to 40 percent—this despite increasing company success over that period.
- Trust declined at three of four US workplaces in 1996 and 1997, dropping to a low point in corporate history there.
- Between 1995 and 1997, the number of workers who felt their company considered their interests in decisions that affected them dropped from 50 to 41 percent.
- During a one-year period (1995 to 1996), the number of Americans who indicated confidence in the people running big business dropped from 19 to 12 percent. At the same time, 81 per-

cent said they believed that senior executives were benefiting from company profits on the backs of employees.

- In a survey of downsized firms, 74 percent reported that workforce morale was low and distrust of management high, 9 percent reported an associated increase in absenteeism, and 13 percent noted an increase in disability claims.

"I've found leadership to be more important than ever. By leadership, I mean not simply the articulation of vision and values, but also a continuous dedication to being brutally honest – with yourself, with your employees, and with your customers – about the realities of this new business environment," says Samirarora, cofounder and CEO, Netobjects Inc., Redwood City, California.

Finally, then, let's see where these results have left the current workforce. It's not a pretty picture, and many of the issues appear to revolve around rank, a situation that can surely be eased by the continued flattening of hierarchical management styles.

- Only 37 percent of employees rate the level of honesty in their workplaces as high or very high, although 95 percent rate their own honesty level as high or very high.
- Only 14 percent agree that "people trust each other."
- As we've mentioned earlier, 54 percent of senior managers think the level of trust between corporate ranks is good, while only 27 percent of their employees agree.
- Sixty-four percent of employees believe management routinely fails to tell the truth, and 43 percent believe that their managers cheat and lie.
- The level of trust is best between front-line workers and their immediate supervisors and worst between front-line workers and top-level executives.

But surely, by now trust is beginning to show signs of recovery? Alas, no. According to a survey of executives at 215 companies, 75 percent say trust is declining, and only 15 percent believe it is improving.

Why is the level of trust between people and their organizations not rising? The answer is twofold. First, perhaps many leaders have failed to grasp the key practices that build trust in the new entrepreneurial age. We attempt to help with that understanding throughout this book.

But there is another key reason for the robustness of this mistrust. Many times we have referred to what we call "value imprinting," the idea that at a certain age, an entire generation takes on a world view based on certain sets of events occurring around them. Anyone born after 1967 or so came of age during the downsizing era, and that includes most of Generation X and the Net Generation. When today's college graduates were ten years old, the worst of the downsizing craze was drawing to an end. It's highly likely that their parents or siblings experienced this mistrust directly. These children's images of the "greedy corporate machine" will die a hard and slow death.

As proof, we point to one person in that group, Murray Dobbin, author of *The Myth of the Good Corporate Citizen: Democracy Under the Rule of Big Business*. He kicks off his anti-corporate, anti-globalization tome with the following dedication: "To my father, whose downsizing by Eaton's after twenty-five years as a dedicated employee was the seed of my activism, and to my mother, whose unfailing sense of right and wrong have helped to guide it."

Connect the dots; contemplate the picture. Then build a strategy, pour on commitment, and groom patience.

New-style loyalty

Despite the stress and devastation that downsizing wreaked on the personal lives of employees, the process was not without its upside. First of all, years of hiring too many middle managers had been slowing down organizational efficiency, and quite apart from whether some firms overreacted or whether the process could have been conducted more fairly or humanely, observers agree that for many corporations downsizing was the salvation that enabled them to stay afloat in an ever faster-moving, more global economy. Further, survey after survey shows that despite the foul-tasting medicine, most surviving employees felt better about their jobs (although not about senior management) afterwards: The redesign of functions responded to their hankering for less supervision, more teamwork, and more cross-training or diversity of tasks. But most interestingly, despite underlying resentment and lack of trust, employee productivity rose or held constant in 70 percent of downsized companies. (Less surprisingly, *short-term* profits rose or held constant in 80 percent.)

How could this be? How could employers who restructured have reported adverse effects on employee workload (62 percent), morale (56 percent), and commitment (52 percent), and yet an *increase* in productivity, service levels, and the competence of the workforce? The answer, in a word, is *fear*. Knowing that they, too, could be axed at any moment and that casualties were heavy as far as the battlefield stretched, surviving employees swallowed their pride and soldiered on. It may also be true that during downsizing, any adverse connection between commitment and productivity, any subtle acts of sabotage, any small increase in absenteeism or disability claims, may have been compensated for by the new efficiencies. (Acknowledging this is not the same as declaring the downsizing exercise an unqualified success.) And some of the resentment may have been watered down by employees' observation that almost all companies were involved, not just theirs, which implied external rather than merely internal forces.

The point is, none of these factors are decorating today's landscape. Rather, neighboring armies are roaming the territory actively soliciting recruits. Nor do employers *or* employees want a full-scale return to security and loyalty. Even if employers could offer these perks again, most employees would resist, and not just due to broken trust. Workers have long since realized that their best investment is in growing their own skills, not growing the company's profits. (Which is not to say that both groups would not welcome back a *degree* of renewed loyalty and security.)

Dennis Bakke, CEO of AES, told us, "The security thing is a natural extension of the dependency thing. I just try to convince people that security is a false god, not something they should desire. Security is a

> Several firms in southern California launched a program known as Lending Employees for National Development as a way to avoid layoffs. When a company lost a contract, it would subcontract a team of employees with expertise in that area to the company that won the contract. The work team being "loaned" would remain employees of their company. This way, companies retained their investment in employees, avoided layoffs, and helped employees broaden their skills.

horrible thing. What are the most secure places you can have? Prisons and Indian reservations. What happens in those kinds of places? All kinds of problems because you are treated like an animal, a kid, an asset. The line 'People are our best asset' is my favorite. What do you do with assets? Sell them, throw them away. The most irresponsible thing we can do is keep one extra person in a business when they're not needed. Some companies think they're doing a nice thing keeping them a little longer, but it prevents anyone else in the organization from growing."

And so we return to our one-legged stool and realize that trust is all that's left to support retention, engagement, and productivity. A sense of entitlement has replaced fear, thus eliminating any interference to the natural linkage between trust, commitment, productivity, and retention. Make no mistake: Commitment, productivity, and retention are increasingly influenced by the degree of trust coursing through the halls at work. Trust allows employees to speak up, take risks, and apply all their skills to resolving company challenges. Distrust influences them to contribute little and invest all their energy in keeping their rears covered.

"In a work world where post-boomers see few traditional rewards left for them, honesty on the part of employers about what they can offer is at a premium. Post-boomers have a completely unvarnished view of corporations, and of the world," says Barbara Moses, author of *Career Intelligence*.

So, too, do boomers. Middle managers of the downsizing era reflect the sharpest declines in morale, especially in areas that measure trust in the organization. In fact, only 2 percent of middle managers name dedication to their firm as the key to success. Instead, 56 percent cite individual ambition as the key. Similarly, a study of *Fortune* 500 managers found that those who survived restructuring focused more on their own careers and less on organizational goals.

> Years ago, Home Depot hired a former homemaker to run an outlet's millwork department. They promised her the required technical training if she would commit to meeting the needs of the demanding and often impatient contractors who formed her customer base. Both sides kept their bargain, and the story has become a Home Depot legend, reflecting the organization's commitment to honesty between senior management and the front-lines.

People's new loyalty is to their professions. In other words, workers are less "IBMers" or "Microserfs" and more "software developers" or "systems analysts." In fact, workers seem to be staying in the same occupation longer now than in the past, even as tenure with a particular employer has declined sharply since 1993 (the length of tenure is currently at its lowest level in twenty years). All of which hearkens back to the days before the Industrial Age, when most workers, from cobblers to fishmongers, were proudly independent. Although this situation stems from lowered levels of trust, is it all bad? Not necessarily. If professional rather than corporate accolades are what drives today's employee, employers can work with that, if only by trumpeting employees' professional standing and awards to their workmates. Certainly, it's something that insightful employers can support through training and "vertical" community-building even as they attempt to spin the wool that will re-knit unraveled corporate identity and trust.

But be aware that the demise of lifelong corporate careers has undercut the need for corporate loyalty. Individuals are now committed to the organization's goals out of self-interest. Loyalty to one's profession, division, colleagues, work team, or project is what should be encouraged, instead. Put another way, leaders must accept that there is only so much a corporation can do to re-sprout corporate loyalty or security—they'll be stumpy legs on the new-economy stool regardless of retooling efforts. But trust is an entirely different matter. A work environment rich in trust and respect has been linked with less stress and greater productivity. Trust also minimizes in-house unethical or criminal behavior, which costs US industry up to $400 billion annually.

All of which begs three questions: What is corporate trust, how can one seed one's firm with it, and how long does it take to grow to maturity?

The ingredients of trust

We believe that Jack Lowe, CEO of TDIndustries, has summarized it best: Tell the truth, do what you say you will do, make decisions with people's best interests in mind, and hold to your code of ethics and values in day-to-day actions so that people can truly believe in them.

Frank J. Navran, a downsizing consultant and author of *Truth &* *Trust: The First Two Victims of Downsizing*, puts it more practically: "It is better to underpromise and overdeliver than to make promises that cannot be kept.... You won't always win. You will not get them everything they want. You will not protect them from every inequity or injustice. It is sufficient that they believe that you are making a good faith effort and that your intentions are honourable. It is also quite acceptable for you to honestly disagree with your employees—to choose not to support a particular cause or to tilt against a particular windmill. But do so honestly, with integrity and full candor."

Co-author Pam Withers, while working as a middle manager in a publishing firm that had taken a financial turn for the worse, was offered a promotion and asked to "boost morale" among the ranks. Although the offer was tempting, she instead made a difficult decision to leave because she perceived that the tools for fixing the leaking ship were not on board, the power to order them was not being given to her, a mandate to be honest with crew about the seriousness of the situation was not being granted, and her influence with fellow employees stemmed from years of being open and honest with them. In short, she ranked her personal values and industry reputation above the new title and responsibilities. As many a consultant has emphasized, it is this perceived values gap between company and employee that often ushers employees out the door. And yet, how often are corporate values discussed, how clearly are they spelled out, and how closely are they guarded? How many leaders realize that although trust can come crashing down in an instant, it takes years to rebuild through daily, consistent actions and a dedication to extracting any weeds that threaten to choke its progress?

When television's *Sixty Minutes* exposed the fact that children were using products by Minnesota adhesive manufacturer HB Fuller to get high, HB Fuller launched an extensive research and development effort to produce an adhesive without hallucinatory properties.

An Arthur Andersen study identifies the key success factors of an ethical culture as leadership, consistency, fairness, open talk about ethics, and employees' perception that ethical behavior is rewarded (and presumably, that unethical behavior draws consequences).

A colleague of ours was taken aback when a brand-new senior manager casually broke a long-held hiring rule to bring a crony on board. A member of the support staff said she felt sick when she overheard this boss tell one person one thing and—seemingly unconcerned that she was once again at his side—another person the opposite. Story upon story began to filter out about this administrator's lack of ethics.

"Watching him operate, I don't believe he has ever been schooled in right versus wrong," said one incredulous observer. Within weeks, this colleague noticed that other people in the department he had never before pegged as dishonest were trying out questionable political maneuvers. Morale plunged, old friends became wary of one another, work output slackened, and at least one senior executive threatened to resign. Meanwhile, everyone waited tensely to see whether the top boss, informed by a brave team of whistle blowers, would cover up or discipline this new executive. Sadly, a cover-up ensued.

At Dana Corporation, the industrial manufacturer, a bulletin board known as the "hat trick," in reference to suggestions popped into an old hat, allows employees to post suggestions, complaints, and queries. Dana asks employees to post at least two items per month, and has a policy of implementing or acting on 80 percent of them. The system is used throughout the firm's US plants and foreign subsidiaries.

"[Unethical] behavior will be mimicked by those who aspire to senior positions," say Terence E. Deal and Allan A. Kennedy. "The most difficult challenge in shaping a company's culture is recognizing that you have to put yourself and your beliefs on display all the time; otherwise you have little hope of influencing others.... Strongly held and consistently practiced beliefs give culture its power to raise human expectations and performance to truly extraordinary levels."

When whistle-blowers are treated as valuable reporters of problems that have gone undetected by other methods, rather than as liabilities, positive things happen. Organizations that have implemented procedures that encourage individuals to step forward say that company integrity and efficiency improve as a result.

Valour Pulse, a weekly electronic reporting system developed by a university professor who specializes in human resources studies, has employees answer a weekly e-mail questionnaire that gauges their "energy level." The questionnaire is designed to serve as an indicator of morale and an indirect measure of trust. The method is objective because employees submit their answers through Valour Inc. of Ithaca, New York, rather than to direct supervisors. The president of San Francisco-based Indus International, a software company that has used Valour Pulse, has said, "Employees can voice their concerns and not worry about retribution. It helps management know what the issues are." He attributes the system with fending off the poisonous results of personality conflicts that erupted during a corporate merger. "The problems were evident on the surface, but it would have taken months for it to boil up. This way, we knew right away about the problem and what to do."

As our colleague witnessed, distrust and dishonesty can spread as fast as one rotten apple spoils a barrel. "Trust and distrust create upward or downward, self-perpetuating spirals," confirms Sandra Robinson, a University of British Columbia lecturer often quoted on corporate trust.

Dennis Bakke, CEO of AES Corporation, told us that he visited one of his company's plants once a month for five years and sat in the control room chatting for four hours at a time with the individuals on the night shift. "Not because I was trying to educate them about what we were trying to do, but to gain their respect and trust." Years later, when Bakke was faced with a financial crisis, he found that the union leader of this plant was willing to propose an alternative pay package, "because he believed he'd be treated like we said he would." The end result was that workers in a five-generation unionized environment agreed to be paid like managers.

"We don't spend a lot of time thinking about trust. We just try to live with integrity.... Nothing matters but the willingness to give up power," Bakke says.

There's that reference to hierarchy again. As the old saw goes, it's hard to trust someone who has power over you. Or, as Daniel Oestrich wrote in *Driving Fear Out of the Workplace*, "Control seems necessary to people when they don't trust each other.... The need for protocol stems from the lack of belief that I can trust others and myself to behave in the right way." Conversely, then, letting go of control and loosening protocol bequeaths a new sense of trust, an extreme example of which is portrayed in our Dennis Bakke profile on page 147. Entrenched hierarchy is

why surveys show that front-line workers are the least trusting of senior management. This is perhaps why progressive CEOs choose to woo them directly, through "listening" lunches and pool-table sessions mentioned in previous chapters.

Not only does hierarchy depress trust but so, too, can an overemphasis on speed. As Edward Marshall said in *Building Trust at the Speed of Change*, "The sense of what is right and fair in work relationships seems to have given way to what is expedient."

Stephen Covey likes to say, "We're good at efficiency, but have you ever tried to be efficient at finding out what's bothering a troubled teenager?" There are times to slow down, times to heed a long-term commitment to build trust over shorter-term goals. Witness Tylenol's willingness to pull massive numbers of bottles off store shelves and engineer a new seal for them when someone poisoned a few bottles after they had reached retail outlets.

Researchers who studied seventeen million employees in forty countries found that people value eight distinct behaviors:

1. Treat others with uncompromising truth.
2. Lavish trust on your associates.
3. Mentor unselfishly.
4. Be receptive to new ideas, regardless of their origin.
5. Take personal risks for the organization's sake.
6. Give credit where it's due.
7. Do not touch dishonest money.
8. Put the interest of others before your own.

Business consultants tend to agree on the following five keys for leaders to create a trustworthy relationship with employees:

1. Create dialogue.
2. Ensure consistency of action.

3. Tell it straight even when the news is bad.
4. Accept criticism and admit when you're wrong.
5. Carry through.

Carrying through is never easy, as Lew Stern, a senior vice-president at Manchester Consulting in Pennsylvania, discovered. When reports complained that he didn't always keep his promises, he began writing down his obligations to avoid faulty memory negatively affecting trust.

Ken Lizotte, director of CareerScape in Concord, Massachusetts, has three rules for building a trusting environment:

- **Listen:** "Let go of your ego and listen to what your employees are saying."
- **Tell:** Inform employees of changes and the rationale for your decisions. "It's slower and messier to keep everyone involved, but it helps create trust."
- **Act:** Don't just seek feedback from employees. If their criticisms or recommendations are justified, act on them. If you choose not to, tell employees why.
- **Be dependable:** Consistent behavior helps employees know what to expect from you.

For organizations that have lost trust, another step must be added: Determine if particular managers may have burned too many bridges, and if so, consider reassigning them so you can create an environment in which the new seeds of trust can germinate.

One way to think about building trust is to contrast the practices of leaders who lose trust with those who win it. How do leaders lose trust in the first place? A study has made that clear, too. They:

- act inconsistently in what they say and do
- seek personal gain above shared gain
- withhold information

"I'm not here to win a popularity contest…. But I always do what I say. I feel very strongly that you can't pay lip service to that," says Mick Burkart, general manager of RailTex's Indiana/Ohio railroad company. RailTex has set up grievance panels comprised of managers and subordinates, in which the majority rules. And when temporary layoffs loomed after a mineral mine collapsed, management sat down with employees to work out how to shift as many field workers as possible to administrative tasks during the shutdown.

- lie or tell half-truths
- are close-minded
- are disrespectful of employees
- withhold support
- break promises
- betray confidences

And how do they rebuild trust? Although it takes twice as long to build trust in a leader than to lose trust in one, here is the blueprint for a successful reconstruction:

- maintain integrity
- openly communicate vision and values
- show respect for fellow employees as equal partners
- focus on shared goals more than on personal agendas
- do the right thing regardless of personal risk
- listen with an open mind
- demonstrate caring and compassion
- maintain confidences

Guess which industries get the highest and lowest ratings for trust? On a scale of one to ten, manufacturing comes out top with 6.1, then banking, marketing/communications, insurance, government/non-profit, healthcare, retail, financial services, computers/high-tech, and telecommunications (the latter bottoms out at 4.8). Of course, different stages of a corporate cycle can also affect trust levels—a time of expansion being highest at 6.2, and a time of downsizing being lowest at 4.7. In between are periods of acquisition, change initiative, re-engineering, mergers, and restructuring.

Trust is easier to build in a homogenous workforce than a diverse one. Diversity means sharply varying world views, work styles, and behavior patterns. And trust is earned in different ways in different cultures. North Americans tend to be quickly trusting, although with a "what's in it for me" layer. Overseas employees, or foreign-born employees, are often put off by the short-term profit orientation, youth emphasis, self-boastfulness, lack of understanding of nonverbal cues, and overfamiliarity of North American managers, which works against the building of trust. North Americans, for their part, often become impatient with the lack of trust initially shown them, or the more laid-back regard for deadlines, thereby crimping the natural process of building trust. One observer found that Vietnamese workers, who composed about 40 percent of the workforce in one company, "were especially fearful of the team concept, which they likened to Communist work teams." As these and many more challenges show up in domestic workplaces as well as multinational work teams, it's time to break out some reading on the topic and/or indulge the workforce with seminars —whatever it takes to build workforce trust. For starters, we recommend *Promise of Diversity*, by Elsie Cross.

Proactive caring is a less obvious but key ingredient of trust. We've talked before about the importance of preventing star performers from burning out. *Fortune* magazine recently related the story of Yolanda Perry-Pastor, a thirty-four-year-old customer service manager of a large plant nursery, whose entire life revolved around the company. She worked long hours, bought into the "we are family" pep rallies, moved to within a few blocks of the office, vacationed with co-workers, dressed her children in company-logo clothes, and didn't mind answering her pager at three a.m. or hauling her children to the company daycare center on weekends. Then a round of layoffs forced a more demanding workload on her. When she asked for a break due to health concerns, it was refused. At her doctor's urging, she took an extended sick leave.

"I felt betrayed," Perry-Pastor said. "Now I see it so clearly. All that family stuff was fake. They were just using me to get that bottom line."

Did it need to come to that? Of course not. Years of investment in a loyal and hard-working employee were lost to the lack of a watchful leader, a proactive anti-burnout policy, a careless moment. Trust is not earned as much by company-wide policies as by the behavior and attitude of individual

"We have an open environment. We avoid smokestacks. People talk across business divisions," says CEO Jim Chesterton of AW Chesterton Company, a family-owned manufacturer of industrial valves and seals in Stoneham, Massachusetts. He's referring to quarterly meetings where employees can talk to him about anything, and the fact that departments, divisions and subsidiaries meet and exchange information on a regular basis.

managers. This makes the process of creating a trustworthy environment more complex and dependent on a consistent pattern of driving a set of values.

Increasingly, trust today also entails resisting the use of technology to monitor employees, or setting policy for how it will be handled. Here, as we mentioned earlier, all the advances that a more democratic and open work environment seem to offer are on the line. Today's technology allows employers to eavesdrop on job applicants, employees, suppliers, and partners through any number of electronic means, from voice mail to the Internet. And as we related in Chapter 2, several British companies are discussing implanting microchips in employees to monitor their whereabouts and timekeeping. But in doing so, they risk felling trust faster than downsizing ever did. Tazeem Nathoo, senior vice-president of operations with VanCity, the Vancouver, Canada-based credit union that has won numerous mentions as one of the best companies to work for, says this issue is not complicated. VanCity's policy is simply not to monitor employees without their knowledge, and when monitoring is put into effect with prior notice, supervisors will explain carefully why they feel it's appropriate. Again, control and trust make poor bedfellows. Or, as Dennis Bakke said, giving up power is everything.

"This is one of tomorrow's issues," Nathoo says. "People in positions of responsibility are going to have to think very carefully about privacy." (See the profile of Tazeem Nathoo on page 70.)

The cynical executive will say, "We try our best to be trustworthy, and if the rank and file don't believe us, there's not much more we can do. Anyway, our first obligation is to keep up with market challenges and changes."

Precisely. Today's organizations must produce unparalleled amounts of change, from reorganization and new products to the day-to-day shifts that characterize business. All of this requires buy-in, and buy-in is facilitated by trust. Jack Lowe of TDIndustries put it succinctly: "Every change we have to make in business today is made easier by trust. When people don't trust you it takes so much effort to get people to go along with changes. They are always skeptical and wondering what you are really up to. Around here, people may ask questions when we say we want to go in a new direction, but not a lot of time is wasted having to convince people that we aren't up to no good. That's what happens when you have trust." It is not difficult to imagine the long-term financial implications of change implementation slowed down by mistrust.

Jack Lowe, CEO
TDIndustries
Dallas, Texas

The year is 1992 and the setting is TDIndustries, the mechanical and electrical construction and service company in Dallas, Texas. Researchers are nosing around in preparation for the second edition of *The 100 Best Companies to Work for in America.*

"We were coming out of some difficult times—off life support but still limping," recalls Jack Lowe, CEO. "They came to see us and spent the day talking mostly to front-line people; they didn't seem much interested in talking to senior executives. At the end of the day, they met with us as a senior team and said that there was obviously a very high degree of trust in our organization, and they wondered what we did to create it.

"I started talking about newsletters, communication, open-book management, participatory management. Finally, Ben Houston interrupted me and said, 'Jack, I know why people trust us. It's because we're trustworthy.'

"What he meant was that it wasn't the 'techniques'; it was the same things that make you trust someone in your life: You do what you say you will do. If you make a mistake, you tell them so and apologize. You give them the straight goods, and you care about their lives beyond simply what they can do for you. It may manifest itself in programs and things, but it is more about character, who we are as opposed to what we do." (When you meet executives at TDI, as we have on several occasions, it's hard not to see what he meant. Their very presence speaks of trustworthiness.)

At TDI—employee-owned since 1952 because Jack's dad decided it was the right thing to do—trust seems lodged in every pore, from the mission statement to strategic planning, even to layoffs. A few years ago, when TDI decided to sell off a few businesses because they did not fit in with company strategy, senior executives offered the employees involved a chance to buy them, which they often did. When employees declined at one of these businesses, however, TDI took the offers to these workers and asked them to select the best buyer. "They did not pick the highest bidder. The one they wanted was offering us 20 percent less, but we sold it to the one they felt good about. What we would have done if the difference had been millions of dollars, I can't say, but people knew we tried to do the trustworthy thing."

The same can be said for TDI's employee-development focus. "Our strategic thinking is to provide a place for people to retire at TDI." TDI is part of an industry in which turnover and temporary layoffs are taken for granted, so the company's focus on helping people stay employed creates a lot of goodwill.

"We do lots of cross-training so that if a particular part of the business slows down, people can do something else." The company, with 1,200 employees and $200 million in revenue, has seventy-five employees who have been with the firm for more than twenty years.

"How do you build trust?" Lowe asks. "You allow people to have peaks and valleys. You show that if they give you the extra mile when you need it, you'll do the same for them. Treat them with dignity—like there is more to life than work and that we know it. I think of a man who works for us who is a Muslim, who said he really appreciates the fact that he can take fifteen minutes out of his day at a construction site to say his prayers. A lot of companies would not make time for that, but trust is about honoring who people are."

Assessing your company for trust

The statements below allow for an initial assessment of how your organization, division, and/or department are doing at responding to the employee search for trust. The assessment is meant to guide your thinking, not provide a definitive quantitative assessment of your progress. For each question below, answer how true the statement is of your work environment using the scale provided:

_____ When tough decisions are made around here (e.g., reorganizations, layoffs, etc.), people can count on hearing what's going on in an honest and timely manner (most of the time with some notable exceptions, 1 point; 3 points if you can't remember when it was last perceived that "management was up to no good").

_____ There are very few unmentionables in our organization. That is, people are fairly honest and straightforward across ranks (2 points).

_____ Our company has a strong set of published values that emphasize ethical responsibility to customers and community (1 point if these things are considered "real" by most people; 3 points if they are at the center of most corporate decisions and a topic of frequent conversation—sorry, no points for published values that draw mostly cynicism from employees).

_____ On a number of occasions in recent memory, the company demonstrated actions, putting the interests of its employees over near-term profits (2 points).

_____ Our company makes a significant and consistent effort to avoid layoffs through cross-training, project shifting, and other means (2 points if it has happened on a number of occasions; 3 if it is a religion).

_____ People who raise ethical issues in our organization are seen as adding value to the organization (2 points).

_____ When there are rumors that our products or services are harming customers or the community in some way, there is a genuine interest in fixing the problem immediately (1 point).

_____ Leaders are generally seen as saying one thing and doing something else.(lose 3 points).

_____ TOTAL

SCORE:

6 or under: Take a full week's management retreat for brainstorming policies that address these concerns.

7–9: You're beginning to look responsive.

10–12: You are above average in meeting today's workers' needs, but there is still room for improvement.

13–16: You are an inspiring example, and probably have the best workers and a strong bottom line to show for it. E-mail us: **izzoinc@aol.com**.

PART THREE
Getting started

10

Leading in the wake of the shifts

"If treated well, people are intensely loyal."

— STEPHEN SMITH, CEO, WESTJET

Years ago when John was giving a workshop for a corporate client, he noticed that participants suddenly started taking copious notes halfway through the morning. "The real workshop doesn't begin until they start taking notes!" he reflected ruefully.

Hopefully, you have been taking notes throughout the process of reading this book and identifying ways that you can put these insights to work in your company. For now, we will focus directly on a few simple questions: Where does one go from here? What do these shifts mean for an organization? How can a leader get started? How can this knowledge be tapped to increase retention and reduce turnover? And finally, are these shifts temporary, and if so, where are employee expectations headed next?

The decision of whether to act on the insights contained in this book rests on statistics we've already revealed. *Sobering statistic No. 1* is that the average cost of losing an employee is between 200 and 250 percent of that person's annual salary. So, if your organization employs three hundred people making an average of $35,000 per year, and has a turnover rate of 10 percent, the annual cost of that turnover is between $1 million and $2.6 million. Did that grab your attention? *Encouraging statistic No. 1*: Gallup found that businesses with the most engaged employees enjoyed 29 percent higher revenue, were 50 percent more likely to boast above-average customer loyalty, and were 44 percent more likely to turn in above-average profits.

Sobering statistic No. 2: Tight competition for good people, whether for front-line or high-tech positions, will continue for at least the next decade—a fact guaranteed by the sheer demographic volume of retiring baby boomers and reinforced by a growing world economy.

So, how does one lead in the wake of these shifts?

Retention is a philosophy before it's a strategy

In most of this book, we have focused on what employees want and expect from work today, and what strategies leading companies are employing to win their commitment. To respond effectively, one must first realize that most of the companies we've held up as having creative responses to these shifts have at their core a *philosophy*, not just a set of tactics. Practices and benefits may entice employees in, but without a philosophical anchor for the company, the same employees will drift away with the next tide. Before your organization can start brainstorming its own innovative approaches, it must first believe in the employee-topped "inverted pyramid" we discussed in Chapter 1. That is, today's companies must be built around employees' wants, needs, and, ultimately, their expectations. To determine the strength of your organization's core philosophy towards people, ask yourself: Are employees regarded as an expendable resource or the gold mine of our enterprise? Is responding to their shifting values a priority or a nuisance to be dealt with by human resources? Does this organization care at a deep level about creating a great and fulfilling place to work?

A clear trend today is that the best workplaces are getting better; a few companies are leading the way in building entire enterprises around employees. How important does your organization feel it is to join these leaders?

One company we've mentioned a few times in this book is Synovus Financial (and its subsidiary, Total System Services) in Columbus, Georgia. Years of consulting have made us a bit jaded about using superlatives in describing workplaces. After all, we've seen enough warts on the faces of supposedly leading-edge companies to breed plenty of skepticism. So when front-line people at Synovus started telling us how much they loved this company and how much it meant to them to work there, we were—well, skeptical! And yet, once John met and conferred with Jimmy Blanchard, the company's CEO for the past thirty years, he became a believer. Toward the end of their first meeting, John squeezed in the question, "Obviously, you have built something special here, something many leaders would die for. What advice would you give leaders who want to create the kind of loyalty you have?"

Blanchard replied unflinchingly, "I would tell them you have to want it. You have to wake up in the morning wanting to create a place where people love to work, and you have to care about that as much as you care about all the other things a leader must focus on—market share, sales, costs, and so on." John nodded, impressed, said his good-byes, and was almost out the door when Blanchard added, "Oh, and you have to want it as an end in itself, not merely as a means to an end!"

Dennis Bakke, the CEO of AES, echoed the same philosophy when he warned John about companies that respond to people's values merely to win them over: "That begins with the wrong premise."

These corporate giants understand the importance of tracking and respecting employees' values. They also understand that while retention may offer an incentive for building an organization around people's values, if retention is the organization's only motivation for doing so, the resulting changes will likely not run deep enough to have a major impact.

Synovus has coined the term "value chain" to describe how people and culture drive strategy and tactics, which ultimately drive performance and shareholder value. This thinking is squarely in the realm of philosophy. When was the last time your organization defined its core philosophies? And does the desire to make the company a great place to work keep leaders up at night?

One of John's mentors is Mark LeBlanc, a leading small-business strategist in San Diego, California. LeBlanc advises consultants to focus on something that keeps clients up at night. He built his own business around how to start and grow a small business because just about every owner of a small business loses sleep worrying about how to grow. Most executives of the companies featured in this book worry about creating an environment that people will want to work in, stay in, and give their very best to while there. Business leaders can apply this same approach: What keeps your management team anxious? How much time and priority is given to people issues?

Jack Lowe of TDIndustries, a construction company that has been on *Fortune's* "Best Companies to Work For" list for several years running, is pretty clear about its people priority. Lowe says, "I want this to be a great place to work. This is the reason we are in business. This is our No. 1 goal." That commitment may explain how TDI has lowered turnover in new hires from 100 percent six to eight years ago, to 40 percent today—with total turnover at 15 percent (of which 10 percent is voluntary). If these figures sound high, rest assured that they are not for the construction industry. And yet, Lowe isn't finished. "I'm striving for 5 percent. Well, I don't know the exact figure, but I just want it to keep getting better. The shape of the [retention] curve has been very dramatic. We are focused on retention and on meeting the needs of our people."

Posted at the entrance to many a Zen Buddhist temple is a sign with three simple words: "Watch your step!" This is Zen masters' way of saying that paying attention is very important. In our experience, the business leader's most important role is to pay attention to the steps ahead of them—in other words, to prioritize challenges. Jack Lowe is focused on retention. Jimmy Blanchard is focused on the first link of the value chain—people. Before launching into a strategy around the values found in this book, re-examine your company's priorities, its root philosophies. We've seen many a corporate brochure that includes the platitude, "People are our most important asset," but winning and keeping people is not a public relations exercise. The companies winning at the retention game have been bold in actually making people a daily commitment.

Will the shifts shift?

Before committing to new philosophies or strategies in light of the shifts we've discussed, some readers are wondering if, or when, those shifts themselves might shift. Where will employee values go in the years to come? Are these shifts an artifact of a red-hot economy, or are they more enduring changes? To know the answer is to understand where values come from in the first place. In much the same way basic personality gets stamped on our psyches early in childhood, cultural values—the way we see the world around us—are formed during our teens and twenties and tend to travel with us the rest of our lives, even as the world changes drastically around us. Values shift very little and very slowly, only a few times in each generation.

Consider John's grandmother, who was born in 1899 and died in 1985. She was a simple woman from Nova Scotia who settled in New York during the Great Depression. Raised in a farming community, she grew up in a time when loyalty was a core value, and she witnessed a world that went from horses and buggies to space shuttles. During her eighty-six years, the world around her changed immensely, as did her personal circumstances. She grew up poor, and although she never became wealthy, money was not a worry in her later years. Yet her values barely budged as her life changed. Years after the Depression, she would follow people around the house to turn lights off behind them, chanting, "Waste not, want not." And years after the Brooklyn Dodgers left New York, she remained a Dodgers fan, chanting, "I am no turncoat!" Having lived and sacrificed through two world wars, she would forever give both politicians and her country the benefit of the doubt. So she, like many of her age group, was slow to grasp younger people's disenchantment with the Vietnam War. She would chant, "America: Love it or leave it." Her values, from thrift to loyalty to politics, were forever imprinted in her psyche. As the world and her personal circumstances changed, her values remained stable.

So it is with the shifts we have identified in this book, and that is why we are confident that they will endure for some time. The boomers who "sold out" their flower-child heritage for corporate perks will forever have a soft spot for an environment that entwines a noble cause with one's livelihood. Gen Xers, who were initially blocked from the corporate world, and who watched older siblings or parents suffer the indignity of unanticipated downsizing, will forever doubt the corporation's loyalty and intentions. Netters who experienced parental divorce and precious little family time will as a generation always hold family a little dearer than most, and will forever seek the integration of their personal and work lives. And kids who grew up pressing the reset button whenever boredom threatened will forever expect, on some level, the world of work to meet that need for newness, instant growth, and excitement.

Exaggerations? Yes. Generalizations? For certain! But values do not change overnight, and the trends we've discussed will ring true long after the next generation's equivalent of a Dodgers exodus is over. Not only are these basic expectations unlikely to change anytime soon, but some will intensify. Here are our educated guesses as to how:

Balance

When the crunch of balancing family and corporate life hits Netters and Xers—who already have stronger values around time than boomers—the expectation of flexibility and balance will accelerate greatly.

Personal and professional development

As the new economy puts increasing pressure on keeping one's credentials up to date, and as Netters and Xers move into what we call the Peggy Lee phase of life ("Is that all there is?"), the desire to combine personal and professional development will grow. Both the aging of the population and the growing affluence of elite workers will accelerate this shift. Meanwhile, as the next wave of post-teens arrives at the workplace—a generation wowed by technology and newness since birth—the odds that they will be satisfied staying in one place without growth for long is slim at best.

Partnership

As more and more workers get a taste for being consulted in decision-making, and having a stake in the game, paternalistic management weakens. And the more educated people are, the more they expect to be able to make choices. Welcome to the new business world, in which there are more partners than employees!

Noble cause

There is growing evidence of a "green shift" in values among Western societies, as in Home Depot deciding it will sell only "certified lumber," and Nike's fall from grace over the childhood labor issue. As the world moves toward holding corporations accountable for integrity and environmental awareness, star talent will be increasingly inclined to pick and choose employers whose values appear to align with their own.

The A versus the B Team

An increasing number of people are drifting away from the influence of the retention craze discussed in this book. While star performers come to expect partnership, balance, noble cause, personal/professional development, community, and trust, workers less attractive to the new economy will struggle to find any work, let alone a meaningful or profound calling. The solution: Extend the same perks inspired by star performers' expectations to the entire workforce. Let janitors become millionaires through stock options. Let dishwashers enjoy the same free massage therapist as the top salesperson. Remember the business consultants who studied the US Marines for secrets to commitment? One recommendation was to take the time to bolster anyone who is floundering, in order to reinforce that individual's sense of belonging *and promote an intense loyalty from everyone else.* Breaking the chain breaks trust and dampens workers' belief in corporate support of partnership.

Diversity

Little has been written about the work values of newly landed North Americans, never mind the hundreds of thousands born, raised, and still living overseas who work for North American interests. As the working population grows more diverse and the more homogenous workforce retires, the need for organizations to attend to these differences will grow. Non-Westerners are, of course, "imprinted" with an entirely different set of experiences, based on what was happening in their culture as they came of age. The fact that workers throughout the world share a growing number of similarities will not greatly alter this imprint.

The first step: An honest assessment

Years ago, John met a salesman on a commuter flight. From the moment this man sat down beside John, he did nothing but complain—about his wife, his boss, the client he was going to visit, the airline, the weather, and anything else that crossed his radar screen. He even had a favorite phrase he uttered numerous times during the brief flight: "People are so stupid!"

As the plane drew near its destination, the salesman finally turned to John and asked what he did for a living. A somewhat peeved John replied, "I give speeches and workshops to corporations about the importance of being positive. I talk about how, if you live and work in a positive manner, great things will come your way." The man brightened and replied without hesitation, "It's so refreshing to sit next to a man who thinks like me!"

Years of consulting have convinced us that many leaders are as misled about themselves and their companies as that man on the plane. Undoubtedly, that salesman would slam shut this book and comment, "This is for other people, other companies, but not for me!"

So, to him and to anyone else about to pass this book along, we advise, "Do an honest self-assessment of how you and your company are responding to these shifts, before shrugging off the matter."

Begin by taking the self-assessments found at the ends of Chapters 4 through 9. Better yet, have each member of your leadership team (which, in truly non-hierarchical companies, means most employees!) fill out the assessment, then discuss the results as a group. Alternatively, assign the book to every member of your management team and have them meet weekly to discuss each expectation, how the company is currently addressing it, and what other measures could be introduced to enhance policy in that area.

A more thorough way to meet these challenges is to conduct a formal assessment of your current corporate culture and practices. The aim: to gain a clear picture of the vital few policies that must change to ensure that your company becomes an employer of choice. When meeting with prospective clients, John likes to ask leaders whether they know the two or three key issues they must tackle to win greater commitment and engagement from their people. Amazingly, many have no idea, or only a vague, intuitive sense of what those priorities should be. A formal assessment can start them down the road to greater things.

Several years ago, John was asked to conduct an engagement and retention assessment for a company considered by many to be a "good" place to work. Although the company's retention rate was above industry average, turnover had been increasing and recruiting new hires was becoming more difficult. Wisely, the leaders of the organization wanted to know why this was happening and, more importantly, what they could do about it. John recommended they conduct an assessment using both a survey and a qualitative focus-group process to determine how vulnerable they were to losing people and what would entice people to stay. John insisted on the qualitative study so that the leaders would hear the real stories and desires of their people—an invaluable supplement to the reams of reports on means and normative comparisons. John's assessment pointed to three critical issues that, if addressed, would cause retention to soar:

1. People wanted to feel that the company was concerned about their personal and professional growth; they wanted more opportunities for learning and expanding their skills.
2. People wanted to feel that the work they were doing was important, was making a difference in some tangible way.
3. They wanted more recognition from management.

Sound familiar? That's right: growth and development, noble cause, and community. (Presumably, this company already excelled at balance, partnership, and trust!)

Over the next year, John's client worked hard at communicating heretofore "hidden" noble causes, bringing in customers to talk to employees about the impact of the company's products. Executives crafted a new mission statement with greater input from associates. Leaders pondered the deeper meaning of work and began to talk about it with their people on a regular basis. They also initiated discussions on the need for greater partnership and personal/professional development. By the end of the year, the results were in: a 35 percent decrease in turnover, and a tangible new spirit throughout the company. What's the lesson here? Taking the time to ask and listen is critical. Surveys are helpful, but real conversations will tell listeners far more.

When was the last time your organization held frank conversations with colleagues as to why they stay and what would make them leave? What key values or needs are not being met at this time?

Imitation: The worst form of strategy?

Imitation may be the best form of flattery, but it is the worst form of strategy. It's tempting, of course, to simply imitate the examples of what other companies are doing to respond to these shifts. We can even hear a few readers thinking, "If informal barbecues create community, let's have a few. If giving work teams power spells partnership, count us in. And if bringing customers in to talk about what a 'difference' our products make illuminates noble cause, we'll bring them in by the truckload. In fact, let's just gather up all the best practices listed in this book and start checking off which ones we'll do. Will five within each category be enough?"

While the examples listed in this book are excellent for pre-strategizing inspiration, duplicating them en masse is not a strategy. Strategy requires focus, or knowing what the critical issues are for your particular enterprise. Before you adopt new perks, ask yourself which values your company has already responded to effectively and which need a new focus. Which practices are most likely to be enthusiastically implemented by the workforce itself and which might meet resistance? In the spirit of partnership—keeping in mind that partnership is one of the new expectations—ask your people for their own creative solutions to their own wants and desires—new policies that would make them want to stay. Again, asking is often as important as implementing new practices. Besides, imitation unaccompanied by a deeper pondering of your basic philosophy may lead to barbecues to which no one shows up, or flex time that no one dares take.

Nonetheless, assuming your organization's management philosophy and values are in the right place, the examples in this book form an excellent jumping-off place. Try discussing each expectation as a leadership team, exploring the practices listed. Using them as a springboard, brainstorm ideas more amenable or specific to your organization, department, or division. Above all, don't feel limited by the examples we've gathered together; use them instead as the foundation for your own creativity. Oh, and don't forget to send us your best solutions, so we can mention them in our next book! **izzoinc@aol.com**

GETTING STARTED

Step One	Have the leadership team read each expectation chapter.
Step Two	Meet and talk about each expectation. Talk about how you understand it, what it means for your type of organization, and how you think your division or company is doing.
Step Three	Using the examples for inspiration, brainstorm all the ways your organization or division could respond to that shift.
Step Four	Identify a few new policies to get you started or to deepen your progress on that shift. Choose only as many as you can commit to implementing.

Doing something is more important than waiting for perfection

We hope this book has stimulated lots of ideas about what your company can do to respond to the changing expectations of your people and to stoke the fires of commitment. The real danger is not a lack of ideas but the chance that those great ideas will never translate into action. In seminars, John often asks attendees to close their eyes and imagine they are stepping over a line between intention and commitment. At first, he worried that they would consider this exercise silly, but more and more came up after seminars and expressed how helpful it was and how often they intended to do things but never got around to them.

Why is it that we read a book like this and never act? George Leonard, a martial arts expert turned leadership guru, explains in his book *Mastery* that at the edge of any new path, we often stand for a long time waiting for the perfect plan and steps to emerge. Analysis replaces action, as we imagine that we can map out the journey in detail before taking a step forward. In reality, the best way to get started is to get started. Once we do something, those actions lead to self-corrections and then to other, more lasting practices. The point is, take a few moments and write down three to five ideas you can put into immediate practice regarding what you have just learned about changing expectations at work. Then instead of worrying whether these are the perfect steps, just get started. It's more important to take some action based on what you've read, than to consign today's thoughts to that great stack of insights never yet passed on to commitment.

A final benediction

The kind of life we lead and the kind of workplace we create are never the product of one life-changing decision, but of thousands of decisions made every day. A few years ago, the entire workforce of the US.Postal Service was told that it was now empowered! How important was that organizational proclamation? Not nearly as important as the small decisions leaders make every day. As in the type of decision a leader must make when people ask if they can attend their child's school play during work hours (balance). As in, the tone of daily conversations those leaders have on the meaning of work versus making the numbers (noble cause). As in, the times that leaders resist making a decision, handing it instead to people weary of having decisions made for them and then asking those newly delegated decision-makers to return and broadcast what they accomplished (partnership). As in, next Monday when you take the time to meet with some of your people, simply to ask how they are doing, or next Friday, when you make the effort to ask what they're up to on the weekend and then follow up by asking them how it went (community).

Stephen Smith, the CEO of WestJet Airlines, told us, "One of the most important things a corporation can do is align the interests of the business with the interests of its people." This book has taken the first step in that process. Now that you know their expectations, the rest is up to you.

Credits

Page iii: Opening quote, "To turbocharge retention...": *Harvard Business Review,* September/October 1999; page 152

CHAPTER ONE CREDITS

Page 3: *Seattle Post-Intelligencer* quote: March 5, 2000; page G1: Page 4: Unemployment is at its lowest rate in 30 years: *Economist,* January 15, 2000; page 25: Page 6: Kinko's quote: *HR Magazine,* December 1999; page 8: Page 6: Mark Sussman quote: *Megagtrends 2000,* page 221: Page 7: 98% of population growth is occurring in countries without a strong education system: *National Geographic,* October 1998; page 4: Page 8: Human resources issues have leapfrogged to employers' No. 1 concern: *Globe & Mail,* November 15, 1999; page D1: Page 9: Number of voluntarily unemployed at 15%, highest in 10 years: *Fortune,* February 7, 2000; page 199: Page 9: Average job tenure in information technology has shrunk to 13 months from 18 months two years ago: *Fortune,* February 7, 2000; page 199: Page 9: Cost of losing and replacing an employee is between 50 and 150% of the salary of the leaving employee: *HR Information Matters,* September/October 1998; page B10: Page 9: Taco Bell outlets with lowest employee turnover produced 50% more in sales: Page 9: "Morale Boosters," *Marketing,* London, September 24, 1998; pages 36-38: Page 9: A significant improvement in recruiting new talent can produce a 10.1% increase in a company's market value, and key HR practices can increase shareholder values 30%:, *HRDM,* March 2000: Page 10: 510,000 full-time information technology jobs are vacant: *Training & Development,* January 1999; page 62: Page 10: By 2006, half of all workers will be employed in information technology positions or within industries that intensively utilize information technology: *Fast Company,* March 2000; page 217: Page 10: US Congress raised the number of visas from 1999 through 2001 for skilled technology workers by 142,500, a 73% leap: *Training & Development,* January 1999; page 62: Page 11: National Manufacturers Association survey (48% unable to read and interpret drawings and diagrams): *Workforce 77,* March 1998; page 48# 004 17% of American MBA students polled by Stockholm-based Universum planned to leave their first position after one or two years: *Fortune,* March 16, 1998; page 167

CHAPTER TWO CREDITS

Page 15: Angus Reid quote: *Shakedown,* page 310: Page 16: Stephen R. Covey re: the new economy needs leaders in every rank: *BC Business,* January 2000; page 38: Page 17: Half of women with small children work, 77% of women with children work: *Megatrends 2000,* page 217: Plante & Moran: (*Fortune,* Jan. 10, 2000 page 98): Page 17: Claire Raines quote: *Beyond Generation X,* page 40: Page 17: Plante & Moran: (*Fortune,* Jan. 10, 2000 page 98): Page 18: Toxic handlers: Peter Frost and Sandra Robinson, "The Toxic Handler: Organizational Hero – and Casualty," *Harvard Business Review,* July/August 1999, pp. 96–106: Page 18: Americans were exposed to six times as many advertising messages in 1991 as in 1971: *Fast Company,* March 2000; page 218: Page 18: SAP-AG: *Industry Week,* August 16, 1999; page 106: Page 19: CDW Computer Centers: *Fortune,* January 10, 2000; page 84: Page 19: Stonyfield Farm: *Making a Living While Making a Difference,* page 13: Page 20: Percentage of 20-somethings living with their parents has doubled since 1960: *Jobshift,* page 228: Page 20: Half of Generation X comes from divorced families, and the divorce rate has shot up since they were growing up in the 1970s: *Rational Exuberance,* page 161: Page 20: McCormick: *Fortune,* January 12, 1998; page 94: Page 21: A recent survey of graduating MBAs showed that a large percentage of new graduates has vowed never to let their work life overwhelm their personal life, a clear backlash against an over-devotion to work: 1997 survey of 1,792 MBA students at 20 US and Canadian schools by Universum, a consulting firm in Stockholm: Page 21: 40% of employees always have their resume up to date and 60% have taken courses to upgrade their skills in the last year alone:

Royal Bank 2000 survey: Page 21: Edward Jones: *Fortune*, January 10, 2000; page 83: Page 22: Companies are lucky to keep an employee the current average of three and a half years (men, 3.8; women, 3.4): *Across the Board*, January 2000; page 17: Page 22: The good risk-taker dwells for large parts of every day in ambiguity, uncertainty and vulnerability, and too much of this diet eats away at one's sense of character: Richard Sennett, *The Corrosion of Character*, pages 84, 85: Page 22: Kinko's Inc.: *HR* Magazine, December 1999; page 88: Page 24: 93% of corporate and human resources executives...: *Training & Development*, October 1999; page 12: Page 24: People born after 1945 are 10 times as likely to suffer from depression as people born 50 years earlier, in a less materialistic era: *The Good Life*, page 144: Page 24:Alcoa Inc.: *Industry Week*, August 16, 1999; page 45: Page 25: Simon Zadek quote: *The Good Life*, pages 129 & 144: Page 25: Two-thirds of experts at the Open University's Futures Observatory...: *Future Revolutions*, page 81: Page 25: "Primary measures of success" chart: *Making a Living While Making a Difference*, page 3: Page 26: Michael Hammer quote, "It is thrilling to be part of a revolution...": *Beyond Reengineering*, page 259: Page 26: Direct democracy and personal happiness: *Economist*, April 17, 1999; page 122: Page 27: US growth from 5% of total capital spending...: *Training & Development*, November 1999; page 38: Page 27-28: Americans are working 163 hours longer per year than they were in 1969: *Fortune*, January 10, 2000; page 68: Page 27: Just over one-third of Britons work on weekends, and 54% work into the evenings: University of Manchester, *The Times*, September 24, 1998: Page 27-28: Americans are outworking the Japanese: *Fortune*, January 10, 2000; page 68: Page 27: Internet chat group about "electronic leashes": *Fortune*, January 10, 2000; page 68: Page 28: One in five American workers will telecommute by 2010: January 25, 1999 web site of IBM Advanced Business Institute, "Five Myths Regarding Leadership, Culture Change and Technology," by Patrick G. Brown & Robert M. Goett: Page 29: Oracle anecdote regarding Intranets and employment perks: *Financial Post* DataGroup, March 6, 2000: Page 29: Regis McKenna quote: "Technology's effects on us today are different...": *Real Time: Preparing for the Age of the Never Satisfied Customer*, pages 15, 16

CHAPTER THREE CREDITS

Page 31: Barbara Moses quote: *Career Intelligence*, page 54: Page 32: 20% of workers are non-white, median age will surpass 40 in the year 2003 for the first time ever, 48% women: Families & Work Institute web site, January 21, 1999: Page 32: 44% of Generation X, 36% of boomers toying with the idea of starting their own business: *Rational Exuberance*, page 11: Pages 32-33: Ellen Gee information: *BC Business*, March 1998; page 26-28: Page 33: PricewaterhouseCoopers' mentoring program, etc.: *HR Information Matters,*: Page 34: Boomers total more than 60 million Americans, etc.: *Workforce*, November 1999: Page 36: games2train.com: *Training & Development*, November 1999; page 20: Page 38: Boomer manager quote: *Civilizing the Workplace*, page 207: Page 39: 54% of 18-24-year-olds highly interested in starting businesses compared with 36% of 35-64-year-olds: *Rational Exuberance*, page 11: Page 38: *Workforce* tips for retaining Gen Xers: *Workforce*, November 1999; page 14: Page 39: Unusual job titles at Play, the marketing agency: *Fast Company*, January/February 2000; page 172: Page 39: 8 of 10 US adults trying to start a business are in the 18 to 34 age group. In contrast, only 2% of the Harvard graduating class of 1942 showed any interest in self-employment: *Career Intelligence*, page 49: Page 39: One out of eight employees moonlights; between 35 and 57 of these own their own moonlighting business: Inc/Gallup survey of 1997: Page 39: 19% of 50-plus crowd, 30% of under-30s are on-line, but users 55 and older spend more time online than their younger counterparts: *Fast Company*, March 2000; page 214: Page 40: Young adults suffered an unemployment rate twice the national average for most of the 1990s: *Rational Exuberance*, page 11: Page 40: By 2003, for the first time ever there will be more workers over 40 than under 40: *Fortune*, February 1, 1999; page 50: Page 40: Computer ownership among individuals over 50 has grown 38% in four years: *Workforce* November 1999; page 29: Page 40: 40% of over-50s own computer: *Training & Development*, November 1999; page 20: Page 40: CEOs believe age 43 is productivity peak: *Fortune*, February 1, 1999; page 52: Page 40: 46% of Gen Xers identify their jobs as an "expression of themselves," compared with 56% of boomers: *Rational Exuberance*, page 12: Page 40: Trainers should change message or activity every 8, 10 or 15 minutes: *Training and Development*, February 2000; page 29: Page 41: Three-quarters of college students say that making a difference in the lives of others is very important, and more than half say doing volunteer work is a worthy cause. Gen X volunteers more than any other generation in America: *Rational Exuberance*, page 16: Page 41: One expert has said of the Net Generation, "They want spirituality incorporated into the company culture, more flexibility than even Generation X wants, and more information, more quickly": *Across the Board*, February 2000; page 55: Page 41: Gender has more power to determine a pay gap than ethnicity: *HR* Magazine, February 1998: Page 41: Human resources professionals believe minorities encounter barriers to career advancement, etc.: *Training & Development*, October 1999; page 12: Page 42: 90% of attendees said they planned to start a family, and 78% of those said they would keep working: *LA Times*, March 6, 2000; Part E, page one; regarding UCLA's Anderson School conference: Page 42: Most women return to work within six months after giving birth, according to Catalyst: *Megatrends 2000*, page 233: Page 42: One-fifth of all complaints received by the Canadian Human Rights Commission in 1998 involved allegations on the basis of sex, and a disproportionate number of those concerned women who suffered adverse consequences when their employers learned they were expecting: *Worklife*, Volume 11, Number 4, 1999: Page 42: By 1990, the number of women working outside the home had leapt to 57 per cent, and today, it stands at 61 per cent. Meanwhile, two-thirds of unmarried mothers with a child under three are now in the labour force, compared with just over half in 1995: *Economist*, January 15, 2000; page 25: Page 42: While only 3% of the most senior jobs in *Fortune* 500 companies are currently held by women, more than 400...: *Globe & Mail*, December 11, 1997; page A14: Page 42: Women have taken two-thirds of all the new jobs in the information economy: *Megatrends 2000*, page 47: Page 42: Ernst & Young's women's network and mentors: *Fortune*, January 11, 1999; page 136: Page 43: "There are not nearly enough people with college degrees...": *Megatrends 2000*, page 48: Page 43: 59% of working mothers would relinquish a day's pay for extra time off, while only 43% of fathers would do so: *Black Enterprise*, June 1993: Page 43: Women like praise in writing, boomers like it more than they get it, and small companies are quickest to hand it out: *Inc.*, May 2, 1997: Page 43: Women are more receptive to and appreciative of detailed feedback and assistance from others: *Across the Board*, January 2000, page 13: Page 43: Women are more receptive to and appreciative of detailed feedback and assistance from others: *Across the Board*, January 2000; page 13: Page 43: Female managers in organizations offering flexible work hours experience a significantly higher level of organizational commitment and job satisfaction: *HR Information Matters,* September 1997; page 3: Page 43: Deloitte & Touche, well known as a progressive company, boasts at least ten part-timers who have achieved partner status: *Fortune*, January 10, 2000; page 90: Page 44: No. 1 predictor of job satisfaction for women is the relationships they form at work: US Bureau of Labor study, 1996: Page 44: David Thomas quote: "Effective management of a diverse workforce...": *HR* Magazine, December 1999; page 67: Page 44: Companies with diverse boards reap greater market returns: Kinder, Lydenberg, Domini & Co., a New York-based investment research firm: *HR* Magazine, December 1999; page 68: Page 45: Almost a third of the Silicon Valley's scientists and engineers are now Asian-born: *Economist*, April 17, 1999, page 69: Page 45: Of the 36,000 Chinese students who have gone to the US to study, only 8,800 have returned since 1979: *Megatrends 2000*, page 201: Page 45: Phyllis Swersky quote: *Megatrends 2000*, page 225: Page 45: Alagasco's $500 prize for diversity suggestion: *Fortune*, January 12, 1998; page 95: Page 46: Five approaches companies take...: "Valuing Differences at Digital Equipment Corporation," *Diversity in the Workplace Human Resources Initiatives*; pages 119-137: Page 46: 1993 article in *Advertising Age*: Regis McKenna, *Real Time: Preparing for the Age of the Never Satisfied Customer*, page 34: Page 46: Companies with greater diversity make better business partners and merge more smoothly with other companies, according to Amy Hillman, management professor at the University of Western Ontario's Ivey

School of Business: *HR Magazine*, December 1999; page 69: Page 47: Regis McKenna quote: *Real Time: Preparing for the Age of the Never Satisfied Customer*, page 35: Page 47: Etec Systems anecdote: *HR Information Matters*, March 1998: Page 47: "Minority-friendly companies tend to be superior performers": *Fortune*, January 10, 2000

CHAPTER FOUR CREDITS

Page 51: "The key to *The Good Life* lies in balance and integration in all facets of our lives." – *The Good Life*, page 87: Page 52: CEO's wife could tell lower-ranking corporate wives how to decorate their homes: *BC Business*, August 1998; page 22: Page 52: American Management Systems: *Fortune*, January 12, 1998; page 87: Page 52: Deloitte & Touche: *Fortune*, January 11, 1999; page 121: Page 53: Workers willing to give up 21% of their work hours *and salary* to achieve more balance: 1996 poll by staffing services firm Robert Half International, Menlo Park, California: Page 53: A lack of balance between work and personal life is one of the top six reasons why 65% of employees on flex schedules would have left the firm without the flextime: Ernst & Young, *Fortune*, November 9, 1998; page 250: Page 53: 60% of men and women under age 25 with children say they would make "a lot" of sacrifices in money and career advancement in order to spend more time with their families: *Rational Exuberance*, page 12: Page 53: 55% of 18- to 34-year-olds identify the freedom to take extended leaves or sabbaticals as a key workplace benefit: *Chips & Pop*, page 175: Page 53: 1995 report of "the new work ethic" by Demos: *Chips & Pop*, page 176: Page 53: Need to increase the over-55's labour participation by 25%: *Age Works*, page 124: Page 53: AFLAC ill-relative time: *Fortune*, January 10, 2000; page 84: Page 54: Genetech: *Fortune*, January 10, 2000; page 90: Page 55: Time spent on the job in a given year has increased by 163 hours in the last 20 years: *Beyond Generation X*, page 45: Page 55: Jamba Juice: *Inc*, June 1999; page 42: Page 56: 41% of British managers disappointed with work/life balance, 85% believe vacation should be compulsory, yet 48% feel guilty when they leave on time: *Management Today*, Work Life Survey, August 1999, UK; page 51: Page 56: SAP-AG: *Industry Week*, August 16, 1999; page 106: Page 57: Dr. James Maas, author of *Power Sleep*, advocates allowing workers to take power naps :"Sleep Deprivation," *Vancouver Sun*, March 17, 1998; pages D1-D2: Page 57: Over the past five years, percentage of workforce sharing jobs has risen by 81%; number that work from home up 70%; 90% of large companies expect more to work from home; three-quarters predict more job sharing: 1997 survey by international management consulting firm Watson Wyatt Worldwide: Page 58: Study of 800 employers indicates that 79% of employees have formal policies for regular part-time employment, and 38% for flextime arrangements. Another 34% provide for compressed work schedules and 26% have job-sharing programs.: Page 58: Telecommuting programs are offered by 17% of employers, with an equal number considering or developing them: 1996 study of 800 employers by consulting firm William M. Mercer Inc.: Page 58: By the year 2010, one in every five Americans will be telecommuters: Advanced Business Institute web site, "Five Myths Regarding Leadership, Culture Change and Technology," by Patrick G. Brown and Robert M. Goett, January 25, 1999: Page 58: Job stress estimated to cost US industry $200 billion to $300 billion annually in absenteeism, diminished productivity, employee turnover, accidents, workers' compensation, and direct medical, legal and insurance fees: *Fast Company*, March 2000; page 219: Page 58: Defining characteristics of Attention Deficit Disorder increasingly prevalent and perhaps due to environmental factors such as the information explosion: *Fast Company*, March 2000; page 219: Page 58: Gemcom Services: *BC Business* Magazine, March 1998; page 28: Page 59: A *Fortune* magazine poll of headhunters recently determined that the employees most likely to turn down job offers had flextime: *Fortune*, January 12, 1998; page 69: Page 59: Fannie Mae "Healthy Living Day": Fannie Mae Web site: Page 60: Deloitte & Touche, well known as a progressive company, boasts at least ten part-timers who have achieved partner status: *Fortune*, January 10, 2000; page 90: Page 60: Dawson Personnel Systems survey: *Inc.*, August 1999; page 112: *Your Money or Your Life* graph: page 282: Page 60: DDC Inc and Medela regarding Mothers at Work program: PRNewswire, August 6, 1998: Page 62:

Republic Bancorp: *Fortune*, January 10, 2000; page 88: Page 63: In 1935, the average working man had 40 hours a week free. By 1990, it was down to 17 hours: *The Sibling Society*, page 36: Page 63: The number of managers working 49 hours or more a week has risen by 37% since 1985: Bureau of Labor Statistics 1998: Page 63: 72% of British managers surveyed said that long working hours affect their relationship with their partner, etc.: *The Times*, September 24, 1998; Quality of Working Life survey produced by the Institute of Management with Manchester School of Management at the University of Manchester Institute of Science and Technology: Page 63: Nearly one in five employed parents is single, 27% are men, and two-thirds of employed parents with pre-kindergarten children rely on partners and relatives as the primary childcare source: Families & Work Institute 1997: Page 63: One of six primary-age children and two out of five grade-school children arrive home after school to an empty house: *The Sibling Society*, page 136: Page 64: The majority of babies born in the US are placed in full-time daycare within a year; nearly half of babies today suffering from a lack of attachment to their parents: *The Sibling Society*, page 136: Page 64: Nearly a third of the population suffers from a definable psychological problem depression in particular growing; may be due to a lack of deep friendships...: *The Good Life*, page 26: Page 64: A company of 1,000 employees loses $1 million per year in stress-induced absenteeism alone: *BC Business*, May 2000; page 81: Page 64: Amgen: *Fortune*, January 10, 2000; page 90: Page 65: Edward Jones: *Fortune*, January 10, 2000; page 83: Page 66: Family problems are one of the top five reasons that relocations fail:1997 survey by Right Management Consultants in Philadelphia, Pennsylvania: Page 67: *Beyond Generation X* quote: "Members of the X generation...have witnessed firsthand a work ethic that eats people up: page 46: Page 67: Computer Associates International item: *Industry Week*, August 16, 1999; page 52: Page 68: WRQ: *Fortune*, January 11, 1999; page 122

CHAPTER FIVE CREDITS

Page 75: *Corporate Celebration* quote: page 101: Page 76: Grand Metropolitan: *The Hungry Spirit*, page 166: Page 76: Fannie Mae: Fannie Mae Web site: Page 76: Lenscrafters: *Fortune*, January 11, 1999; page 136: Page 77: Oxfam receives a constant stream of resumes from high-powered executives looking for a change: *The Hungry Spirit*, page 160: Page 77: Volunteer work and Gen X: *Rational Exuberance*, page 16: Page 77: 72% of corporate and human resources executives polled said their companies' values motivate them personally: *Training & Development*, October 1999; page 12: Page 77: Bright Horizons quote: *Fortune*, January 12, 1998; page 92: Page 77: The Body Shop item: *Megatrends 2000*, page 236: Page 78: Environics International poll: *Across the Board*, January 2000; page 28: Page 78: Associates III: *Beyond Generation X*, page 89: Page 79: Every 100 pounds of product manufactured in the US creates at least 3,200 pounds of waste: Paul Hawken, *The Good Life*; page 129: Page 79: The world's population nearly quadrupled between 1900 and 2000: *National Geographic*, October 1998; page 4: Page 79: The world's income is now less evenly distributed than it was one hundred years ago: *Globe & Mail*, "Amazing Facts," April 3, 2000; page 2: Page 79: Results of a survey of graduating MBAs: 1997 survey of 1,792 MBA students at 20 US and Canadian schools by Universum, a consulting firm in Stockholm: Page 79: Even more recently, respondents responded marriage, health and ethics: *Making a Living While Making a Difference*; page 3: Page 79: Pledge programs: *Making a Living While Making a Difference*, page 167: Page 80: Dayton, Ohio flood in the early 1900s and John Patterson: *Discovering America's Past: Customs, Legends, History & Lore of our Great Nation*, The Reader's Digest Association, 1993; page 288: Page 80: Medtronics: *Fortune*, January 11, 1999; page 136: Page 82: IKEA's driving purpose: *The Natural Step for Business*; page 48: Page 81: ICN Pharmaceuticals Inc: *The Mission Statement Book*, page 242: Page 82: Johnson Wax: *The Mission Statement Book*, page 253: Page 82: Borg-Warner: *The Mission Statement Book*, page 100: Page 82: Pre-IPO stock pledges: *Fast Company*, March 2000; page 166: Page 83: Pfizer: *The Mission Statement Book*, page 343: Page 83: AES: *CMA Management*, October 1999; page 50: Page 83: Jostens Inc: *The Mission Statement Book*, page 262: Page 83: Shaklee US: *The Mission Statement Book*, page 384: Page 83: Tandy

Corporation: *The Mission Statement Book,* page 412: Page 83: Patagonia: *Fortune,* January 12, 1998; page 86: Page 85: Bell Canada item: *Making a Living While Making a Difference,* page 39: Page 86: The Endangered Species Chocolate Company: *Making a Living While Making a Difference,* page 12: Page 87: Placer Dome item: *Chips & Pop,* page 179: Page 87: 90% of *Fortune* 500 companies have formalised ethics codes, and 30% of those have ethics officers or specialists to support their ethics programs. Canada alone employed 60 ethics officers in 1998, while another 60 Canadian companies boasted corporate ombudspersons: *HR Information Matters,* April 1998; page B5: Page 88: *Fortune* magazine reporter and Container Store: *Fortune,* January 2000; page 76: Page 88: DaimlerChrysler AG: *Industry Week,* August16, 1999; page 47: Page 89: The Body Shop broadcasts: *Corporate Celebration,* page 100: Page 89: Paul Hawken quote: *The Natural Step for Business,* page 202: Page 89: Four companies profiled in *The Natural Step for Business:* pages 192, 193: Page 89: Scandic Hotels: *The Dance of Change,* page 532: Page 90: Coalition for Environmentally Responsible Economies (www.ceres.org), representing more than 80 businesses, non-profits and public agencies: *Making a Living While Making a Difference,* page 56: Page 90: David Packard quote: *The Hungry Spirit,* page 77: Page 90-91: Michael Dell quote: *Fast Company,* December 1999; page 116: Page 90: Nike Canada's P.L.A.Y. program: *Report on Business,* August 1999; page 22: Page 90: The Body Shop item: *Megatrends 2000,* page 236: Page 91: Worldwide survey of managers' values: Charles Hempden-Turner, quoted in *Corporate Celebration,* page 13: Page 92: Psychotherapist Francis Hope quote: *The Good Life,* page 47 *USA Today* survey: April 22, 1997: Page 92: HB Fuller: *Fortune,* January 12, 1998; page 94: Page 93: Homestead.com anecdote: *Fast Company,* April 2000; page 76: Page 93: Bain & Co. anecdote: *Globe & Mail,* April 17, 2000; page M1: Page 93:Computer Business Associates International Inc: *Industry Week,* August 16, 1999; page 52: Page 94: General Mills anecdote: *Industry Week,* August 16, 1999; page 103: Page 94: *Industry Week* quote: *Industry Week,* August 16, 1999; page 103: Page 94: Marriott International: *Fortune,* January 12, 1998; page 87: Page 95: Whole Goods Market: *HR Magazine,* December 1999; page 92: Page 95: Finova Group: *Fortune,* January10, 2000; page 84: Page 95: Timberland: *Fortune,* January 10, 2000, page 90 and *Fortune,* January 12, 1998, page 90: Page 95-96: Michael Hammer quote: *Beyond Reengineering,* pages 267, 268: Page 96: Three parts of one's soul: Charles Handy*The Good Life,* page 127: Page 97: Three factors common to *Fortune* magazine's 100 best companies: *Fortune,* January 12, 1998; pages 72-74

CHAPTER SIX CREDITS

Page 101: *The Natural Step for Business* quote: page 10: Page 101: Kinko's Inc: *HR Magazine,* December 1999; page 88: Page 102: 1968 study: *The Affluent Worker: Page* 102: 3M: *Built to Last,* pages 157, 158: Page 102-103: Net Generation's itchy feet: *Chips & Pop,* page 194: David K. Foot's four kinds of career paths: *Boom, Bust & Echo,* pages 61, 62: Page 103-104: Foot quote: *Boom, Bust & Echo,* page 64: Page 105: James Dyson anecdote: *Industry Week,* June 21, 1999; pages 42, 43: Page 105: Sears Competency Transformation: *Network World,* February 21, 2000; page 66: Page 106: Royal Bank of Canada survey: April 2000: Page 106: Employer-sponsored training attracts recruits: Business Wire, September 7, 1998: Page 106: *ComputerWorld* survey: *Technical Training,* March/April 1998; pages 16-19: Page 106: 1999 Gallup poll: September 3, 1999 from Internet: Page 106: *Chips & Pop:* page 191: Page 106: June 1997 survey of workplace benefits valued by Netters: *Chips & Pop.* page 175: Page 106: 70% of companies believe that phased retirement offers solution to growing labour shortage, and three of four older workers prefer to reduce hours gradually: *Seattle P-I,* March 5, 2000; p G1: Page 106: Intel: *Fortune,* January 12, 1998; page 87: Page 107: 1998 Watson Wyatt survey of employers: Strategic Rewards Survey of 614 US employers: Page 107: 75% of higher performing companies linked training programs with strategic goals, compared with only 67% of other organisations: *HR Information Matters,* 1999; page 46: Page 108: Employment in the information technology services sector is expected to nearly double between 1999 and 2005, from a current 1.1 million workers: *Training & Development,* January 1999; page 62: Page 108: Technology-delivered training expected to account for 55% of corporate training, up from 20% in 1999: *Training and Development,* November 1999; page 38: Page 108: Web-based training has produced 50% savings in time and cost: *HR Information Matters,* July/August 1998; page K8: Page 108: Charles Schwab: *Fortune,* January 10, 2000; page 83: Page 109: Design the training around the task, not the language: Kevin Kavanaugh, *Training & Development,* April 1999; page 15: Page 110: Employee career development account: *Career Intelligence,* page 205: Page 110: Mercer Management quote: *Fortune,* May 1, 2000; page 336: Page 110: 86% of US employers surveyed found recruiting qualified workers difficult, and 60% reported problems retaining employees: *HR Focus,* July 1998; pages 11, 12: Page 110: Motorola: *Fortune,* January 12, 1998; page 94: Page 110: SAS turnover rate: *Fortune,* January 10, 2000, page 98 and *The New York Times* Magazine, March 5, 2000, page 82: Page 110: Chick-fil-A: *Beyond Generation X,* page 89: Page 111: Land's End: *Fortune,* January 12, 1998; page 88: Page 112: David K. Foot quote: *Boom, Bust & Echo,* page 65: Page 112: HB Fuller: *Fortune,* January 12, 1998; page 94: Page 113: LifeCenter web site anecdote: *Fast Company,* October 1998, page 201: Page 114: Wall Street firm: *Harvard Business Review,* September/October 1999; page 149: Page 114: *The Harvard Business Review* quote: September/October 1999; page 146: Page 115: Joan Mara and peer mentorship information: *BC Business,* November 1999; page 52: Page 115: Up to 70% of employee knowledge is obtained informally on the job: Jack Stack, "The Training Myth," *Inc.*August 1998: Page 115: *Fortune* survey re employees who had resisted headhunters' offers, as to why they had stayed put: *Fortune,* January 12, 1998; page 69: Page 115: The Tandy Corp./RadioShack: *HR* Magazine, December 1999; page 90: Page 116: 1960s study in Great Britain: *The Affluent Worker:* Page 117: A match of life and work interests is the most important of the three for long-term career satisfaction: *The Harvard Business Review,* September/October 1999; page 147: Page 117: Silver Diner: *Nation's Restaurant News,* February 7, 2000: Page 118: Paula Lawlor quote: *Inc,* February 2000; page 78

CHAPTER SEVEN CREDITS

Page 123: Charles McGrath quote: *The New York Times* Magazine, March 5, 2000; page 17: Page 124: Kinko's quote: *HR Magazine,* December 1999; page 8: Page 125: 61% of senior managers feel they treat employees as valued business partners; only 27% of employees agree: *Report on Business,* February 1999; page 3: Page 125: Dyson Appliances: *Industry Week,* June 21, 1999; page 42: Page 126: Schwab: Schwab Web site: Page 127: Donnelly: *Fortune,* January 12, 1998; page 94: Page 128: Only 10 % of workers say they are part of a participatory environment: *Training & Development,* February 1998; pages 58-61: Page 128: US employees rate two-way communication and individual recognition as highly important to job satisfaction, second only to salaries and benefits, but fewer than 35% frequently share opinions with top management: *HR Information Matters,* September/October 1998; page E7: Page 128: Microsoft: *Fortune,* January 12, 1998; page 84: Page 129: BrainBank anecdote: *Washington Post,* July 15, 1998, page C09: Page 129: At Medi-Health Outsourcing, employees who pass on a lead that generates money can collect $500 to $1,000: *Inc.*February 2000; page 81: Page 129: 3M: *Built to Last,* pages 158, 159: Page 130: Best ways to engage workers: *Across the Board,* November/December 1999; page 52: Page 130: *Megatrends 2000* quote: "People who are difficult to supervise...": page 223: Page 130: Irshad Manji anecdote: *Risking Utopia* and *BC Business* Magazine, March 1998; page 26: Page 130: Imagination Ltd.: *Fast Company,* April 2000; page 168: Page 131: "Hungover" quote: *Beyond Generation X,* page 40: Page 131: Noel Tichy & Ford: *Fast Company,* April 2000; page 148: Page 131: Imagination Ltd.: *Fast Company,* April 2000; page 168: Page 131: Kinkos: *Beyond Generation X,* page 79: Page 132: Teknion Corporation: *Globe & Mail,* March 3, 2000: Page 132: AES Corporation: *CMA Management,* October 1999; page 50: Page 132-133: Peter Senge quote, "Sooner or later, executive leadership becomes crucial...": *Dance of Change,* page 566: Page 132: WL Gore: *Fortune,* January 12, 1998; page 84 & January 11, 1999; page 127: Page 133: Marriott: *Harvard Business Review,* May/June 1999; page 117: Page 133: Southwest Airlines employee quote: *Fortune,* January

12, 1998; page 84: Page 133: Medi-Health Outsourcing: *Inc.*, February 2000; page 76: Page 133: Harley-Davidson: *Industry Week*, February 1, 1999; page 6: Page 134: Dallas-based Texas Instruments: *Fortune*, January 12, 1998; page 92: Page 134: Continental Airlines: *Fortune 500*, January 10, 2000; page 88: Page 134: Granite Rock: *Fortune*, January 12, 1998; page 86: Page 135: Adrian Woodridge quote: *New York Times* Magazine, March 5, 2000; page 83: Page 135: *Dance of Change* description of open-book management: page 181: Page 135: International Harvester: *Dance of Change*, page 381: Page 136: The Container Store: Container store web site: Page 136: TDIndustries' monthly meeting: *Fortune*, January 12, 1998; page 84: Page 136-137: Open books lead workers to see and understand the big picture: *Canadian Manager*, Summer 1999; page 27: Page 136: Nordstrom Inc: *HR* Magazine, December 1999; page 87: Page 137: Royal Bank study on employee attitudes: April 2000: Page 137: 36 of 58 publicly held companies offered options: *Fortune*, January 10, 2000; page 83: Page 138: "The new economy is about unlimited opportunity...": *Fast Company*, March 2000; page 166: Page 138: Compensation pies: *BC Business*, September 1998; page 47: Page 138: Pay-for-performance history: *New York Times* Magazine, March 5, 2000; page 46: Page 139: AT&T, Blue Cross Blue Shield, and Owens Corning: *Fortune*, February 1, 1999; page 64: Page 139: Whole Foods Market: *HR* Magazine, December 1999; page 92: Page 139: Synovus: *Fortune*, January 10, 2000; page 1998: Page 139: The millionaire clubs: Southwest Airlines, *Fortune*, January 10, 2000; page 82: Page 140: Mary Parker Follett quote: *Report on Business*, April 1999; page 91: Page 140: John Kotter quote: *Report on Business*, April 1999; page 92: Page 141: Andrall E. Pearson quote: *Fast Company*, January 1999; page 73: Leadership business generates $15 billion US annually: *Report on Business*, April 1999; page 91: Page 142: Task of today's leaders: *Fortune*, March 6, 2000; page F9: Page 142: The Container Store: *Fortune*, January 10, 2000; page 75: Page 143: Robert Wright quote: *Megatrends 2000*, page 229: Page 143: Four qualities that characterise effective leadership: *Harvard Business Review*, May/June 1999; page 111: Page 143: Nordstrom Inc: *HR* Magazine, December 1999; page 87: Page 144: US Marines study: *Harvard Business Review*, May/June 1999; page 107: Page 144: Herman Miller: *Fortune*, January 11, 1999; page 142: Page 145: Ingram Micro: *Fortune* January 11, 1999; page 140: Page 145: Ernst and Young: *HR Information Matters*, September/October 1998; page E7: Page 145: Whole Foods Market: *Fortune*, January 12, 1998; pages 87, 89: Page 145: Vigilance: *CMA*, October 2000; page 51: Page 146: Dyson Appliances Ltd.: *Industry Week*, June 21, 1999; page 40: Page 146: Pfizer: *Fortune*, January 10, 2000; pages 88, 98

CHAPTER EIGHT CREDITS

Page 151: Ken Blanchard quote: *Corporate Celebration*, page 65: *Page* 152: Wegman's Food Markets quote: *Fortune*, January 12, 1998; page 85: Page 152: 26 of *Fortune's* 100 Best Companies offer personal concierge services: *Fortune*, January 10, 2000; page 64: Page 154: British study in the early 1960s: *The Affluent Worker: Page* 154: McCormick: *Fortune*, January 12, 1998; page 94: Page 155: 77% of employees get more satisfaction from time they spend away from their jobs than from work hours: Gallup, September 3, 1999: Page 155: 85% expect to continue with some kind of work, and 69% say they will work only because they want something to do, not because they will need the money: Gallup, September 3, 1999: Page 155: 47% of senior citizens work because they need the money, 86% work because they like being with other people, and 82% work because they need to be productive: *Training & Development*, June 1999; page 12: Page 155: Amgen Inc.: *Industry Week*, August 16, 1999; page 46: Page 156: P&G anecdote: *Built to Last*, page 132: *Page* 157: 1958 *Mill & Factory* magazine survey: *SM's Roundup of Recent Research Findings*, August 1958; page 35: Page 156: Amgen: *Fortune*, January 12, 1998; page 92: Page 157: "This new workplace ...": *Fortune*, January 10, 2000: Page 157: Catapult Systems Corp: *Inc 500*, 1999; page 11: Page 158: Southwest Airlines quote: *Accountancy* 121, February 1998; pages 40-42: Page 158: PeopleSoft: *Fast Company*, January 1999, page 80: Page 158: Container Store quote: *Fortune*, January 10, 2000; page 75: Page 158: BMC: *Fortune*, January 10, 2000; page 63: Page 158: DeMarini Sports: *Inc*, June 1999; page 42: Page 159:

Great Plains Software of Fargo, North Dakota quote: *Fortune*, January 12, 1998; page 90: Page 159: Four dimensions of community: *Chips & Pop*, pages 200-203: Page 159-160: Maintenance staff emergency fund: *Dance of Change*, page 383: Page 159: WRQ: *Fortune*, January 10, 2000; page 90: Page 160: Baptist Health Systems: Fortune, January 12, 1998; page 94: Page 160: Marriott International: *Fortune*, January 12, 1998; page 87: Page 160: BE&K: *Fortune*, January 11, 1999, page 136 and *Fortune*, January 12, 1998, page 89: Page 160: Michael Hammer quote: *Beyond Reengineering*, pages 264, 265: Page 160: Lawrence Management Services Inc: *HR* Magazine, December 1999; page 88: Page 161: Empire Blue Cross and Blue Shield: *Journal for Quality & Participation* 21, January/February 1998; page 56: Page 161: Employees in companies with five or fewer workers are more satisfied than other employees: Royal Bank of Canada Study of worker attitudes in Canada, April 2000: Page 161: Petro Canada manager quote: *Chips & Pop*, page 202: Page 161-162: Charles Handy quote: *The Hungry Spirit*, page 192: Page 161: Four Seasons: *Fortune*, January 11, 1999; page 140: Page 162: Thomas L. Friedman quote: *New York Times* service, *International Herald Tribune*, March 10, 1999; page 9: Page 162: Jack Hartnett, the president of DL Rogers Corp.: *Inc.*, July 1998; page 64: Page 162: Mountain Equipment Co-op: *BC Business*, April 2000; pages 47, 50: Page 162: Peoplesoft: *Fortune*, January 12, 1998; page 86: Page 164: Liechtenstein Global Trust, *Corporate Celebration*, page 9: Page 164: MTW Corp.: *Fast Company*, December 1999, page 86: Page 164: JM Smucker: *Fortune*, January 10, 2000; page 88: Page 165: McKinsey and Co. quote: *Chips & Pop*, page 201: Page 165: ObjecTime: *Chips & Pop*, page 203: Page 165-166: Cisco: *Fast Company*, February/March 1998; page 56: Page 166: Kingston Technology: *Fortune*, January 12, 1998; page 84: Page 166: Kingston Technology: *Fortune*, January 12, 1998; page 84: Page 167: SAS Institute: *Fortune*, January 12, 1998; page 84: Page 167: SAS turnover rate: *Fortune*, January 10, 2000, page 98 and *The New York Times* Magazine, March 5, 2000, page 82: Page 174: Joe Demarte quote regarding Nordstrom: *HR* Magazine, December 1999; page 88: Page 175: Leonard Berry quote regarding The Container Store: *Fortune*, January 10, 2000; page 78

CHAPTER NINE CREDITS

Page 176: 87% of North American organizations and 86% of companies abroad (especially in the UK, Germany and Japan) downsized between 1986 and 1993: Lisa Baggerman, *Industry Week*, January 18, 1993: Page 176: Between 1987 and 1993, large companies like IBM, Sears Roebuck, and GE shed a quarter or more of their workforces: *Forbes*, April 25, 1994: Page 176: One-third of households contained someone who lost their job, and nearly 75% of all households experienced a close encounter with layoffs between 1980 and the late 1990s: *New York Times* as reported in *Rational Exuberance*, page 148: Page 176: On average, workers who lost their jobs but found work elsewhere earned 15% less, and 25% lost their health coverage as a result of job dislocation: *Revitalizing the Workplace after Downsizing, Mergers and Reengineering*, page 78: Page 176: Quote from *Revitalizing the Workplace after Downsizing, Mergers and Reengineering*, pages 78, 79: Page 177: Between 1988 and 1996, the number of employees who said that they often did not believe what management said rose from 33 to 40%: *The New Deal at Work*, page 238: Page 177: Trust declined at three of four workplaces: Manchester Consulting, *Management Review*, July/August 1998 cover story: Page 177: Between 1995 and 1997, the number of workers who felt their company considered their interests in decisions affecting them dropped from 50 to 41%: Towers-Perrin Workplace Index press release, 1997: Pages 177-178: Number of Americans indicating confidence in the people running big business dropped from 19 to 12%, etc.: *Business Week*, March 11, 1996; page 60: Page 178: A survey of downsized firms found that 74% reported that workforce morale was low and distrust of management high: US Department of Labor, *A Guide to Restructuring*, 1995: Page 178: 9% reported an associated increase in absenteeism, and 13% noted an increase in disability claims: American Management Association Survey on downsizing, 1996: Page 178: Only 37% of employees rate the level of honesty in their workplaces as high or very high, although 95% rate their own honesty level as high or very high: Spring 1998 survey by the American Management Association reported in *Training & Development*, November 1999; page 16: Page 178: Only 14% agree that "people trust each other": *Training & Development*, November 1999; page 16: Page 178: As we've mentioned earlier, 54% of senior managers think the level of trust between corporate ranks is good, while only 27% of their employees agree: *Report on Business*, February 1999; page 3: Page 178: 64% of employees believe management routinely fails to tell the truth: 1994 & 1996, US-based Council of Communication Management, *Worklife Report* 1999, Volume 11, Issue 4, page 6: Page 178: 43% believe that their managers cheat and lie: survey by Mirvis & Kanter, *National Productivity Review*, Autumn 1989: Page 178: The level of trust is best between front-line workers and their immediate supervisors, and worst between front-line workers and top-level executives: Manchester Consulting as reported in *Modern Machine Shop*, December 1998: Page 178: 75% of executives say trust is declining, and only 15% believe it is improving: *Management Review*, July/August 1998: Page 178: Netobjects CEO quote: *Fast Company*, January 1999; page 77: Page 179: Murray Dobbin quote: *The Myth of the Good Corporate Citizen: Democracy Under the Rule of Big Busines:* Pages 179-180: Employee productivity rose or held constant in 70% of downsized companies; short-term profits rose or held constant in 80%: American Management Association survey on downsizing, 1994, AMA, New York: Page 180: Employers who restructured reported adverse effects on employee workload (62%), morale (56%) and commitment (52%), and yet an *increase* in productivity, service levels and the competence of the workforce: *The New Deal at Work*, p 126: Page 181: Barbara Moses quote: *Career Intelligence*, page 74: Page 181: Only 2% name dedication to their firm as the key to success. Instead, 56% cite individual ambition as the new key: *Training* , February 1992; page 74: Page 181: *Fortune* 500 managers found that those who survived restructuring focused more on their own careers and less on organizational goals: *Strategic Management Magazine*, Journal 14, 1993; pages 161-179: Page 181: Home Depot legend: *Harvard Business Review*, May/June 1999; page 110: Page 182: Workers seem to be staying in the same occupation longer now than in the past, even as tenure with a particular employer has declined sharply since 1993; the length of tenure is currently at its lowest level in 20 years: *The New Deal at Work*, pages 134, 135: Page 182: A work environment rich in trust and respect has been linked with less stress and greater productivity: *Worklife Report* 99, Volume 11, Issue 4; page 6: Page 182: Trust minimizes inhouse unethical or criminal behaviour, which adds up to $400 billion annually within US industry: *Canadian Manager*, Winter 99; page 23: Page 183: Frank J. Navran quote: *Truth & Trust: The First Two Victims of Downsizing*, pages 132, 133: Page 183: *Sixty Minutes* & HB Fuller: Revitalizing the Workplace after Downsizing, Mergers and Reengineering, page 5: Page 183: Arthur Andersen study: *Canadian Manager*, Winter 99; page 24: Page 184: Terence E. Deal and Allan A. Kennedy quote: *Revitalizing the Workplace after Downsizing, Mergers and Reengineering*, pages 210, 211: Page 184: Organizations that have implemented procedures encouraging individuals to step forward, say that company integrity and efficiency improve as a result: *Human Resource Management Journal 7*, No. 4, 1997; pages 5-10: Pages 184-185: Valour Pulse: *Management Review*, July/August 1998 cover story: Page 184: Dana Corporation: *Management Review*, July/August 1998, cover story: Page 186: Ciba Specialty Chemicals: *Management Review*, July/August 1998, cover story: Pages 186: Eight distinct behaviors, five leaders' keys to a trustworthy relationship with employees, and Lew Stern & Ken Lizotte mentions: *Management Review*, July/August 1998 cover story: Page 187: How do leaders lose trust in the first place?: Manchester consulting, *Management Review*, July/August 1998; cover story: Page 187: Mick Burkart quote regarding RailTex: *Management Review*, July/August 1998, cover story: Page 188: Industry ratings for trust: Manchester consulting, *Management Review*, July/August 1998 cover story: Page 189: One observer found that Vietnamese workers, who composed about 40% of the workforce in one company, "were especially fearful of the team concept, which they likened to Communist work teams": *Learning and Work*, page 27: Page 189: Yolanda Perry-Pastor anecdote: *Fortune*, January 10, 2000; pages 65, 66: Netobjects CEO quote: *Fast Company*, January 1999; page 77: Page 189: Jim Chesterton quote: *Management Review*, July/August 1998, cover story: "Hungover" quote: *Beyond Generation X*, page 40

Abrahams, Jeffrey. *The Mission Statement Book: 301 Corporate Mission Statements from America's Top Companies.* Berkeley: Ten Speed Press, 1999.

Bagby, Meredith. *Rational Exuberance: The Influence of Generation X on the New American Economy.* New York: Dutton/Penguin, 1998.

Barnard, Robert et al. *Chips & Pop: Decoding the Nexus Generation.* Toronto: Malcolm Lester Books, 1998.

Berry, Leonard. *Discovering the Soul of Service: The Nine Drivers of Sustainable Business Success.* New York: Free Press, 1999.

Bly, Robert. *The Sibling Society.* Reading: Addison-Wesley Publishing, 1996.

Bridges, William. *JobShift: How to Prosper in a Workplace without Jobs.* London: Nicholas Brealey Publishing, 1995.

Cappelli, Peter. *The New Deal at Work: Managing the Market-Driven Workforce.* Boston: Harvard Business School Press, 1999.

Cohen, Eli B. *The Leadership Engine: How Winning Companies Build Leadership at Every Level.* New York: HarperCollins, 2000.

Collins, James. *Built to Last: Successful Habits of Visionary Companies.* New York: HarperBusiness, 1994.

Covey, Stephen. *Seven Habits of Highly Effective People.* Salt Lake City: Franklin Covey Co., 1989.

Darrah, Charles N. *Learning and Work: An Exploration in Industrial Ethnography.* New York: Garland Publishing, 1996.

Deal, Terence E. and Allan A. Kennedy. *Revitalizing the Workplace After Downsizing, Mergers and Reengineering.* Reading: Perseus Books, 1999.

Deal, Terence E. and M.K. Key. *Corporate Celebration.* San Francisco: Berrett-Koehler Publishers, 1998.

Discovering America's Past: Customs, Legends, History and Lore of Our Great Nation. New York: Readers Digest, 1993.

Diversity in the Workplace Human Resources Initiatives, ed. Susan E. Jackson & Associates. New York: Guilford Press, 1992.

Dobbin, Murray. *The Myth of the Good Corporate Citizen: Democracy Under the Rule of Big Business.* Toronto: Stoddart, 1998.

Dominguez, Joseph R. and Vicki Robin. *Your Money or Your Life: Transforming Your Relationship with Money and Achieving Financial Independence.* New York: Penguin Books, 1993.

Everett, Melissa. *Making a Living While Making a Difference: The Expanded Guide to Creating Careers with a Conscience.* Gabriola Island: New Society Publishers, 1999.

Foot, David K. with Danial Stoffman. *Boom, Bust & Echo: How to Profit from the Coming Demographic Shift.* Toronto: Macfarlane, Walter and Ross, 1996.

Friel, John C. and Linda D. Friel. *The Worst Seven Things Parents Can Do.* Deerfield Beach: Health Communications, 1999.

Goldberg, Beverly. *Age Works: What Corporate America Must Do to Survive the Graying of the Workforce.* New York: Free Press, 2000.

Goldthorpe, J et al. *The Affluent Worker: Industrial Attitude and Behaviour.* Cambridge: Cambridge University Press, 1968.

Hammer, Michael and James Champy. *Reengineering the Corporation: A Manifesto for Business Revolution.* New York: HarperBusiness, 1993.

Hammer, Michael. *Beyond Reengineering: How the Process-Centered Organization is Changing Our Work and Our Lives.* New York: HarperBusiness, 1996.

Handy, Charles. *The Hungry Spirit: Beyond Capitalism: A Quest for Purpose in the*

Modern World. London: Arrow Books/ Random House, 1998.

Hendricks, Gay and Kate Lickman. *The Corporate Mystic: A Guidebook for Visionaries with Their Feet on the Ground.* New York and Toronto: Bantam Books, 1996.

Hochschild, Archie. *The Time Bind: When Work Becomes Home and Home Becomes Work.* New York: Metropolitan Books, 1997.

Kaye, Beverly L. and Sharon Jordan-Evans. *Love 'Em or Lose 'Em: Getting Good People to Stay.* New York: Berrett-Koehler, 1999.

Klein, Eric, and John B. Izzo. *Awakening Corporate Soul.* Vancouver: Fair Winds Press, 1998.

Leonard, George Burr. *Mastery: The Keys to Long-Term Success and Fulfillment.* New York: Dutton, 1991.

Maas, James B. with Megan L. Wherry. *Power Sleep: The Revolutionary Program that Prepares Your Mind for Peak Performance.* New York: Villard Books, 1998.

Manji, Irshad. *Risking Utopia: On the Edge of a New Democracy.* Toronto:Douglas & McIntyre, 1997.

Marshall, Edward M. *Building Trust at the Speed of Change.* New York: Amacom, 1999.

McKenna, Regis. *Real Time: Preparing for the Age of the Never Satisfied Customer.* Harvard Business School Press, 1997.

Mercer, David. *Future Revolutions.* London: Orion Business Books, 1998.

Moses, Barbara. *Career Intelligence: Mastering the New Work and Personal Realities.* Toronto: Stoddart, 1997.

Naisbitt, John and Patricia Aburdene. *Megatrends 2000: Ten New Directions for the 1990s.* New York: William Morrow & Co., 1990.

Nattrass, Brian and Mary Altomare. *The Natural Step for Business: Wealth, Ecology and the Evolutionary Corporation.* Gabriola Island: New Society Publishers, 1999.

Navran, Frank J. *Truth and Trust: The First Two Victims of Downsizing.* Athabasca: Athabasca Educational Enterprises, 1995.

Oliver, Richard W. *The Shape of Things to Come: Imperatives for Winning in the New World of Business.* New York: McGraw Hill, 1999.

Promise of Diversity. New York: NTL Institute/Irwin Publishing, 1994.

Raines, Claire. *Beyond Generation X: A Practical Guide for Managers.* Menlo Park, California: Crisp Publications, 1997.

Reid, Angus. *Shakedown: How the New Economy is Changing Our Lives.* Toronto: Seal Books/McClelland-Bantam/Doubleday Canada, 1996.

Ryan, Kathleen and Daniel I. Ostreich. *Driving Fear Out of the Workplace: How to Overcome the Invisible Barriers of Quality, Productivity and Innovation.* San Francisco: Jossey-Bass Publishers, 1991.

Schor, Juliet. *The Overworked American: The Unexpected Decline of Leisure.* New York: Basic Books, 1991.

Senge, Peter. *The Dance of Change: The Challenges to Sustaining Momentum in Learning Organizations.* New York: Doublelday/Currency, 1999.

Sennett, Richard. *The Corrosion of Character: The Personal Consequences of Work in the New Capitalism.* New York and London: W.W. Norton & Co., 1998.

The Good Life. London: The Demos Collection Issue 14, Demos, 1998.

Wright, Leslie and Marti Smye. *Civilizing the Workplace: Corporate Abuse: How 'Lean and Mean' Robs People and Profits.* Toronto: Key Porter Books, 1996.